BUILDINGS FOR THE ELDERLY

BUILDINGS FOR THE ELDERLY

Noverre Musson, AIA, and Helen Heusinkveld

Reinhold Publishing Corporation / New York
Subsidiary of CHAPMAN-REINHOLD
New York—Amsterdam—London

© 1963, Reinhold Publishing Corporation
(SUBSIDIARY OF CHAPMAN-REINHOLD)
Printed in the United States of America
Second Printing, April, 1967
Library of Congress Catalog Card No. 62-19489

Designed by Myron Hall III
Type set by Graphic Arts Typographers, Inc.
Printed by Halliday Lithograph Corporation

CONTENTS

INTRODUCTION

This book is intended as a review of current thinking and current design of housing for the elderly. It is meant to give serious minded and creative thinkers a broad look at what has been done and to inspire in them a healthy respect for—but not automatic acceptance of—the experts as well as a healthy contempt for private or official dogma and ready-made answers. Perhaps we should say of all opinions as Shakespeare has Horatio say, "So I have heard, and do, in part, believe."

The book is written for people who like people. The elderly are people—people who, to quote Cleveland Public Housing Director, Ernest Bohn, are "just like other people, only more so."

If this study can persuade architects and laymen to approach the problem of building for the elderly with hearts and minds geared to discovering and making use of mature resources, they will learn to pursue their goal with enthusiasm rather than pity.

In this decade many new, unthought-of forms of joyous, emancipated living will be discovered by and for the seniors of our citizenry. It is hoped that the text and exhibits found here will help to stimulate new, gracious, and beautiful forms of architecture to interpret this emancipation. This is our objective. Any particular subject of discussion in the book is tributary to and not to be mistaken for the objective.

Certain basic problems face each generation as it comes along. In a rapidly evolving, almost discontinuous culture such as ours, these problems seem new. The fact is rather that these are old basic problems that merely present themselves in new contexts and therefore must be handled in new ways.

Within the memory of people alive today, our American social structure has gone through a complete changeover from an agrarian to an urban civilization. This has forced upon us new situations which we are philosophically and therefore functionally unprepared to assess and handle with complete assurance.

In a rural society, a three- and even four-generation family was not unusual. The elderly continued to be useful to the day of their death or to the day of complete disability. Their stored-up experience was respected. There were farm chores to be done which they could perform, and young children they could look after and even train in the ways of the farm. So the sense of their value to the community was continuous even if reduced. (The same social framework automatically gave meaning to the life of the growing children in a way unknown to the city child today.) There were few unattached, indigent elderly persons to be provided for. Such care as was needed was provided in a meager but businesslike way in the county "Infirmary," the "Poorhouse," or similar institutions. No one tried to be euphemistic about the fact that these were institutions. The residents of such "homes" were perhaps unfortunate, but this was life; and such folks were expected to be grateful for the charity they received. In the cities of a generation ago the same attitudes obtained.

Today the three-generation family is not the norm, although statistically it is still a going institution. Many grandparents do look after the house while the father and the mother both work, and grandparents in such homes are often grudgingly tolerated as built-in baby sitters or dishwashers.

But there is an increasing separation of the generations. Even parents feel keenly the separation from their own teenagers; and the gulf between these young folks and their grandparents, particularly the dependent ones, is almost unbridgeable. Not that such separations did not exist before. But the lack of shared experiences, as a result of the kaleidoscopic changes in technology and social patterns marking every decade of this century, has tended to heighten the separation.

The individual today therefore more and more seeks comradeship in his own age group outside the family circle—small fry with small fry, teenagers with teenagers, young marrieds with young marrieds, oldsters with oldsters. This is the cause for the burgeoning of Golden Age Centers. There the retired elderly —cut off functionally from usefulness to family and community, lacking a basis for rapport with a broad segment of the society as well as their own kin, separated from others by gulfs of education and experience, no longer the repository of wisdom for the young—can find solace and real contact with people of their own age and circumstances.

The incredible mobility of the American population is another factor which militates against families staying together as they once did. The young adults move with great frequency in an effort to advance in employment. Either changing employers or moving up within an organization often means a move to another city or state. The oldsters may not wish or be able to follow, and it may be desirable to keep an old home base as a central location for several migrating children.

These factors are stimulating a whole new set of criteria for residence after 65 and presage a demand for a new kind of senior living—imagined, but seldom available before. The answers to these urges and felt needs have been expressed in volume in such manifestations as warm climate trailer camps, retirement subdivisions, and even whole towns of retirees —for the most part in mild and warm climates. But in colder climates, we see the development of apartments, row houses, and even subdivisions populated primarily by folks over 65. Some of these are inadequate, or worse. Some are badly located. Some are unsafe and inoperable because they are poorly designed. Some are out of reach of the necessary health facilities. Some call for a pioneering spirit from people no longer equal to living the pioneer life.

These may or may not be temporary circumstances. But a new factor that is not temporary, and that is only just beginning to be felt, is the greater financial independence the next generation of elderly will have. Federal Social Security added to the proliferating pension plans of business and industry will see the average worker retiring into security instead of into dependence or real need as many do now and most did in the past. This factor is giving more and more elderly people the choice of whether they wish to live with relatives or maintain independence of residence.

From these circumstances we see flowing new attitudes toward the old-folks homes. The alert and enlightened elderly in unprecedented numbers are seeking personal security in kinds of senior-years residences unknown in the past. More able to buy what they want, they are dreaming of, seeking, and finding new ways of living in retirement.

The purpose of this book is to examine the kinds of residences for the mature years now available and popular, to take a look at the kinds of residences now being planned and built, and to evaluate current concepts. The authors approach their task with the humble feeling best expressed by Olive Randall, Vice President of the National Council on the Aging, when she says that "while we plan the problem is changing," and we are all "expressing opinions out of deep ignorance." We proceed, however, with the conviction that if satisfactory answers are to be found, they will be architectural ones inasmuch as history proves that any "way of life" has finally found expression in buildings and that these buildings have unavoidably molded the way of life of the people who have lived in them.

The authors would like to give credit for the inspiration, assistance and invaluable information they received from Dr. Wilma Donahue, architect Bo Bousted, the officers and staff of the National Council on Aging, all the dedicated and informed people who attended the N.C.O.A. 1960 Conference, architect Douglas C. Weiss, Mrs. Eunice Lynd, and Mr. William Sohl.

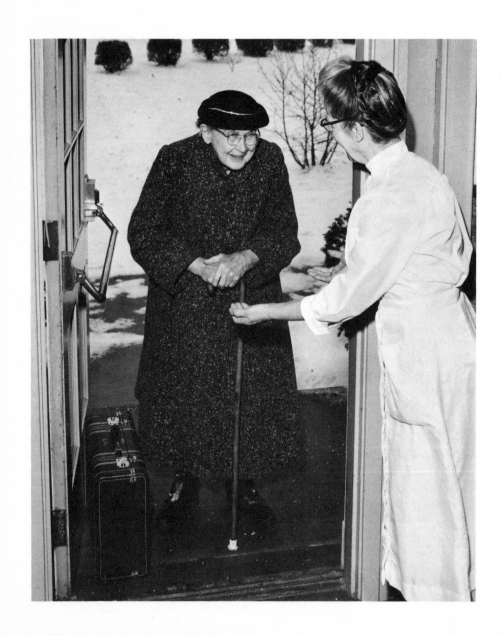

CHAPTER 1

WHOM TO BUILD FOR

Who are the elderly?

Government statistics define the elderly as people 65 or over. Actually the elderly are *ALL* of us—only a little older. They are not a specific type or kind of person; they are our neighbors, our relatives, our friends, the widow down the street, with great diversity of background, education, abilities and interests. Some of them may have, or in the foreseeable future may develop, varying degrees of physical and mental limitation.

Because of the changing pattern of family life, with the happy three-generation home gradually fading from the scene, the elderly person of today has lost his time-honored function in the family. He is no longer the story-telling "bridge to the past" adored by grandchildren, nor does he hold prestige for wisdom once accorded him by his own sons and daughters. Compulsory retirement has cut him off from many friends of all ages, his companions at work perhaps for years. Reduced income limits his social life. He has a great adjustment to make; if he has lost his mate, that adjustment is even more difficult. Hence in spite of added years, and in spite of the many modern conveniences afforded by science, he is not necessarily a happy person. Yet retirement from work and separation from family need not mean giving up interest and satisfaction in living. The right retirement home may be the key to years of contented, fruitful living.

How many of them?

The 1960 United States Census figures give a total of 16,559,580 in the 65-and-over population of our country. This represents one in eleven of the total population. The number is constantly increasing because more people are today surviving the diseases once fatal to childhood and youth (diptheria, pneumonia, scarlet fever, tuberculosis, poliomyelitis, etc.) and are living into the eighth and ninth decades. The prediction for the year 1975 is that there will be 21,872,000 people 65 and over, and for the year 2000, 30 million in that age bracket.

The figures in the accompanying table show the increase in the 65-and-over population in the United States from 1900 to 1960 by decades.

Increase of Population 65 years of age and over

Year	Total Population	Population 21 years and over	Population 65 years and over	% of elderly to total population	% of elderly to 21-and-over population
1900	75,995,575	42,112,917	3,080,498	4.1	7.3
1910	91,972,226	47,332,277	3,949,524	4.3	8.3
1920	105,710,620	60,887,000	4,933,215	4.7	8.1
1930	122,755,046	72,944,000	6,633,805	5.4	9.1
1940	131,669,275	83,997,000	9,019,314	6.8	10.7
1950	150,695,361	97,403,000	12,267,527	8.1	12.6
1960	179,323,175	107,377,000	16,559,580	9.2	15.4
Predicted for 2000			30,000,000		

U.S. Census, 1960.

The 1960 Census shows that 45.3% of the total population 65 and over are men and 54.7% are women. The disproportion increases with age, as the following table indicates.

	Men	Women
65 to 69 years	47	53
70 to 74 years	45	55
75 to 79 years	43	57
80 to 84 years	41	59
85 years and over	39	61

What is their urban-rural distribution?

Like the rest of the population, the aged are largely city dwellers. Seventy out of every 100 live in cities, 30 being men and 40 women. Thirty out of 100 live in rural areas or small communities up to 2,500 population. Fifteen of these 30 are men, and 15 are women.

For each 100 people aged 65-and-over

	Live in city	Live in rural area
Men	30	15
Women	40	15

What is their marital status?

Of the 45 men in every 100 people 65-and-over, 25 are living with a spouse, 16 are widowed, and 4 have never married. Of the 55 women in every 100 of this age group, 25 are living with a spouse, 22 are widowed, and 8 have never married. The differential shown by these figures has its effect on housing and living arangements of the elderly. Married couples are likely to maintain their own households longer that the unmarried; women without husbands generally have lower incomes and are more likely to live with their children than are single men.

For each 100 people aged 65 and over

	Total	Living with spouse	Widowed	Never Married
Men	45	25	16	4
Women	55	25	22	8

What is their economic situation?

The generally low income of the 65-and-over group is due basically to retirement from employment. Only one in five men, and very few women, are employed the full year round. The median income of all elderly couples living independently in urban areas has been estimated at $3382 for the year 1959. The median income of the elderly living alone in the same year was $1176.

Whereas elderly persons as a group have higher average savings than younger people, most of these savings are in their homes and in life insurance and are not always readily convertible to cash. Owning a house that is mortgage-free can mean an average saving in housing costs of about 30% over what those who must rent would pay and thus help make a small income go farther. But like other forms of saving, home ownership is found more commonly among those with higher income. Among beneficiaries of the Social Security program about two out of three of the married elderly and one out of three of the non-married studied in 1957 owned a nonfarm home. Most of these homes were mortgage-free, but the equity was relatively modest. The median amount was about $8,000.*

Will this situation be static? It could well improve, contingent of course upon the state of the national economy. More and more people are being covered each year by the Social Security program. Today's group aged 75 and over have the least income because fewer of them are covered by this program. Whereas today approximately 72 per cent of the 65-and-over group are covered, we can anticipate as many as 95 per cent being covered in the foreseeable future. And because education is definitely correlated with higher income, the ever increasing enrollments in our institutions of higher education will certainly be reflected in larger benefits for the retired because of higher earnings during their working years. Further, the amount of money one may earn without penalty and with less penalty while receiving benefits under Social Security is moving upwards. There is a question whether Social Security should include some automatic provision for benefit adjustment to meet cost-of-living index. This plan has been tried by nine European countries, some using the average wage level as basis of adjustment, some the cost-of-living and wage level, and still others merely the cost-of-living index.

An additional source of income for the elderly may be the increasingly popular business pension. Relatively few in today's 75-and-over group receive such benefits. At a hearing in July, 1961, before the Sub-

*Lenore A. Epstein, "Income, Retirement and Security for the Aging," Proceedings, Eighth Planning Conference for Architects, U. of Illinois, 1961.

committee on Retirement Income of the Special Committee on Aging, United States Senate, testimony was introduced to the effect that pension plans in business and industry are currently on the rise and attracting new adherents. There were 1000 pension plans operating in 1940; in 1960 there were over 60,000. Over 20 million people are now covered by private pension plans; the number is increasing by better than a million a year.

Also showing continued increase are profit-sharing plans, providing for deferred payments after retirement, and group life insurance programs providing protection after retirement.

So the future for the elderly citizen may be much brighter economically. And although compulsory retirement today abruptly curtails the income of this group, some do have equity which could be transferred from an unsatisfactory home to something more suitable for their declining years. This might be a smaller, more easily managed home for continued independent living, or the entrance payment for a selected group-living arrangement.

What is their political potential?

The 65-and-above group constitutes 15.4 per cent of the voting power of the nation, and although unorganized (as yet) its influence must be recognized. Already some states, notably California, but also Washington and Colorado, are responding to pressures of the elderly group with plans for more generous aid.

Which categories of the elderly need housing?

Since the war, building emphasis has been on homes for young couples. FHA programs, Veterans' preferential loans, all have been geared to house new young families. There has been no general concern about housing for the elderly until the past five years.

With the current trend of many United States industries to move their younger personnel from one section of the country to another, we note that some 35 million people moved in the year 1961. The elderly parents of these young people do not generally go along; it might mean only another uprooting in just a few more years. So they choose to stay where their roots are. But as they become older, and more infirm, it is increasingly difficult to find a place to live that is convenient, safe, and within their price range. The reduced income of compulsory retirement affects practically every older citizen. And with the changing social order, of parents living independently of their married children—even when the children are not on the move—a vast need for housing for older people has arisen. Just what is needed, and how much in each category in any one community can be determined only by some sort of survey.

New housing will probably be required by those elderly people who now live

(a) With married children, but prefer independence

(b) In walk-up apartments, but need elevators

(c) Alone, but want some group-living arrangement with sociability at hand

(d) Independently, but want to relinquish responsibilities

(e) In substandard housing.

For these different groups the following types of housing would find ready markets:

(a) Small, single dwellings, easy to care for, economical in upkeep

(b) Elevator apartment buildings

(c) Various types of group arrangements for housekeeping, with shared facilities and opportunity for sociability at hand (including trailer parks)

(d) Full care retirement residences, with meals and various services

(e) Public housing.

What do they need in a retirement home?

The elderly person needs security, independence, involvement and last, but not least, privacy. To some extent the building can provide all of these.

1. *Security*—He needs a sense of physical safety—safety from falling; safety from the alarms of rushing children, bicycles, automobiles; safety from the danger of fire. He wants to be sure that in time of any emergency he can get help. He wants to know that he can get health services should he become ill. His desire for financial security is equally strong. He doesn't want his money to run out. He wants to live within his income, whatever it may be. His retirement home can and should meet these needs.

2. *Independence*—To help him retain his dignity and self respect, he needs the maximum leeway for coming and going and doing as he pleases. In other than completely independent living, the administrator can meet this need by careful attention to house rules, especially dining room hour and seating flexibility.

3. *Involvement*—He needs acceptance for himself by people with whom he can find intellectual rapport. He needs involvement in the life about him so that he will be encouraged to give of himself. This can prevent the unfortunate tendency to withdrawal, so common in elderly people. He needs adventure, a spark, something to look forward to, something to make tomorrow different from today. Anticipation helps to keep people young.

4. *Privacy*—He needs a place to be alone when the mood directs. Even greater than the obvious need for physical recuperation is the need for the opportunity to think through his personal problems and develop spiritual and intellectual resources to meet them. Life deals us all varied experiences of both joy and sorrow, for which we need the quiet mind to remember and the courage to forget. For this, and for personal meditation, the true source of spiritual strength, privacy is essential.

The later years can be fruitful ones. The right atmosphere in the retirement home can offer opportunity for continued growth in the realm of the mind and the spirit, although of course it cannot guarantee the individual resident's response to that opportunity.

CHAPTER 2

WHO SHOULD BUILD

Who should assume responsibility for building for the elderly? Since the problem is national in scope, it is clearly everyone's responsibility: (1) the individual elderly person for himself; (2) the group of friends who want to enjoy the mature years together; (3) the church or fraternal group concerned with the welfare of their own aging members; (4) the builder and developer for profit; (5) local and state governments for the benefit of low-income citizens.

When we realize that the life span of all of us is increasing and that our children are marrying earlier, it becomes evident that most of us will live a third of our lives after our children leave home. Compulsory retirement will doubtless limit our income too in our later years. As intelligent citizens, we all have a responsibility to see to it that there is adequate housing to meet the needs of the increasing number of aging citizens. Such housing should be of sufficient variety to meet their varying tastes and be available at prices they can afford to pay.

The 1960 census figures indicate that 11 per cent of all new dwellings should be planned to meet the needs of the aging. According to New York architect Sidney Katz, 300,000 new units will be needed per year for the next 15 years to serve our 65-and-over citizens. And because people of 65 and over have as varying tastes as do people of 30, we ought to build a variety of living arrangements from which elderly people may choose their retirement homes.

Those who should consider building for the elderly include: churches, fraternal groups, builders and developers, citizen's groups, government, and private individuals.

Churches

Church boards are committed to see to the well-being of their members. Traditionally they have built homes for the aged and infirm and for those who have no families to care for them. Today a new trend in church homes for the elderly is sweeping the country, offering an exciting, venturesome way of life for the retired person which is a far cry from the custodial care of the church home of yesterday. There is great variety of type, cost range, and services. Homes of great charm abound on the West Coast, in Florida, and in the Southwest, with scattered projects throughout the whole country. Waiting lists testify to their popularity and the satisfaction of their residents. Church boards everywhere have the responsibility to plan now for the happy later years of their members.

Fraternal, professional, and labor groups

Boards of fraternal groups have the same responsibility and the same opportunity to plan retirement homes for their members as do churches. Masonic homes are traditional throughout the country. The P.E.O.'s have two new homes in California. There are a number of very successful projects for retired teachers: Gray Gables at Ojai, Calif., one in Omaha, one in Portland, and a new one planned in Denver, to mention only a few. The Upholsterers' Union has a village for its retired members at Jupiter, Fla. Being built in two stages just outside Denver is Geneva Village, a 100-unit project for retired members of the International Waiters' Union.

The fact that there seem to be more projects in certain sections of the country does not mean people prefer to live in these regions. A country-wide poll of representative retired people by the Retired Teachers' Association and the Douglas Fir Plywood Association in 1960 indicated that the general preference of retired people is to stay in their own communities, where they have lifetime friends and associations, if they can find what they want.

The builder or developer

Health statistics tell us that one-half of the elderly have good enough health to live independently; another third could manage such living with special features to meet individual handicaps and with supporting community services available.

Although one-half of the elderly have incomes under $3000 per year, the other half have incomes over that amount. The total income of the over-65 group is about 25 billion dollars per year—5 per cent of the gross national product.

Mr. S. M. Bourland, 1st Vice President of the First Federal Savings and Loan Association of Peoria, Ill., says older people are a preferred credit risk. Their incomes generally may be reduced, but they are stable—Social Security, pensions, annuities, interest, etc. Moreover, this group has less other heavy expenses to meet than do younger people; the children are educated; no costly household furnishings are needed. His building and loan association will finance a loan to an older person or couple of satisfactory financial background in an amount requiring monthly payments equal to 40 per cent of income; normally they limit a loan to an amount on which payments do not exceed 25 per cent of the monthly income. In case of the death of the mortgagor, says Mr. Bourland, the heirs can be counted on to finish payments.

Moreover, the 1961 Amendments to the Housing Act give building and loan associations more leeway in financing homes for the elderly. Such loans may be made in amounts up to 90 per cent of the appraised value and run for thirty years. Building and loan association financing is less costly than financing through Federal Housing Administration insurance programs.

The builder or developer should find the field wide open for imaginative private enterprise to build for retired people, either single dwellings scattered through residential communities of the general public or special group projects. Freedom House, Horizon House, and Golden Age House are examples of special design of single dwellings for older people. Orange Gardens, in Kissimmee, Fla. (see Section VI), and Ormond-by-the-Sea, Fla., as well as Youngtown, in Arizona, to mention but a few, are retirement villages built by private enterprise. A cooperative apartment building can also be developed by the entrepreneur for the retiree market. Senior Homes, Denver, is a cottage cooperative development sponsored by several Protestant churches.

A dream for the future was expressed by George Kassabaum, A.I.A., of the firm of Hellmuth, Obata & Kassabaum in St. Louis. His dream is for the developer of new subdivisions to plan one out of every seven homes for the use of elderly people. He would have a neighborhood community of 750 families, with a shopping center, elementary school, church and professional offices, all in the center within walking distance of all the residents. The single house for the elderly would not look different from the outside, but special features for safety and convenience would be incorporated within—multiple electric outlets, low cupboards, maximum storage space for a lifetime of accumulations, etc. Special projects for older people would house not more than 30 couples and 30 singles, and would have central dining room, recreation facilities, laundry and basic infirmary. Such central services would be available also to the elderly living in single dwellings.

Some builders have considered conversion of older hotels into accommodations for older people. Such efforts have met with varying degrees of success. A number of them operating in the eastern part of the country seem to be able to keep costs down. One operator even makes it possible for residents to earn part of their living expenses.

Carmel Hall is the largest and most elegant of such conversions. Its once sinister reputation, earned when a notorious gangster was slain within its portals, has been completely erased by its current humanitarian dedication. This was formerly the Detroiter Hotel, located downtown in that city. It is now owned and operated by the Carmelite Sisters and cares for upwards of 500 elderly people. Leo Bauer, A.I.A., Detroit, is the architect. Carmel Hall has a particularly well equipped rehabilitation center and adequately staffed and fully utilized occupational therapy department. The total cost of this conversion gave a per resident cost about equal to the average for new construction.

The builder and developer in every community has a responsibility to investigate local needs and to help meet them.

Citizens' groups

An interesting venture by a citizens' group has taken place in Oklahoma City.* In recognition of the complex needs of elderly citizens, limited studies were conducted by the Altrusa Club and a small group of community leaders. Housing was found to be the paramount need. Because it was recognized that no religious, fraternal, or civic organization could finance adequate services to residents of in-evolved to build a service area for a retirement village and to make land available to different groups to build housing. A committee of sixty citizens representative of community-wide church, fraternal, and civic organizations organized the nonprofit Foundation for Senior Citizens, Inc., to implement plans for a retirement village. A master plan will provide zoning restrictions and minimum construction standards. Community living units, apartments, and cottages are planned to meet varying requirements of the residents.

A beautiful 320-acre tract of land at the edge of the city was purchased by the Foundation. The village will have a park-like setting with no through streets, to minimize traffic problems. Four small lakes contribute to the beauty. Informal recreational facilities will be provided throughout and a larger formal recreational center with specialized facilities in the central area. Because the village is at the edge of the city, a small shopping area is planned. An interfaith chapel will serve those residents unable to maintain participation in their own churches. There will be an auditorium, library, music library, and hobby shops. Guest houses for visitors will have adjacent playgrounds for children.

For those with financial or psychological need for productive work, sheltered workshops will employ residents on piece-work contracts. Greenhouses will give employment and aid in landscaping the village.

*Information on this project was provided by Fanny Lon Leney, M.D., member of the original planning group.

A 50-bed rehabilitation hospital with potential for any desired expansion will serve not only the patients hospitalized, but also numerous residents of both the village and the larger community. Intensive physical and occupational therapy is planned, to return each patient to maximum activity at the earliest possible time. The services of the therapists will be utilized in all recreational programs, the hobby shops, and the sheltered workshops, but their primary program of rehabilitation will be conducted in the hospital. The hospital nursing service will provide village residents with visiting nurses during minor, short-term illnesses. In case of emergency, a signal from any residence will bring a nurse at any time of day or night.

The Oklahoma City Appeals Review Board authorized an initial public fund drive for $350,000 for this project.

Government

Local government can be helpful in solving the housing problem for its elderly citizens. Zoning ordinances can be changed to permit small single houses on smaller lots, perhaps in the currently popular cluster arrangement; restrictions can also be relaxed to permit small shops carrying basic needs to operate within the area. Government also can stimulate private enterprise to venture into this field of building by special tax privileges. Building might be encouraged by a government-financed survey to determine the specific local need (see directions for survey in Chap. 6).

Members of city councils are probably aware that public housing authorities are now building projects with units designed especially for the elderly. If the city does not have federally assisted public housing, local government, through preferential FHA programs can sponsor housing for its elderly citizens in the low or middle-low income brackets (see Chap. 9).

"County home problems can be met, as some counties have proved, providing aged persons with cheerful, homelike surroundings. County commissioners have traditionally had the responsibility of housing the completely indigent. The inhabitants of such homes were once called "inmates." Today we have many county nursing homes and they are inhabited by "residents" or "patients" and more important, they are treated as such. Old county homes in many states are being replaced by new structures, built especially to accommodate the needs of aging persons requiring care, and at the same time to give them attractive, homelike surroundings in which to round out their years. Many homes not replaced have been modernized and enlarged to meet new standards. Occupational therapy and planned activities are routine in these new homes, and every effort is made to interest residents in activities as well as in each other. Individuality is recognized, but planned recreation and crafts keep residents alert and interested, and shared activities foster congeniality."*

Some state governments have assumed responsibility for helping with the problem. "New York has had for several years a Limited Profit Housing Act to help finance housing for its middle-income aged. Under this act the City of Rochester built Cobbs Hill, a 70-apartment project for elderly citizens who did not qualify for public housing but could not meet costs of available decent housing on the regular market. This project does not cost the taxpayer anything. Average rents are $17 per month per room. There has always been a waiting list since completion, and another such project is under way. Now New York State also charters membership corporations to obtain mortgage loans to build housing for the aged. Thus employee organization retirement groups, labor unions, religious groups, veterans' groups, fraternal bodies, and the like, can now sponsor housing for their aging members under state auspices. This involves meeting a 10 per cent equity investment, often the cost of the site for the proposed project. The state housing finance agency will advance a 90 per cent mortgage loan at low interest rates.

"Colorado has built a cottage project for elderly citizens in Trinidad. State aid for elderly citizens in Colorado is $106 per month. Board, room and laundry is furnished at the Trinidad Home for those living on state aid alone, with the operational deficit met by the state. To those with larger income the cost is $145 to $170 for one- and two-bedroom cottages respectively. This cost includes meals, recreational facilities, etc."†

New Jersey, Connecticut, and Massachusetts have also pioneered in this field.

Individual citizens

Last, but not least, an individual or a couple still living in the house that was right for the family, but now just a bit (or a lot) too much to manage, could profit by talking to the architect about building something that will take less housework, less work in the yard, that won't cost so much to operate, and that will incorporate all the new safety features. Such a home would afford freer living for the later years.

Or, a group of close friends could consider a cooperative project. Each could have independent living quarters, and the cooperative could be designed to create a beautiful integrated environment where the individual unit gains from the over-all effect. The particular recreational facilities the group enjoys could be incorporated. Facilities like laundry and heating could be shared, and maintenance costs reduced. Best of all, the friends could look after each other in any emergency. Good friends who feel a responsibility toward each other would be wise to plan ahead.

The client

This book purports to discuss the design of residences for the elderly. Design is the architect's function. In order to proceed with building therefore, the above groups of people, who, we have said, should build for the elderly, first engage an architect and then become his "client."

When any individual, group or agency actually proceeds to build a residence for the retired, he assumes in the process the role of owner in contradis-

*"New concept of County Homes," State of Illinois.
†"Senior Citizens at the Crossroads," What's New?, No. 214, Abbott Laboratories, Chicago, 1959.

tinction to the architect and the contractor or "builder." This triumvirate, owner, architect, and contractor, makes up the building team—each of whom has a separate role. But the drama does not start until the owner—the client—gives the word.

Architects do not perform without clients. An architect needs a client to set his activities in motion. Furthermore, he cannot begin to act until the client tells him what he wants. The client has a need, and he has the impulse to satisfy that need. These are the two most important functions of a client: (1) to understand his need, and (2) to know how to take the proper steps to satisfy it, enough to keep him busy right through the building process. A third function is similar: to follow through with proper maintenance and use of the building once it is completed. This function may be taken over by the owner in another guise or as another person, the manager or administrator of a project.

The client, therefore, is the motivator and the formulator of the project, whether he is an individual with a private need or member of a committee with a group or public need. His job will be to comprehend in depth the meaning of the need to be satisfied; then his commands for action will be clear, wise, and decisive. Confusion and indecision will obtain in the degree that this comprehension is lacking. To be effective, he needs also to know and respect the abilities and functions of the members of the team he gathers around him; to know where his job starts and stops and the exact dimensions of the job of the others. This calls for an analysis at some point to distinguish (1) social problems, (2) policy problems, (3) management problems, (4) architectural problems, and (5) construction problems in order to determine who best can handle them.

A word about committees might not be amiss here. A committee of architects is impossible. We all remember the quip that defines a camel as a horse designed by a committee. In the same way the larger body the client becomes, the less effectively does he function. Building committees of seven to 10 or even 20 are not uncommon, and a memorial project in Ohio once had a building committee of 50. The results were abortive. An experienced architect will tell you that there should be a rule to limit building committees to five. This limit might well be made statutory. A certain well-known church architect adds $1,000.00 to his fee for every member of a building committee over three. If an organization cannot find five members for a building committee whom they can entrust with the handling of a project, they are beginning in uncertainty, and adding members to the committee will only add to the confusion.

The client needs to give his architect practical help like budget information, a topographical survey of the property, and data on accommodations to be provided. He should also make clear less concrete things such as his image of the project, his idea of the people who will occupy it, and what he hopes to do for them. How well these latter ideas are communicated may be the key to the success of the project. Much of the rest of this book deals with the identification, dimensions and communication of these ideas.

The client sets the tone of a project and he sets its limits. He should be certain then that his limitations are wise, that he is stimulating the full possibilities of the project, and that he is not limiting the opportunities it presents.

CHAPTER 3

WHAT TO BUILD

What to build is a question we can answer when we have determined exactly for whom we will build. The answer is also influenced by who does the building.

In Chap. 1 we identified statistically and in general groups who the elderly are. We determined who among them need residences. This statistical identification, however, we found to be only the barest beginning of a program for the design of architecture. It is necessary to have a clear and detailed acquaintance with the elderly—with their natures, their physical limitations, their social and psychological demands and their aspirations—before we can formulate a suitable environment.

But with the statistical data in hand, we can establish the range of possibilities of living arrangements needed by the growing elderly population and perhaps evaluate the types. This range of need spans the economic spectrum from low-cost subsidized shelter to de luxe accommodations; it spans the geographic situation from apartments in the central business district of our big cities to residences in open country; and it spans operational types from the completely independent house to living arrangements providing almost complete physical care and supervision.

We speak of living arrangements. This terminology is used to focus attention on the life to be lived in the "what" we decide to build.* A building does not exist independently of people, and therefore any thinking about a new building must focus on the people who will occupy it, on how they wish to live, and on how the building can make the life in it more felicitous and satisfying. If we thus focus attention on the life to be lived in a building, we answer many questions which otherwise might be perplexing; in fact, viewed in this way, many questions answer themselves.

Although the percentage of people at the bottom of the economic graph is greater among the elderly than among any other age group, these are not the only elderly people needing help in finding suitable homes. Traditionally the indigent elderly were the ones provided for. However meagerly their needs are met, they still get first attention today. It is only in this decade that widespread attention is being given to the needs of the elderly in other income brackets. The well-to-do and those of modest income appear to need help just as much as the indigent. This need has been uncovered by the new examination of the functional aspect of living arrangements and its meaning to the elderly, and this analysis has revealed that most houses and apartments are poorly adapted to serve the elderly.

The burgeoning market for luxury retirement homes and for retirement villages of all economic levels is an index of the demand, and of the willingness of the elderly to seek out accommodations they consider acceptable and can afford.

The demand for special accommodations for the elderly as an acceptable and desirable way of living, surprisingly enough, has created a new and still evolving field of design: residences for the elderly, as opposed to storage-for-old-folks in the traditional "old folks home" sense. The demand has risen out of sociological changes taking place in America today and can be implemented by current economic and technological changes. We must be careful, therefore, not to freeze our concepts to types of housing already available which appear to be popular. Variety of choice should be as open to the elderly as to any other age group. Architect George Kassabaum emphasizes this point in the Missouri Report for the White House Conference on Aging of 1961.

The almost universal phenomenon of waiting lists at homes for the elderly may not indicate they are the most desirable or preferred facilities. It may indicate that these are simply the best or the only thing now available. We may see as great a change in our con-

*For a definition of the terms of semi-technical nature used in this book, see "Terminology" at the conclusion of Section VII.

Menlo Park Retirement Apartments, Menlo Park, Calif. Architects: Skidmore, Owings & Merrill.

Royal Oaks Manor, Duarte, Calif. Architects: Orr, Strange & Inslee.

El Rancho Trailer Park, Bradenton, Fla.

Presbyterian Homes, St. Paul, Minn. Architects: Armstrong & Schlicting.

First Community Village, Columbus, Ohio. Architects: Tibbals-Crumley-Musson.

cept of desirable living arrangements for the elderly in the ensuing decades as we have seen in what makes desirable sleeping for automobile tourists—from the "tourist home" of the thirties to the posh motor hotel of the sixties. Fortunately, there is likely to be less untrained improvising in this field than we saw in the field of tourist lodgings.

Types of housing available

People who can and want to live independently, as well as people who prefer varying degrees of group living for companionship or for physical assistance, must be accommodated. Living arrangements for the elderly may thus be looked at in two ways: (1) in terms of the type of living offered, be it independent, assisted, or protected; and (2) in terms of the type of residence provided, be it dispersed, proximate, or congregate. The grouping of projects presented in Section VI follows the second set of categories. Here living arrangements are considered in relation to both categories.

We apply the term "dispersed" to residences for the elderly to identify individual units especially designed for the elderly but mingled with other residential types without special relation to each other. These may be individual houses or they may be individual flats, apartments, or row houses included among units for other families in the same building, group, or neighborhood. This type of housing represents the ideal of integration with the community. Observation, however, does seem to bear out the fact that all but the most resourceful elderly living in this situation do gradually retreat into isolation.

"Proximate" residences—that is, groups of housekeeping units gathered together into retirement villages, apartment houses for the elderly, trailer cities and the like—represent a kind of home construction which should have great appeal to the merchant builders. This type of housing has been exploited in the South, Southwest, and West. There appears to be a first-rate opportunity in other parts of the country for any builder who will analyze, design, and merchandise a product for this market which shows taste,

flare, and real understanding of the basic needs of his prospective customers. Undertaking a project of this sort entails a moral obligation to see that the special requirements of the elderly in the way of health services and daily shopping needs are fully met. The builder planning a typical new dormitory suburb should be concerned about schools and shopping centers, but he knows that if he disregards them, the public will eventually provide the schools and the residents will drive some distance to the nearest shopping center until the demand brings one closer. But the health and other services needed by the elderly are not automatically provided as are schools, and public transportation or a shopping center half a mile or a mile away may present a critical hardship to an elderly person. A retirement village has as great a need for a social hall or meeting center as another type neighborhood has for a school. It may even need a community center where daily meals may be had. Such things usually do not concern merchant builders, but in this field of home construction they are as vital as sewers and water.

The field of "congregate" home construction is a foment of activity. New and beautiful concepts are emerging. Some represent a blend of proximate and congregate arrangements which is creating a whole new category of living for retired people. The development of these new concepts is changing the universal attitude toward housing for the elderly so that "living for old home makers" will begin to have, as Prof. Walter Vivrette of the University of Minnesota has pointed out, all the attractions of "living for young home makers." To date, congregate homes have been built almost exclusively by churches, lodges, unions, and governmental agencies. This will probably continue to be true. However, FHA has a provision for builders for profit to enter this field. We will watch the development with interest.

In the proximate and congregate field, hotel and motel conversions have been tried as a way to find an economical kind of accommodations for elderly living. Carmel Hall in Detroit is an outstandingly successful example. Others have been less successful.

Frequently the location of the hotel or motel ripe for conversion is poor. Perhaps the poorest is the motel available on a disused highway, left stranded by highway rerouting. Generally the building does not convert readily, is beyond the reach of public transportation, is not well located for shopping or social activities, and is woefully distant from the necessary health services. The atmosphere such locations create of being stranded and of sinking into innocuous desuetude is not a healthy one.

1. *For Independent Living* (individual housekeeping residences for unassisted, completely independent living):

Dispersed—Scattered elderly individuals or families, integrated with or submerged in the community, and living in:

    Individual residences

    Double houses

    Duplexes

    Party wall row houses

    Apartments of all kinds

    Apartment hotels

    Hotel rooms (non-housekeeping).

Proximate—Grouped housekeeping units for the elderly living independently but in groups (sometimes with optional provisions for meals and maid service and sometimes with a self-generated program):

    Trailer camps

    Retirement villages

    Retirement row houses

    Apartments catering primarily to the elderly

    Hotels catering primarily to the elderly.

Many of the above accommodations could be owned outright by the individuals occupying them, owned on a cooperative basis, or rented.

2. *For Assisted Living* (Non-housekeeping; moderate independence with varying degrees of service, food, and care provided):

Hospital for the aged, Queens, N.Y. Architect: Joseph D. Weiss.

Congregate—Groups of elderly under one roof, or at least one management, receiving food service, housekeeping service, etc., and assistance with group activities:

    Hotels for the elderly
    Motel conversions
    Homes for the elderly
        Lodge sponsored
        Union sponsored
        Church sponsored
        Entrepreneur sponsored
        Industry sponsored
        Community sponsored
        State sponsored
        Federally sponsored (veterans, etc.).

The congregate home is never owned outright by the individual residents and only rarely on a co-operative basis.

3. *For Protected Living* (Minimum independence, with services, food and full care provided):
    Congregate—
        Nursing homes (chronic and convalescent
            conditions)
        Hospitals (acute conditions)
        Institutions for the physically disabled
        Mental institutions.

(Building types included in this group for protected living are specialized to varying degrees and will not be considered in this work. Many good treatises are available on these types.)

Some of the accommodations mentioned for independent and assisted living are more suitable than others. All will benefit immeasurably from careful attention to location, site selection and architectural design, including site plan, building plan, and engineering design. Anything built today is likely to meet with success. But as the range of choice is broadened, the elderly will become more and more discriminating in their preferences. Therefore, the most complete architectural analysis and enlightened design are of paramount importance.

Deciding on the type of housing

In determining what to build, a market survey is important. This will help turn the general statistics found in Chap. 1 into specific statistics for a given organization, neighborhood, city or area. These in turn will need interpretation and evaluation. Most surveys reveal a high demand for nursing facilities. It is important not to be sidetracked by this very real and vocal demand so that we lose sight of the larger population whose present make-do arrangements may even hasten their need for the special treatment facility. The market survey is treated in Chap. 6.

Sociologist William C. Loring, speaking primarily of independent living, has pointed out the astonishing size of the untapped market for housing for the elderly.* The people who form this market obviously are living somewhere now. But the building industry has yet to sense the opportunity this field offers to the developer who will engage qualified professional help and do a sophisticated job of locating, siting, designing and merchandizing retirement residences of quality. Locations which require dependence on private automobile, or too long a walk to satisfy daily needs, are to be avoided on pain of failure to serve the residents for whom the project is undertaken.

Churches and other non-profit organizations could do an inspired service if they would build carefully located dispersed or proximate residences for independent living in combination with a congregate home program. Such housekeeping units may be, but need not be, on the same site. They could be scattered around in the immediate neighborhood. Locating them so that they are convenient to the social, recreational, and health facilities of the congregate home would stimulate acquaintance and acceptance of the home by the individual who later might choose to relinquish independent living for the convenience it provides at the home. The congregate home might make a base from which to render minor services to these people living independently, such as home-

*Architectural Forum, Dec., 1960, and March, 1961.

maker assistance, which would enable them to maintain independence longer.

One of the major cleavages in thinking about how the elderly should live is the debate on integral versus segregated living.Should the elderly be mingled with the rest of the community or should they be gathered together into separate communities of varying degrees of detachment from the community? Lewis Mumford eloquently states the case for integration with the community; he finds it the most normal and happy circumstance for the elderly.

Acting on this philosophy, Public Housing authorities in certain cities have provided scattered units for the elderly throughout their projects. Subsequent research revealed that these elderly formed new friendships only with the nearest other elderly people. They had not made acquaintance or real friendships with people of other ages. They liked to look out on children playing, so long as they were far enough away that the noise was dissipated. They did not like children rushing up and down their own halls. They were physically integrated with the community but socially isolated. This would seem to have refuted Mr. Mumford's contention. The current tendency in public housing is to provide separate buildings exclusively for the elderly which are inserted as a unit into multi-building groups of non-elderly housing. However, questions lurk in the background of this data:

1. Were these people not already socially isolated individuals when they joined the public housing community?

2. Is not public housing an economically stratified community and therefore a segregated one in itself?

3. Does this kind of sampling represent a basis for an opinion about the elderly at large?

4. Is not Mr. Mumford talking about a larger, less easily identifiable group of people who are in fact already integrated with a community and who would seek this same way of life in seeking a new residence?

Albert Mayer, noted architect and city planner, perceived a unique opportunity when he designed the Gaylord White Houses for the New York Metropolitan

Housing Authority. Here was a complex of housing with a community center which was to include units for the elderly. He came up with an astonishingly subtle but simple plan which integrates the elderly with the community but allows them an option of as much isolation or segregation as they might choose individually. This kind of opportunity is all too seldom given an architect. His design (shown in Section VI) is worthy of study as is the architect's commentary on his objectives.

Basic design characteristics

Certain characteristics will be found in all good residences for the elderly whether the units are minimum-cost or luxury construction, whether they be for independent or assisted living. These special characteristics which may distinguish them from residences for other family types are quite specific but will not render their design undesirable for folks of other ages. These characteristics have to do primarily with size, location, and functional details. A brief list is given here. Each item is covered in detail elsewhere in the book. The relative importance of these items will vary with the housing type, but all obtain.

1. Size of individual living unit (whether one room or five):

a. Small enough to be easily managed.

b. Large enough not to be cramped or over-crowded with normally required furniture so that cleaning, etc., is difficult.

c. Adequate to accommodate part-time help if nursing care is needed.

d. Attention to the space requirements necessary for maneuvering a wheel chair, if need be.

2. Location: Carefully related to the shopping, services, health facilities and activities most important to the elderly (see Chap. 4).

3. Functional details: Special attention to design for safety, with regard to lighting, stairs, floors, baths, cooking facilities (see Section V).

The building

The end product of the type of undertaking explored in this entire book is a building. It is hoped that the end product will also be architecture so that it will be worthy of the investments of time, devotion, aspiration, and cash it represents. Such a building starts with an idea—we might even say an ideal—and if the idea is not lost in the shuffling of minutiae along the way, there is a chance the building will express that ideal when completed.

Frank Lloyd Wright stated the case unequivocally when he said, "No building has a right to be erected unless it is the working out of some idea, the practical demonstration of some principle at work."* In this he eschewed the purely functional approach to building which designs primarily for traffic flow and easing the work of the housekeeper. There is nothing wrong with such considerations, but they are only limited objectives and when these objectives assume undue importance, in all likelihood the *Idea* has escaped. Wright demolished the house-is-a-machine-for-living theory by saying, "yes, insomuch as the human heart is a machine for pumping blood." Our concern must be with what we really feel the heart of the matter to be. A fine surgeon may keep a human heart pumping but leave the affections untouched. There is great danger of paralleling this operation in building for the elderly—we may be maintaining the semblance of life without regard to the essence of life—construction but not architecture.

It may be urged that attaining the ideal life in a residence for the elderly is a matter of administration, organization, or program, but it must be remembered that if the ideal is not present as an objective from the very start, it is unlikely that it can be injected into the project as an afterthought. There is nothing that brackets a standard of living so inevitably as a building; and the standard it sets should be something to measure up to instead of to overcome.

It may be interesting and useful to the reader to evaluate how he thinks the projects included in Part VI of this book measure up in respect to starting with an idea and achieving it. Every building is a clear, readable expression of the quality of thought that

*My Father Who Is On Earth, John Wright, G. P. Putman's Sons, New York, 1946.

went into the process of its conception. More readable than some other forms of modern art, modern architecture is a language worth learning.

So far the new examples of residences for the elderly are free from the exhibitionism seen in a surprising share of the new churches being built. The latter trend is not necessarily to be deplored, for at least it denotes a striving for dynamism in church thinking. The danger is perhaps the opposite in the field of building for the elderly: a spiritless, prosaic thinking. Because it must be sought with humility, genuine architecture eludes both these kinds of thinking, both the assertive as a substitute for meaning and also drab, joyless functionalism. Genuine architecture neither comes to us gratuitously nor is it taken by storm.

How do we start to seek the idea which shall illuminate our end product, the building, and make it architecture? By focusing on the individual life to be lived in it. By bringing to our thinking about the ideal life all the perception, imagination, and zest we can. By forging the idea so as to comply with and enhance that ideal. We must plan real homes for real living with vigor and joy by real people. Architecture can give the life lived in it a sense of dignity; it can color every activity from washing clothes to entertaining guests with a sense of fitness and beauty; it can evoke a sense of pride; it can establish a sense of comfort and security; and it can bring a sense of satisfaction in living.

CHAPTER 4

WHERE TO BUILD

Where-to-build is linked to what-to-build just as what-to-build is linked to for-whom-to-build. These three considerations—where, what and for whom—are not mutually exclusive, and each is subject to adjustment in terms of the other two. But here, as throughout our study, the individual to be accommodated must be the overriding consideration.

Types of location available

The choice of where to build residences for the elderly will be made from a broad range of urban and non-urban milieus. These include:

Urban

1. Central city
2. Declining gray areas adjacent to the central business district
3. Near-in old residential areas of the last century

Suburban

1. Old suburbs, turn-of-the-century
2. Pre-war suburbs, built between 1920 and 1940
3. New suburbia, of post-war creation

Non-urban

1. Exurbia, that non-urban, interurban area which will be the next target for urbanization
2. Small country towns
3. True rural open country
4. Special geographical locations, such as the seaside, or the mountains.

The choice of location should be guided by a set of criteria which embrace city planning principles, sociological and psychological factors, and esthetic considerations—each interpreted for its significance to the elderly themselves. These three ways of looking at the criteria are co-equal in importance when making judgment.

A building should integrate with a neighborhood. This means it should be an addition to a neighborhood and should be at home in it but not that it should be absorbed by it or vanish into it. It means that the uses and users of the building should be compatible with the surroundings. Therefore, a residential project seems best located in or adjacent to a residential neighborhood. Due to the economic stratification of land in U. S. cities, which is manifested in the economic segregation of neighborhoods, we must consider whether the new resident of a new building will feel at home in a given neighborhood.

An already established community seems to offer most to elderly people seeking a residence. The established community has the transportation, services, utilities, commercial center, and health facilities they need.

The importance of accessibility

We considered in Chap. 2 what the elderly want and need in a building. Now let us consider what they want and need in a site for the building. We present here two check lists for evaluating a site.

Check list 1 categorizes the wants and desires most often expressed by the elderly in terms of physical access to various facilities. The more important the facility is to them, the greater their demand for ease of access to it. These requests reflect in many ways psychological needs as well as physical. They are critical to persons living independently. Their equivalent, however, is important in a degree to the person in a sheltered living situation.

One thing the elderly do not want is peace and quiet as represented by the rural setting considered desirable for them in years past. But Checklist 1 remains an area for continued research. Its categories of access are based on broad samplings, but these samplings may be grossly influenced by the type of people to whom questions were addressed. The relative importance of the items on this list must therefore be evaluated in terms of the individual or the group to be served and the type of building being proposed.

The cultural and educational background of the

Check List 1 — Access

Direct access desired to:
  Grocery store—a necessity
  Church—spiritual and social satisfactions
  Drug store—sundry shopping pleasures
  Post office — important means of communication and even doing business
  Laundry
  Restaurant—a social facility as well as convenience
  Movie house—entertainment
  Other elderly people
Easy access desired to:
  Shopping—the greater the variety, the better
  Bank
  Doctor
  Library
  Senior Citizen Center
  Utilities' office—for payment of bills

Feasible access desired to:
  Podiatrist, dentist, oculist
  Health services
  Cultural and educational facilities—museums, concerts, theater, lecture series, etc.
  Social services
  Government offices
Of indefinite importance:
  Nearness to family
  Nearness to friends
  Nearness to children
  Nearness to parks
  Public recreation
    facilities

Studies show that these are apparently of less importance to the elderly than is assumed by casual observation, providing compensating elements are in the picture.

individual (or group) and his economic status, temperament, or physical condition may render some items on the list of negligible importance or make others of overriding importance. A person of meager education may not feel drawn to museums and lecture series but rather to a Senior Citizen Center.

Access to facilities also needs individual definition. For some individuals or groups it may mean by automobile, either self-driven or chauffeured by relatives, friends or employees. Furthermore, access will change meaning if the individual changes physically and mentally. Needs diminish as capability is curtailed.

Evaluation of specific urban and nonurban locations

Let us now take a look at possible locations for residences for the elderly in specific urban and nonurban contexts and rate them in terms of how readily they satisfy the desires expressed in Checklist 1. For ease of reference, "shopping" will be considered to include the restaurant, bank and post office; "community services" will cover private doctors, public health services, governmental services, private and public social and welfare agencies; "cultural facilities" will cover educational facilities such as libraries, schools and universities as well as museums, art galleries, concerts and theater; and "recreational facilities" will cover movies and Golden Age centers. We will also rate the locations in terms of certain practical considerations which affect the choice. These considerations are given in Checklist 2. The locations considered are all prototypes and the observations about them are therefore generic. The term "near" is intended to mean "within walking distance."

Checklist 2—Practical Considerations

Land—the cost, availability, and size of plot
Utilities—the availability of gas, water, sewerage, and electricity
Zoning—is there need for a change? Will it entail a fight?
Transportation—public (important to the resident and employees)
Ambiance—the look and feel of the neighborhood

Central city:
Land—cost high; large sites seldom available; high-rise construction almost inevitable. Utilities—fully developed. Zoning—usually favorable. Transportation—excellent. Ambiance—lively urban, with heavy traffic and noise. Shopping—excellent. Community services—excellent. Cultural facilities—excellent. Recreation—excellent.

The Central City offers a concentration of advantages which offset the disadvantages of congestion and traffic, but a site must be chosen with care so as to include as many desirables as possible within walking distance. Churches are usually scarce in the central city. The mixture of land uses and enterprises here is usually no disadvantage.

Grey area (surrounding the central city):
Land—costs lower; large sites difficult to assemble because of estate ownership. Utilities—available. Zoning — easily obtained. Transportation — good. Ambiance—lively but inclined to be depressing, combined with heavy traffic and noise. Shopping—available but spotty. Community services — good. Cultural facilities — not really near. Recreation — spotty.

The mixture of land uses in this area is likely to include industrial activities unsatisfactory to a residential situation. Churches are even more scarce than in the central city. A careful search for a site

in this gray area may uncover one well oriented to the real advantages of the city core. This area is most likely to be, or about to be, a slum. But through the Federal Urban Renewal Program, many cities are currently restoring these areas to top quality usefulness and sometimes in the process producing neighborhoods ideal for residences for the elderly.

Old dense residential areas (75 to 100 years old)
These are the dense, close-in old residential neighborhoods most likely to be slums today. Urban renewal is providing opportunities in these neighborhoods. Without it, the chief advantages are favorable land cost and fully developed utilities. Transportation may be good. The ambiance is usually not satisfactory.

Old suburbs (50 to 75 year old mansions and fine houses):
Land—costs vary considerably with location. Utilities—available. Transportation—available. Zoning—may need a change. Ambiance—may be excellent. Shopping—varies. Community services—vary. Cultural facilities—accessible. Recreational facilities—spotty.

This is an area where sizeable pieces of ground may be assembled. Trends in changing city character should be examined to assess the future of the neighborhood. It may be full of rooming houses now or changing to an office-commercial area. If the assumed move of suburbanites back to the city is valid, these areas may hold their own and even be in for upgrading as residential neighborhoods.

Pre-war suburbs (pre-1940):
Land—costs moderate. Utilities—available. Transportation — usually available. Zoning — a change will be needed and may be hard to obtain for group housing (this is the part of our cities where Joseph Weiss says, "Zoning is guarded more preciously than motherhood"). Ambiance—most satisfactory.

These suburbs represent the first stages of modern urban sprawl and therefore walking distances may be extended. Care will be needed to select sites near shopping, community services, and with feasible access to cultural and recreational facilities. Churches are abundant. Many elderly live here but the individual residence, if not well located, can produce isolation. Due to young people moving out to the F.H.A. ranches, some such neighborhoods are gradually, imperceptibly becoming villages for the aged, and very satisfactorily so where social services and community institutions are well established.

Post-war suburbs:
Land — costs moderate but rising. Utilities — often overloaded and inadequate. Zoning—adverse to group residences. Transportation — poor. Ambiance—may be visually attractive but socially segregated, to the disadvantage of the elderly. Shopping—may be distant. Community services—undeveloped. Cultural facilities—non-existent. Recreational facilities—distant.

In this "up and coming" world of G.I. loans and young white collarites primarily oriented to the producing, care and feeding of young children, the elderly person may be socially isolated because of age segregation and physically stranded by the expanded distances of urban sprawl.

Exurbia, open country, the mountains, and seashore:
Urban values are non-existent here. Isolation will be complete for the individual elderly. Group residences may develop their own sense of community and provide on their own the services, values, and amenities freely available in urban situations. Often these services and amenities are self-developed and very makeshift. The ambiance can be rewarding or depressing, depending on the texture of the group, and this factor alone can far outweigh the value of geographical situation.

Summary of steps to be taken

The critical steps to take in analyzing a choice of site for a residence for the elderly are finally three:
1. Establish a clear picture of who will live there.
2. Determine the type of building or buildings they need.
3. Check the site against the two checklists.

Establishing an answer for one of these points may alter your thinking about the other two. One reason a clear answer to the first is important is that in an urban context it may be extremely desirable to serve people where they are, and where their need is. Therefore, it may be expedient or even salutary to provide for some people in the gray areas, the old neighborhoods, and even the declining areas, locations which might not for other reasons rate so highly on our scale of desirability of location. Close liaison with your Urban Renewal agency may pay dividends in these cases.

A word of warning: keep an eye on the demographic forecasts; consider what the need will be in ten years; and in almost every case pick a site which will allow for expansion within a decade.

Role of architect in choosing site

The land chosen on which to build residences for the elderly probably has more effect on the physical characteristics of the finished building than any other single factor outside of the mind of the architect.

It is urgent that the architect be engaged and brought into the discussion of site selection as early as possible. He has a practiced eye and background of experience in dealing with sites few laymen can match. Even the layman with experience of this kind is unlikely to view sites with the architect's vision for opportunities or hurdles latent in a site.

Any of the categories of location mentioned at the beginning of this chapter may have interesting or even remarkable geographical features, such as hills, bluffs, a lake, a river, ravines or a gentle slope. A geographical feature may be regarded as an asset or a handicap and so become the prime reason for choosing or rejecting a given site. But choosing or re-

jecting a given site on the basis of geographical features before consulting an architect is unwise.

When an architect is engaged after a site is already chosen and settled upon, he may be reluctant to tell the client that the site has drawbacks. This is natural because of the very talents he has to offer. An architect approaches his work in a creative way and he regards the drawbacks of a site as a challenge to his ability as much as he does budget or personality of a client. Sometimes the results of this approach are brilliant. But had he been offered a choice of sites, he might have rejected one in favor of another.

Your architect will be happy to discuss the sites under consideration with you in terms of all the factors discussed in this chapter or even make a written report, if it is necessary, for a board or a committee. The relative importance of topography to other factors will be revealed through the detailed analysis he will make of many technical matters such as site drainage, water runoff, need for sewage pumps, danger of flooding, soil types and soil bearing conditions, as well as access to utilities, traffic, water pressures available for fire protection, and the like.

Land cost considerations

A project is often sparked by the fact that someone has offered to donate a certain piece of ground or a certain property suddenly becomes available at a very good price. The decision of what site to choose, therefore, may seem ready-made when a project is first conceived. In such a case, it is extremely important that the proposed site be accepted only after it has been analyzed in terms of sound criteria. Its shortcomings should be noted and the cost of overcoming them accounted for. These factors should be weighed against its advantages.

Cheap land may be the most expensive investment an individual or committee can make. The cost of providing transportation for residents and employees to and from a project located off the public transportation lines may alone outweigh the supposed economy represented by the initial acquisition cost. Maintenance of private sewage and water systems may be a burdensome chore as well as expense. A location too far out or in the wrong neighborhood may strongly affect resale value of private property or the attractiveness of a group project to prospective residents. More than one congregate home for the elderly has been poorly located and has suffered over the years — at great cost in money and service — because the land was initially a bargain or a gift.

There used to be a rule of thumb that land cost for a private residence should not exceed 10 per cent of the total cost of the project. But in high quality neighborhoods the land cost may reasonably be as much as 20 or even 25 per cent of the total. Even this figure might be exceeded in some cases. The astronomical cost of tiny lots in San Francisco with a view of the bay is an example. For congregate homes, land costs will run from $150.00 to $600.00 per resident. In any case, the economics of the entire project must be analyzed to determine whether it can bear a given land cost.

Psychological factors of location

As mentioned previously, elderly people do not yearn to go back to the farm. Ex-farmers do not constitute the bulk of the elderly, and even farmers are now drawn to towns and cities. Nearly all surveys show that, by and large, elderly people prefer the peace and quiet of a busy street to the loud silences of rural solitude. A Thoreau-like urge to hermitize comes to few people, young or old.

For the person of advanced years, the degree of ease with which he can reach a store or other facilities may proportionately affect his happiness, mental well-being, and even health. Distance of travel alone may become a critical factor to elderly persons of reduced circumstance. They have been known to skimp on their eating in order to have carfare to go to the Golden Age Center. But when the effort required to go outweighs the motivation to go, a door is closed to the individual with incalculable psychological impact.

Certain physical and mental characteristics of the elderly lend importance to certain characteristics to

be sought in a site for their residences. They may be overly sensitive to noise (due to latent anxieties). Part of the residence, especially the sleeping rooms, should provide isolation from sound. Or they may be hard of hearing. The site should not create hidden traffic hazards to the deaf. Because they may not see well or lack agility, they are easily frightened. They have a natural curiosity and enjoy watching activities, but they are timid about plunging into them. Their balance may not be good and walking may be difficult. Therefore, long walks on busy streets necessary for shopping or for finding companionship and entertainment may be exhausting because of the multiple challenges and alarms as much as the physical exertion. A boy on a bicycle, as architect Joseph

Weiss points out, may seem a major menace.

A site therefore should be sought which provides some of the following:

- A busy life around
- A view of traffic and people
- A view of a river, valley, lake, a playground or a ball park
- Separation from playground if one exists
- Protection but not isolation from the alarms of the street
- Sun and breeze, but shelter from them also
- Possibility of some level ground, walks, or terraces
- Suitably friendly, intimate scale

Sessions Village, Columbus, Ohio. Architects: Miller and Reeves.

Handling of the site

On-site development should be determined by the personal characteristics and limitations of the elderly. For dispersed single and group (proximate) housekeeping residences consider:

- Small lots to limit upkeep
- Simple landscaping that is easy to maintain
- Minimum of grass to cut
- Level walks and drives
- Safe and easy driveway access with good visibility
- Short walks and drives to minimize snow removal
- Entrances, front porches and sitting areas that promote neighborliness and sociability
- Good night lighting
- Patios with privacy
- Preservation of trees and other existing features
- Greatest ease of access to central facilities, such as a social hall, by internal paths if posible
- Design for views from the building as well as vistas from yards and gardens.

Proper scale is a critical problem. Typical recent suburbs of one-story houses on ample lots have a scattered, incohesive look that is unsatisfactory in scale. Distances look even greater to walk than they are. On the other hand, turn-of-the-century middle income residential developments of two-story houses on small lots may be deplored for their ugliness, but they have a closeness and cohesiveness, an intimacy of scale that gives a sense of security not to be found in suburbia. Something of their intimacy and security should be sought in new site plans without their regimented row-house ugliness. Architect E. N. Turano, A.I.A., has provocative ideas on this subject (see New Jersey projects, Section VI). A superb example of imaginative site planning for maximum use and minimum upkeep is Sessions Village of Columbus, Ohio (1926).

The congregate home site plan should take into account all the suggestions above and add a few other amenities. Provision for group activities is essential in these homes. Friendships are by two's and three's. So consider also:

- Very small, private garden plots
- Small scattered sitting areas, both sunny and sheltered
- Seating at entrances where people and cars come and go
- Seating at street for watching the passing show
- Variety of orientation
- Internal protected areas for group recreation
- Drinking fountains
- Intertwining and crossing walks to encourage chance encounters
- Walks wide enough to allow wheel chairs to pass
- If site is large, toilet facilities at distance from the buildings, especially at recreation areas
- Provide movement on site—bird feeding; ponds with fish, running water, fountains; mobiles.

CHAPTER 5

WHAT THE BUILDING WILL COST

The cost of building an individual family living unit of any kind can vary considerably, whether it is a detached dwelling or a unit in a large congregate complex. A congregate home of some size—100 or more units—can be built for as little as $7,500 per resident (construction costs for 1962) and provide in addition to shelter and living space a surprising amount of auxiliary facilities for the resident's pleasure, convenience, and care. The average cost of projects studied (see Section VI) was $9,221 with some running as high as $30,000. A detached dwelling for a single family unit, other than a house trailer, can scarcely be bought for less than $10,000 and may, of course, run many times that.

Basic factors determining cost

The basic factors, or categories of decision, which determine cost are three: (1) size, (2) quality, and (3) budget. Any two of these, within reason, may be dictated by the client and the third will then be determined by the architect. If the client wants living space of a certain size (1), for a certain cost (3), his architect must determine what the building can be built of (2). If the client wants to establish the size of the dwelling (1) and the kinds of building materials (2), then the architect must tell him what it will cost (3).

The budget, of course, must be realistic in terms of the client's other wishes. It should be apparent at once that the client cannot set a ridiculously low budget and ridiculously large size and expect his architect to come up with anything better than canvas for shelter. (The great Frank Lloyd Wright actually built a residence of canvas for himself and his students in the Arizona desert when he wanted to enclose a maximum amount of space for the minimum amount of dollars. The result, characteristically, was architecture of the highest order—a veritable "pleasure dome" of Kubla Khan.)

Usually, the client has a general idea of what he would like in the way of all three—size, quality and budget—so the preliminary discussions serve to reveal to the architect what flexibility he has within each of these categories, and to help the client understand what his other limits are, while maintaining the fixed point of budget, size, or quality he has in mind.

Size

Size is a critical factor in designing for the elderly. Many elderly want to escape from the burden of houses that have become too big. But their problems of operation are just as acute if the house, apartment, or trailer is too cramped. Effective size is not necessarily determined precisely by the number of square feet included. A compact unit which is carefully designed may yield more convenience and livability than one 10 to 20 per cent larger which is poorly planned. This again points up the fact that one design of a given size and cost may be a poor buy in terms of livability even though the unit sizes and unit costs look to be normal, while another design of no greater size and no greater cost may yield immeasurably more convenience and pleasure because it was conceived with greater skill and talent.

Quality

Quality is a term which should be used to cover degree of mechanization as well as costliness of building materials chosen. It is obvious that the cost of the individual house or apartment is increased, without changing its size, if teakwood parquetry floor is used in place of floors of oak or plain asbestos tile. Also it is obvious that adding mechanical refinements such as garbage grinders, dishwashers, electronic air filters, and motorized garage doors increases the unit cost rapidly without adding a single square foot of space. Sometimes including this kind of equipment actually reduces the living space, and one must weigh

its real value in livability against its cost in dollars and space.

Another kind of quality, which can vary greatly without altering the cost in any way, is the quality of architectural design. Quality of design relates directly to the kind of thinking and the talents brought to bear on the project rather than to the amount of money spent. Many a project of shockingly poor design has cost as much, or more, per resident than outstandingly good ones. Oftentimes, the poorly designed project is explained on the basis of its being "practical," to which we can say with Lord Dunsany, "The practical is always the short sighted," for too often the term "practical" is used to justify uninspired, routine, and even dismal lack of design quality, to become in effect the cloak for expediency in thinking. Quality design is not an extra cost. Upon occasion, it may even prove an economy. However, it should never be peddled or hired on the basis of economy, but rather on the basis that hiring the most capable and inspired architect will produce for a given dollar the greatest increase in livability for the user of the building, the resident for whom the design is conceived, promoted, and built.

Determining unit costs

What is meant by cost per square foot or cost per cubic foot? These are terms not generally understood by the public. They are not absolutes. They are, in fact, highly qualified indices. It is extremely important to understand what is included in these unit cost figures when they are used. In the project examples which are shown in the tables of Section VI, you will find both total and unit cost figures quoted for many of the projects. The authors have endeavored to indicate what they include and what they do not include in each case (usually all construction costs and fees but not land and furnishings) and to indicate the year in which the figures were established.

There are standard methods of arriving at total square-foot and cubic-foot figures, but in calculating all but the simplest cubical buildings, individual interpretation of the standards becomes necessary, and

this affects the totals, particularly in a complex building or group of buildings. For instance, how can we equitably make an accounting of retaining walls and screen walls for patios, service courts, etc., in a square-foot take-off? Or for that matter, what is the precise square-foot or cubic-foot rating of various kinds of roof overhangs in such a take-off? These are all real items of cost in the total, but what is their precise reflection in the square-foot and cubic-foot calculations which determine the final calculation of unit costs? (See also Item 7 below.)

Detailed factors bearing on cost

Many factors which have little or nothing to do with the architectural design affect the total cost of a project in varying degrees. Some of them are:

1. *Area of country in which construction takes place* (these variations are not uniform nor are they mutually compensating):

a. Labor costs vary markedly from one area to another.

b. Material costs vary markedly from one area to another.

c. Construction practices vary markedly from one area to another.

2. *Climate of area:*

a. Number of working days available per year varies according to weather.

b. Degree of weather protection and amount of temporary heat needed during construction.

c. Amount of insulation, double glazing, etc., needed in design due to climate.

d. Degree of mechanical elaboration needed in design due to climate.

3. *Size of project:*

a. An individual residence will cost appreciably more than if it is one of a group of 20 or 30 built at one time even if these are not repetitive in design.

b. A tract operation of 100 or more houses of four to six basic designs will produce even lower unit costs.

c. Proximate and congregate residences go down in unit cost as the number of units is increased because the shared facilities for service, recreation, and care do not increase proportionately.

d. Designing for future expansion, particularly in congregate housing, can put a special cost burden on the original residence units, because certain parts of the work are not expandable, so work must be done in the first stage on a scale to accommodate the completed project. The following items are of such a nature:

- Land cost
- Site development:
  Grading
  Landscaping
  Utilities, taps, and entrances
  Wells and sanitary systems
- Public spaces:
  Lobbies
  Meeting rooms
  Dining rooms
- Service facilities:
  Kitchen and auxiliary areas
  Elevators
  Receiving
  Mechanical rooms and some mechanical equipment

e. Careful designing can minimize the cost imbalance of some of these items but they cannot be completely circumvented. The author's Lutheran Senior City was originally designed for 150 residents to be expanded later to 265. A cost analysis showed a difference in estimated construction cost of $8,400 per unit for the first stage as against an estimate of $7580 if the entire project were constructed at once. This difference in cost per unit made a significant difference in the operating cost balance sheet.

4. *Site:*

a. A flat site is generally more economical to build on than a sloping or hilly one.

b. Ease of access to site determined by location or terrain can affect cost.

c. Location determines some important cost factors such as need for private water supply, private sewage disposal, and type of available fuel. In many cases where natural gas is a common fuel, a site remote from the supply may mean that the operation costs will be higher if another fuel is used, as well as the fact that the heating and cooling system will be more expensive.

d. Size of site: If the area is constricted or confined to the size of the building itself, as on a lot in the central city, costs may be higher than if the contractor has space for stockpiling materials on the site and for maneuvering without regard to public traffic.

5. *Codes and regulations:*

a. Code requirements may affect cost of construction noticeably. Codes vary from state to state, city to city, and even among municipalities within a metropolitan area. Sometimes crossing a boundary from one suburb to another or from city to county can change drastically the type of construction required. This may be due to one code's being much older than another; to a desire in certain suburbs to force quality construction; or to a reluctance to accept new construction practices.

b. Other regulatory agencies affect construction costs too. If a congregate home must meet nursing-home standards throughout, the cost is automatically upped. Nursing-home standards vary greatly from state to state, and even if only the infirmary section of a congregate home must meet nursing-home standards (which seems a logical approach), a variation in requirements will be noticeable from one locality to another.

c. Lending institutions may have their own standards of construction which must be met if they are to accept a mortgage, and these standards may or may not be realistic in terms of modern construction.

d. Fire-insurance ratings can affect operating costs appreciably, and it may be that some extra expenditure on construction can reduce the cost of insurance on a long-term basis.

e. FHA has construction requirements affecting cost of construction.

6. *Construction team:*

a. A sophisticated builder can overcome some of the limitations placed on the project because of factors listed above by organizing his work, scheduling deliveries, programming sub-contractor activities, and using modern mechanization of job operation. If by skillful scheduling, programming, and utilizing mechanical equipment to speed operations, a contractor can save one month of construction time on a sizeable project, the savings in construction loan interest alone may offset some of the other costs.

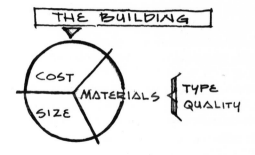

7. *Architectural design:*

a. Design decisions can also affect the unit costs per square foot and per cubic foot. For instance, suppose we raise all the ceilings in a project one foot. We are increasing the cubic-content figure for our building by about 10 per cent. But the added foot may increase the total cost by 3 to 5 per cent. This actually reduces the calculated cost per cubic foot. But we have not changed the square-foot area of the building. So while our cubic foot cost goes down, our cost per square foot increases.

b. A project with a number of large open spaces, such as social halls, a gymnasium, a large dining room, an auditorium or chapel, will show more favorable unit costs than a project which consists primarily of living units with small room sizes and a proportionately higher number of kitchens and baths. On the other hand, a one-story project requiring a fairly low degree of fireproofing may show more favorable unit costs than a fully fireproof project of two or more stories, even though two-story residential construction is usually more economical than one-story. High-rise building costs are expensive at the start and go down as the building increases in height until the optimum is reached when the cost of elevators is balanced out against the number of units. But above a certain height—10 to 15 stories—the construction costs rise markedly, canceling out the advantages of increased height.

Each of the above factors should be carefully analyzed for any proposed project, and a well-informed architect can give great assistance in determining their relative significance to a client's undertaking.

The cost of land for any kind of project is an important factor to consider. If the operating budget of a congregate project will carry the load, it may be advisable to pay a high price for a site, providing it adds greatly to the appeal and desirability of the whole project because of its character or location (see also Chap. 4).

In fact, economy may be wisdom—and usually is—but economy as the sole criterion in any decision may jeopardize the final result. It may prove that a little judicious spending would have gained much for a project in livability, atmosphere, and convenience. It has been said that since the world is daily getting more crowded, and since in this country, at least, the services and conveniences which used to be associated with a life of luxury are the everyday norm for a larger and larger number of people, perhaps the ultimate luxury is space, and to be extravagant with space is the only real extravagance left us. Perhaps what might seem to be a short-term extravagance will make needed expansion feasible in the long run.

CHAPTER 6

FIRST STEPS

The sponsor of the congregate or proximate home for the elderly faces a number of important decisions in organizing to build:

1. Is incorporation desirable?
2. What criteria should govern selection of the building committee?
3. What endorsements of the effort are advisable?
4. How can the sponsor be sure that the type of home envisioned will meet the real needs of the people to be served?
5. What should be the guiding factors in the choice of an architect?
6. Who should approve the site?
7. How will the project be financed?
8. How soon should an administrator be sought?
9. Is it important to budget for professional services for decoration and landscaping?
10. Who will be responsible for the operation of the home after it is built?

The following suggestions on these crucial questions are offered from the experience of sponsors and architects of such homes.

Incorporation

Separate incorporation is a requisite for FHA insured loans. It is desirable also for other methods of financing because it absolves individuals from personal financial liability and fixes responsibility in the corporation. It also establishes a basis for taxation. Of course, the services of an attorney are required.

The building committee

Before selecting this important committee, define the scope of their responsibilities and prerogatives. The building committee should be a small dedicated group. A membership of more than five will prove unwieldy. Members will need to meet often and for many months, so it is most important that the group represent a broad spectrum in point of view. Every member should be a person with business, organization, or community social experience. Persons filled with sympathy for the cause and with all good intentions but without experience in making sound judgments and serious business decisions can be a hindrance or a cipher on such a committee. This is a business undertaking to be executed with all the imagination and good sense required to make an outstanding success of any enterprise.

Endorsements

It is important to secure the backing of the responsible boards of the sponsoring organization. For a Protestant church, this would mean the Board of Trustees or Board of Management of the local church, the city board of the denomination, and the state or regional board of the denomination. Although such boards will not be expected to assume financial responsibility, their endorsement of the venture will be of value to the local group in securing a loan. Their help will be needed also for fund raising and for obtaining wide publicity.

Survey

It is desirable to make, or have a qualified professional organization make for you, a market survey to determine what is needed, for example, what type accommodations potential residents will want and what they can afford to pay. Circulating a questionnaire to determine possible residents in the fifty-plus age bracket might be a first sounding board. Sociology departments of universities are frequently equipped to conduct surveys or to advise a group on how to conduct one. The publication, "How to Make and Use Local Housing Market Surveys," presents a technique with which local groups can conduct sample housing surveys. It can easily be adapted to provide information on housing for older people. This pamphlet was prepared by the Bureau of Business and Social Research, University of Denver (Fitzhugh L. Carmichael, Director) for the Housing and Home Finance Agency, Division of Housing Research. It may be procured from the U. S. Government Printing Office, Washington, D. C. (Catalog No. HH 1.2: H81/23; cost, 55¢).

A survey should tell you:

1. Area studied and to be served
2. Total population over 65 in area
3. Range of incomes represented
4. Number of people in each income bracket
5. Ages represented in each bracket
6. Existing facilities: location, date built, type, size, rental or purchase price of each
7. Number of people in each bracket still needing special accommodations
8. New facilities, what will be needed and popular: kind, size, location, ages to be served, reasonable charges.

However, such a survey is only as good as the people making it and the people analyzing it. It needs to be studied with profound thoughtfulness. The persons interviewed may not have the proper concept of the proposed facility and its advantages. The survey might seem to reveal nursing care as the greatest need, for example, whereas it might be only the most apparent need. Very careful training of the interviewers is essential.

Selecting the architect

This is perhaps the most important of all steps. The best architect available will be the best buy (see Chap. 3). Housing for the elderly is a relatively new field of building, and of course many mistakes are being made. Basically the architect should understand and be sympathetic to older people and their problems; he should be able to project their needs five and ten years hence and plan accordingly. One firm of architects in the Northwest, desirous of building their first project in this field, sent all five members of the firm to visit different congregate homes for the elderly in a large area of the West Coast. They interviewed the architects who had designed the homes, the administrators who operated them, and even the residents who lived there. They amassed a lot of valuable information as to what was and what was not satisfactory, and why, and proceeded accordingly, with noteworthy results.

If no one in your community has built in this field, it would be money well spent to secure a consultant architect who has had such experience to work with your local architect. You may save yourselves expensive or irreparable mistakes.

Once you have selected your architect, come to agreement with him as to what decisions will be his responsibility and what the committee's. It is important to have this clearly understood and accepted. It is also important to establish the lines of communication between his organization and the committee, and the two organizations should appoint a contact person to handle dealings when they are not meeting together.

A clear definition of the architect's fees, duties, responsibilities and extent of services is essential. This becomes important, for example, in the promotion stage when the architect's talents and materials can be very helpful. But services in this area are beyond the usual scope of his duties and should be paid for separately.

Choice of a site

If you find a site which meets the approval of the committee, take an option but do not close the deal until you have selected your architect and he has approved it (see Chap. 4). If you are going to seek an FHA insured loan, the site must also be acceptable to the FHA local official and possibly to the lending agency, so proceed slowly.

The desirability of room for expansion is stressed by many who have undertaken to build for older people. With the increased interest in the new aspects of retirement living, additional accommodations are often needed within a relatively short time. There is a growing group of "younger oldster" couples who want housekeeping cottages on the site of a congregate home. They want to use the various facilities available at the home and be prepared against the day when one of them will be left alone.

Financing the project

Discuss alternate methods of financing with the appropriate boards of your organization and get their views (see Chap. 9). They will be more cooperative in helping you meet possible financial problems if they have been consulted in the planning stage. Consult people with experience in the field. Talk with proper authorities on Federal, state and local taxes to get qualified advice on long term aspects of each method of financing proposed. In making your decisions on financing, have present a Certified Public Accountant or an attorney familiar with problems of financing, taxes, and nonprofit requirements and advantages.

When to get an administrator

When you have selected the building committee, start looking for an administrator. Have him sit in on all meetings of the committee as soon as he has been selected. He should know what thinking has gone into the different decisions throughout the planning of the home, and this detailed knowledge cannot be acquired by even the most careful reading of the minutes. Moreover, by having him become a part of your group at an early stage, the enthusiasm of your committee will be an inspiration to him in the execution of his duties.

As with the architect, there must be a clear understanding as to what types of decisions will be his alone and on what types he will only advise. If he is to work with the architect, the line of communication must be made clear.

Consultant services for interior decoration and landscaping

Just as it is important that the committee secure the best possible architectural services for design of the building, so is it desirable that they consider employing professionals for interior decoration and landscape architecture. The architect can create opportunities for interesting living through purposeful design, and the administrator can effect a warm, friendly and happy home atmosphere through his talents and dedication. But these advantages may both be unapparent to the prospective applicant if the interior furnishings and decorating, and also the landscaping, are haphazard and in poor taste. The amateurish additions of inappropriate pictures, pottery, plants, furniture, garden furniture, sculpture and accessories can downgrade a fine building and reveal instantly to the discriminating visitor, prospect, or resident the shortcomings of the management. Usually, those most sure of their own good taste are the most willing to employ professional supervision. Even if the building is not all that could be wished, often the skilled decorator can mitigate shortcomings in many artful ways not apparent to the amateur. This is not an area for expediency, and the advice of the professional is just as important as if the problem were legal, financial, or medical. Money spent for professional services is more than justified and time will prove it an economy. They will, of course, work with or even for the architect.

Operation and maintenance of the home

The Board of Trustees, set up under the Corporation, will become the official administrative body (see Chap. 18). All policy decisions will come from them. Desirable committees to be appointed will include Finance (and Investment), Promotion, and Admissions. Design must be considered as a prime element of promotion.

Building facilities should be planned in relation to services and facilities in the community (see Chap. 15). If certain services which are properly the responsibility of the community do not currently exist, try to start a concurrent promotion of such services, preferably through some external interested organization or committee.

Operation of the home will be entrusted to the administrator, whose jurisdiction will be carefully spelled out to align with the over-all philosophy and policy adopted by the Board.

CHAPTER 7

THE ARCHITECT

Conceiving, designing, and constructing a building requires the attention, effort, and cooperation of a great many people: laborers, craftsmen, technicians, government officials, consultants, engineers, manufacturers, bankers, and many more. This operation calls for complex teamwork from a production team whose individual roles must be clear, whose areas of responsibility are understood, and whose chain of command is precisely established and observed. Producing a building is too costly an investment to allow hazy, poorly defined procedures.

A skeleton diagram of the team would probably look like the one in the table. The chain of command is unmistakable. The dotted lines indicate lines of communication for transfer of information only — never orders. Other people or lines of communications may be added to the chart as needed but should not disrupt the chain of command.

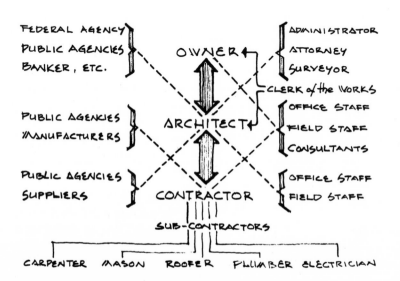

CHAIN OF COMMAND

If there is a clerk of the works, he is an employee of the owner, responsible for job records and accounting. Although he works under the architect's direction, he does not replace, supersede, or circumvent the architect's field staff in the supervision of the construction activities, and his function has nothing to do with construction or materials quality. These are contractual responsibilities of the architect, and for someone else to assume them would be an abridgment of his contract.

The architect of a building is inevitably the most important member of the building team. His insight, inspiration, skill, sensitiveness, and grasp of the problem — or lack of these faculties — is stamped upon every square inch of the product to a degree far surpassing that of any of the other participants. Every member of the team leaves his imprint on the product in some measure, of course, but ultimately all their thinking is channeled through the head, heart, eyes, and pencil of the architect. If the product has shortcomings, he may try in various ways to explain them. He may mollify his conscience by claiming that another member of the team insisted on this concept or that detail, but the responsibility for the quality of the spirit of the project is finally his alone. A good architect would not have it otherwise.

Furthermore, no other member of the team is so well equipped as the architect by background, education, experience, or talent to coordinate and supervise the fabrication of the product once it has been conceived, designed, and committed to working drawings and specifications. Like the score for a symphony, drawings and specifications tell pretty much what is to be done, but the full extent of the vision cannot be put on paper. Choice of the exact brick, roof material, or shade of paint can make or ruin a design. The architect knows his design more intimately than anyone else, and only he can keep all the myriad performers in his orchestra playing in proper relationship to each other. Hence his spot on the team as conductor. On the other hand, the architect deals with subcontractors and individual workmen only through the contractor or his agent.

To use another analogy, the architect acts as the author and director of the show whereas the owner is its angel and producer. The producer may know a great deal about the show but not as much as the author-director, and he doesn't order the actors around. Their relationship is an intimate, mutually responsible one, but the roles are not interchangeable.

This is the reason it is critical for an owner about to build—whether a committee or an individual—to select an architect with the utmost care. The final building results will be determined more by this decision than by any other the owner will make. He should make this selection as soon as possible, moreover, so that the architect may participate in the formulation of the idea from the very beginning. The good architect is highly sensitive to the various aspects of a building problem—the purpose, the people, the physical environment, the budget—and his responses will illuminate rather than hinder a client's progress toward critical decisions.

What does an architect do for his fee? Most people assume they already know; but most people have only a general notion of what the architect does and how he does it. The uninformed will say that he draws blueprints. The informed will say he designs buildings. This can mean to the one that he is a kind of exterior decorator and to the other that he is a mere manipulator of space. The architect, on the other hand, will tell you that he performs a service, a claim which may sound a little vague and perhaps superfluous to someone who wants a new building.

All who have some grasp of the architect's service agree that he must be a good businessman, must keep records and accounts, perform on a schedule, be ethical, deal smoothly with people, and have a sufficient grasp of his craft to know costs, materials, techniques, basic engineering, and the like. He must also be able to create a product that is functional, livable, handsome, individual, and even unique but that is still practical to maintain and operate and costs a specified amount of dollars per square foot (on the nose). They agree that his product should have aesthetic as well as practical attributes. Therefore, although they may feel inarticulate or be shy about discussing such matters, they tend to agree that he should have artistic talent, that he is, in effect, an artistic businessman, a practical operator with an aesthetic sense. This makes him a little suspect to many. Some are suspicious that he is too artistic to be practical, whereas others may fear he is too practical to be aesthetically creative.

There can be no quarrel with the concept that to the degree an architect is not an artist, to that degree he is not an architect. In his book, *The Artist in the Modern World*, Jules Langsner says, "The artist's primary purpose is the intensification of experience..." This is a formidable and accurate statement of the purpose of the genuine architect in creating buildings. It is also the assumed objective (if not always consciously identified) of the architect's client. Every client expects in a new building a new environment created to intensify some experience, and he wants it for a fixed price. Most architects are willing to try.

A list of the architect's specific functions and procedures required to accomplish this end includes the following:

1. Client conferences
2. Client contracts and relationships
3. Design
4. Engineering
5. Selecting engineering consultants, interior design consultants, landscape consultants, and the like
6. Consultant contracts
7. Schematic drawings
8. Preliminary drawings
9. Working drawings
10. Specification writing
11. Job meetings (with staff and technical consultants)
12. Printing and reproduction
13. Cost estimating and control
14. Approval of shop drawings
15. Selection and scheduling of materials and colors
16. Materials design

17. Material samples cataloging and storage
18. Utility, sewer, water, highway contacts
19. Zoning checks
20. Building code checks
21. Health code checks
22. Local, state and national government building regulations checks
23. City ordinance considerations
24. Finance agency contacts
25. Bid taking and bid analysis
26. Tax and legal considerations
27. Contractor liaison
28. Construction supervision

To operate his office the architect also must attend to a multitude of activities all the way from accounting to the maintenance of a technical library. All these activities are directly or indirectly of interest to the client and the competence with which they are performed will affect, in a degree, the kind of service a client receives from his architect. But the fact still remains that the architect's unique commodity is his talent, without which he may perform all or most of the above activities with great competence and still deliver to his client a mediocre product. This talent is unique to the individual, and its quality is contingent on his particular mix of experience, sensitivity, discipline, and vision.

The architect's product is buildings, and if he is fortunate, gifted, organized within himself, and in command of his talent, his product is architecture. According to architectural writer Eldon L. Modisette, the function of architecture is not merely to reflect social conditions but also to transform them. In his words, "This is possible because architecture emerges from the imagination, desires, and dreams of man as well as out of the more mundane social and economic world. The architect, then, not only receives directives from his society, he gives directives also. Thus, architecture becomes a way of shaping the future."

The client understands of course that constructing a new building is, for better or worse, a sharp delimiting of the future of people he may never see. Every wall that is built becomes a divider, a separator. It can also become an enclosure, protector, a shield, a sanctuary, an aesthetic presence. The client must encourage his architect to make every wall perform the greatest good for all whose future it limits.

What must the client do for the architect? A look at Chap. 2, "Who Should Build," will be useful in this connection. The client must play his own role well. He must provide the architect information and data on a number of subjects and pay the cost for doing so. Among the things the client must provide for his architect are the following:

1. Decision-making: Clear directives as to who will make decisions for the owner, especially if the owner is a committee or board. Also, prompt decisions every time these are necessary to the architect's work, both before and after construction begins.

2. Budget: The owner should work out with the architect a clearly defined budget for buildings, site improvements, furnishings, and equipment.

3. Site data: The owner must provide the topographic survey, location of utilities, layout of streets and alleys, access, test borings, percolation tests, a record of trees to be saved, easements, setbacks, restrictions, existing improvements, or presence of remains of past improvements (wells, tanks, foundations).

4. Building program (see Chap. 8).

5. Choice of consultants: The architect should choose the consultants he is to work with or have full approval of the choice.

6. Schedule of work: It is unwise to leave the matter of schedules vague. It is equally unwise to demand a crash performance from the architect, especially during the preliminary design period when a search for the basic concept is being made. If the time schedule is too tight, there is something wrong with the schedule.

7. Pay: The architect's reimbursement may be made in several ways. The percentage of construction cost is not the only means of establishing the fee, nor is 6 per cent the only or necessarily correct fee. The architect may negotiate a fixed fee for the work, or he may work on a direct cost plus 125 to 200 per cent basis, the rate being determined by the nature of the job, the organization of the architect's office, and the price scale of the area for salaries, rent, and other overhead. Or the architect may perform on an hourly or per diem basis during preliminary consultation when a project is in the formative stage before a formal contract is indicated. Prompt payment of the architect's invoices for service, or his certificate of payment to contractors, is a good index of the owner's confidence in and appreciation of the architect's value.

Many of these items will be spelled out in the architect-owner contract and should be fully discussed before services are rendered.

The client should choose his architect on the basis of past performance (not necessarily in the field of design for the elderly), and, as previously mentioned, he should choose him as early in the discussion of the project as possible. If too many factors are nailed down before the architect is engaged—site, program, time table, budget, standards—they will act as a positive discouragement to good architecture, which is the essential thing the client hopes to buy from the architect.

Architects cannot ethically bid for jobs by shaving down fees. The owner who plans to choose his architect exclusively on the basis of the size of the fee may be doing himself out of needed service. For the same fee and the same budget, one architect may build a better or a more commodious building than another. For a higher fee one architect may build a more economical building than another. It costs an architect extra time in study and research to bring down the cost of a building, but as Charles Colbert, Dean of the School of Architecture at Columbia University, says, "Architects are told to cut costs, but they aren't paid to cut costs."

The American Institute of Architects and the National Council on School House Construction have prepared a formula for choosing an architect, which is given here in a form adapted to use for a home for the elderly:

A. *Information to be given the architect:*

1. Name of sponsor

2. Name of person to whom questionnaire should be returned

3. Size of project

4. General description of proposed projects

5. Approximate time table for planning and construction period

B. *Architect's questionnaire:*

1. Name

2. Business address

3. Telephone number

4. Type of organization, whether individual, a partnership, or a corporation

5. Names of principals, professional history, professional affiliation, key personnel, staff organization.

6. A list of completed buildings the architect's firm has designed during recent years. If he has recently established his own practice, he should indicate prior responsible affiliation with other projects, underlining those projects which he feels are examples appropriate to the sponsor's problem and which he would like to have visited. The cost of each building, the type of building, its location, and dates of construction should be included on a separate sheet.

7. Names of persons to whom the committee may write. These persons should have knowledge of the architect's firm and his work.

8. Attachment of any other material which might help the committee. In questions 7 and 8, the board (or committee) is interested in finding out about the architect's integrity, thoroughness, creativeness, adequacy of supervision, business procedures and record keeping on the job, and financial responsibility.

9. If the architect is called in for an interview, he should be asked to furnish information indicating that:

a. his organization is adequate to do the job

b. previous commitments will not prevent expeditious planning of the project

c. he is willing to devote time to planning with designated members of committees, staff, or board

d. contract documents (plans and specifications) are prepared in the proper state of completeness.

This questionnaire will help a committee to do an orderly job of gathering data on architects. If interviews are held, they should not be scheduled too close together, and the interviewees should be treated as the professional men they are. Inspecting an architect's previous work is useless unless the committee makes a genuine effort to evaluate it in terms of the particular problem the architect had to solve in each project and to evaluate the beauty and excellence with which he did so.

Ultimately, the committee needs to make the choice on the basis of the quality of an architect's past work and on the committee's individual feeling as to which architect will bring the greatest insight, talent, and concern to the project in question. August Heckscher, President Kennedy's special consultant on the arts, says that in life ". . . the enjoyment of beauty and excellence is as much a part of the pursuit of happiness as material abundance," a happiness, he says, "which nothing else in our national life, not abundance of gadgets nor free time, has been able to fulfill."

CHAPTER 8

WRITING THE ARCHITECTURAL PROGRAM

We need to take a very hard look at ideas and at the words with which they are expressed
Harold Taylor, Philosopher

It is useful in any design project to put down on paper a list of objectives the design is to aspire to and a list of the requirements it is to meet. These lists are important, no matter how simply they may be prepared. The requirements cover such concrete matters as size, cost, quality and compliance with codes. The objectives are the human values such as convenience, beauty, atmosphere, and architectural merit. They constitute the reality of the project and of course are never 100 per cent attainable. But they are the dividends on the investment, and the percentage of them attained determines whether or not the investment in the project has been worthwhile.

These two lists should be made by the owner of the project whether an individual for his own residence, the owner/builder of a speculative project, or the committee for an organization-sponsored undertaking. In each case, the architect should assist in making, or should edit in detail, and finally should agree to the list proposed by the owner and verify its feasibility and completeness.

The architectural program should then be written from these lists and should cover the three factors of size, quality, and budget as discussed in Chap. 5. It should cover, in as much detail as seems necessary, such things as land use, accommodations required, activities to be provided for, staff to be housed, and services to be performed. For each category, the architect will, by asking pertinent questions and making suggestions, assist in developing balance and completeness in the program, whether the program can be stated on one page or takes a dozen or more.

The first step is for the owner (individual or committee) to "come to terms with the problem." This means to arrive at a list of terms, which may be only single words or statements, that state as clearly as possible the owner's dream for the completed project. The terms we wish to identify, the words we wish to characterize the undertaking with, are the objectives we aspire to. The author has found this process of particular value for building committees. Each member of the committee is asked to "come to terms with the project" individually beforehand, and then in committee meeting they arrive at a composite set of terms. Together they agree upon a joint statement of objectives, a joint description of the vision toward which all will work. This is done before any decision is established about such things as square-foot areas, unit costs, kinds of building materials, or types of kitchen equipment.

At this stage the committee is putting down on paper their feelings about the project. If a committee cannot achieve a minimum commonality of feeling at the outset, they will have no unified position from which to make detailed decisions as they go along. A close look at the process of making a decision about any concrete detail whatsoever will reveal that such a decision is made on the basis of the result we *feel* it will establish. No matter how rationally arrived at or how logically supported afterward, the moment of decision is an emotional exercise, and the decision is more often defended on the basis of that emotion than any other. The average person has seldom given much thought to this process in spite of the fact he uses it daily and hourly. Poets, artists, and architects, on the other hand, are very conscious of the procedure and train their sensibility to operate clearly and effectively in this way. Conscious use of the process by the average person may be illuminating and rewarding.

Once the committee has come to terms with the problem, it will be important to return to this statement of objectives periodically and, if necessary, to revise it as the design emerges and the concrete image takes form so as to avoid conflicts and frustrations later.

It is during this first active stage that those contemplating building for elderly persons need to be certain that they have an understanding of this specialized problem in the light of the best thinking available. Their own observations and pondering on the meaning of aging will be their ultimate criteria for judgment. They therefore dare not be superficial, but should acquire depth by reading the literature available, by careful observation of the elderly, by interviewing them, and by discussion of the phenomenon with people who have more than opinions to offer. It is only thus that they can avoid the "wasteful practice of trying to solve a problem without knowing what the problem is."

Among the human values to ponder in relation to the individual resident are:

1. Security
2. Variety
3. Individuality
4. Independence
5. Privacy
6. Self respect
7. Mastery of environment
8. Respect for environment
9. Adventure
10. Need to combat loneliness, feebleness, lack of motivation
11. Need to feel a part of a community and according to Lewis Mumford, "even the need to withdraw from it upon occasion."

The person involved in building for the elderly, whether for himself or for others, should make his own list. He will add to the above and then edit it to a firm statement of his own view of the problem. Finally, he should assess such terms as these in depth to determine their meaning and importance to the residents of the building and therefore their significance to the concept of the building.

If the meaning of such terms is understood, they can have a profound effect on the functional and aesthetic character of the building design. This un-

derstanding will permeate every specific decision made. For this reason, we consider the analysis of the problem to be Step No. 1. Step No. 2 may be more voluminous, but by no means more important.

Step No. 2 is making a list of the requirements the building is to meet. This list consists of the concrete facts the owner has decided upon about the project. It might simply state how many people the building is to accommodate and how much money is to be spent. The list may, however, be much longer and more complete.

When the program for a large-group residential project is written from these two lists, it may amount to a detailed description of many aspects of the undertaking. It will include something on all the topics discussed in the remaining chapters of this book: Land, accommodations, activities, services, care, staff, budget, administration, and construction.

There are two important things to remember in this process:

1. The owner must not make decisions on matters about which he is not informed or not qualified to judge.

2. The owner is not writing a building materials specification but a set of requirements the building is to meet.

These two warnings overlap. Owners frequently get excited by the advertising for some new wonder material or piece of equipment fresh on the market. The architect is less sanguine about such Johnny-come-latelies. Every year a new and promising crop bursts upon the waiting world of construction. Of the 100 or so in each new crop, all but three have vanished in five years, not having stood the test of time, the only valid test for building materials. In the same way, an owner seldom knows the full range of building materials and equipment available for a specific use and so he operates from a limited knowledge.

The owner therefore should decide what he wants to accomplish for the resident and let the architect decide how the building can best aid this end. In actual practice these are mutual decisions, but a clear understanding of the areas of decision is critical to an efficient, fruitful and happy client-architect relationship.

We present here an "areas of decision" diagram prepared by Tibbals-Crumley-Musson, the author's firm, for the INCO Corporation while developing their long-range master plan. It blocks out for a specific project what the client needed from the architect and what the architect needed from the client, and how their thinking mingled in the product.

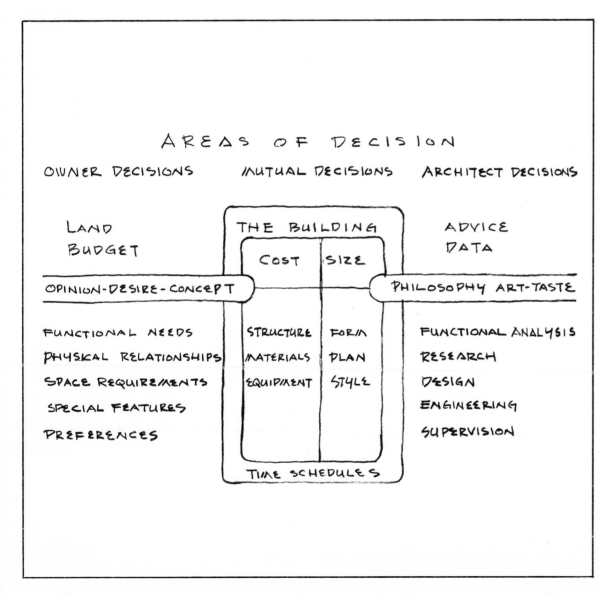

A R E A S   O F   D E C I S I O N

OWNER DECISIONS   MUTUAL DECISIONS   ARCHITECT DECISIONS

LAND   THE BUILDING   ADVICE
BUDGET   COST   SIZE   DATA

OPINION-DESIRE-CONCEPT   PHILOSOPHY ART-TASTE

FUNCTIONAL NEEDS   STRUCTURE   FORM   FUNCTIONAL ANALYSIS
PHYSICAL RELATIONSHIPS   MATERIALS   PLAN   RESEARCH
SPACE REQUIREMENTS   EQUIPMENT   STYLE   DESIGN
SPECIAL FEATURES   ENGINEERING
PREFERENCES   SUPERVISION

TIME SCHEDULES

CHAPTER 9

FINANCING

The recent nationwide upsurge of interest in providing "new look" homes of all kinds for our older citizens has received its chief impetus from the incentive programs for financing offered by the Federal government and certain state governments. Such homes can still be financed with less red tape by conventional loans, however, and sometimes with terms as advantageous. The Federal Housing Administration will also insure loans under a number of programs, each meeting special circumstances. A direct loan is available through the Housing and Home Finance Agency to assist in building rental housing for lower middle income elderly people by partial local tax exemption, low interest rate, and long amortization period loans. Federally subsidized public housing now provides special housing for the elderly of very low income.

We shall discuss (1) conventional loans, (2) loans made with the cooperation of the Federal Housing Administration, (3) the direct loan program of the Federal government, (4) an example of a state aid program, and (5) the Federally subsidized public housing program, including recent changes effected.

Conventional loans

Conventional mortgage loans are made by lending institutions — banks, building and loan associations, insurance companies, trust funds, pension funds, etc.— on the security of property. All the risk is assumed by the lender, and in case of the borrower's inability to meet his obligated payments, the lender must recover the amount owed to him by forcing the sale of the property. Lending institutions are regulated by law as to interest rates. Banks, through FDIC, and savings and loans, through FSLIC, are subject to Federal regulations.* Institutional practices

*FDIC: Federal Deposit Insurance Corporation; FSLIC: Federal Savings and Loan Corporation.

vary greatly and should be checked with the individual bank or lending agency. However, the 1961 Amendments to the United States Housing Act give Federal building and loan associations considerably more leeway in financing homes for the elderly. Such loans may be made in amounts up to 90 per cent of the appraised value of the secured property and run for 30 years. They would be less costly than if financed through the Federal Housing Administration programs. Lenders are generally beginning to realize that the equity is in the building, not the borrower, and are establishing more enlightened lending policies.

If an individual wishes to obtain a conventional loan on a residence for an elderly person, himself or someone else, he should follow the normal procedure used in purchasing a home. He should make the desired down payment and get a loan for the balance from his bank or other lending agency. This would be repaid, both interest and principal, by agreed upon monthly payments.

The same procedure would obtain for a nonprofit group, such as a church, a union, or a fraternal order, undertaking to build a simple housekeeping project, a full-care retirement home, or a combination of several kinds of housing arrangements. To minimize the size of the loan needed as well as to repay the loan, the sponsor might set up a nonprofit corporation to establish tax exemption and solicit contributions to a building fund. Or it might issue bonds and sell them to future residents of the project, to members of the sponsoring organization, to trust or pension funds, or even to the public.

Another method of financing currently in vogue is to accept down payments, or founders' gifts, or entrance fees, from incoming tenants of the project. Such down payments pay for life occupancy of an agreed type of dwelling unit. The amount of such charge varies with the individual home and also within it. Some homes have units whose life occupancy fee is set as low as $500, $1,000, or $2,000; others may run as high as $35,000. Such a method anticipates a continuous source of income as units are re-

sold following the death of tenants. Some projects will also accept interest-bearing deferred-occupancy down payments from younger people who wish to subscribe to future residency. (Mrs. X, at 60, prefers to maintain independent residence now, but would like to assure herself of a unit in the home at say 70 or 75. She therefore pays the life occupancy down payment fee in advance for the type of accommodation she prefers. Management will pay interest on her money until she actually enters the home.) This policy provides management with additional funds.

It is necessary to check different state rulings on the matter of property tax exemption for nonprofit projects. It is also important to check with the regional office of the Internal Revenue Service upon specific requirements for income tax exemption on founders' fees, life occupancy fees, or whatever the name entrance payments are called. Basically the requirement is that the nonprofit motive of the sponsor be established and that a certain amount of charitable work be done by the home.

In addition to founder's fee, the resident in proximate housing or congregate housing is generally obligated to pay a monthly maintenance fee. In proximate housing this may be the rental for the dwelling unit and may include utilities and use of such communal facilities as the project offers. In the congregate home it may include meals, maid service, laundry, and minimum, limited, or complete health service.

Occasionally a full-care residence may offer the incoming resident the option of paying the monthly maintenance fee in a lump sum in advance for life. Life expectancy would be actuarially figured. This method provides management with more working capital.

Loans made with FHA cooperation

The FHA does not lend money or build houses. It insures mortgage loans of private capital by private lending institutions on housing projects constructed by private builders. The projects developed under FHA programs are in no sense government projects

or government-sponsored projects. They are merely government insured. The Government, through the Federal Housing Administration, insures the lender against loss due to foreclosure. The purpose is to encourage the lender to take a risk he might not otherwise feel justified. It is financed by a premium (½ per cent per year) paid by the borrower in addition to interest. Some programs may waive the premium, in which cases the Government assumes the risk. Since its inception, the Federal Housing Administration program has been fiscally sound.

There may be an added cost on FHA loans. The private lender may demand discount to compensate for the low fixed interest rate, currently about 3 per cent on 5¼ per cent thirty-year loans. This discount increases the effective rate from 5¼ to 5.52 per cent.

Among its various programs, the FHA has several for elderly housing. We shall briefly review these:

Section 203 is to help elderly individuals finance private dwellings suitable for their later years. The limit of the loan is $25,000. Maximum maturity of the loan is 35 years for a new building and 30 years for an existing building. Down payment may be made by a second party (relative or friend), and if the older person is not considered a good risk, the FHA may still insure the loan if he has a responsible co-signer.

Section 213 insures mortgages on cooperative housing projects of five or more dwelling units. There are different regulations for management-type and sales-type cooperatives. For manager-type cooperatives, permanent occupancy is vested jointly in members of the corporation or beneficiaries of the trust. For sales-type cooperatives the individual dwelling units may be released from the blanket mortgage of the project. The maximum insured loan on management-type cooperatives is 20 million dollars; on sales-type, 12.5 million. Maximum maturity on management-type is 40 years; on sales-type, 35 years.

Section 221 facilitates sales and rental housing for displaced elderly persons. Projects in urban renewal areas, or those that accommodate persons relocated from urban renewal areas, particularly qualify for this program. Multi-family rental or sales housing may be developed by either nonprofit or profit-motivated sponsors. Loans equal to 100 per cent of replacement value may be insured by nonprofit groups; this figure is reduced to 90 per cent if the group is profit-motivated. Maximum maturity is 40 years. Rents will be regulated by FHA in relation to the nature of the project and its location. Eligible buyers of single-family homes need put up only a nominal down payment, any or all of which may be used to cover closing costs.

Section 231 sponsors may be nonprofit organizations, such as churches, lodges, local governments, etc., or profit-motivated groups. Projects may include not only those of economical construction but also those with the more complete types of conveniences which high income people can afford. Commercial facilities, health services, recreational facilities, etc., may be covered in the insurance. Profit-motivated groups are limited to developing housekeeping projects and may not use founders' fees, etc., as funding devices. This restriction is not placed upon nonprofit groups. Section 231 financed projects may also include conversion of hotels and other residences into permanent housing (instead of transient). The maximum loan is 12.5 million, except for a public mortgagor like a local government, which may insure a loan up to 50 million. One hundred per cent of FHA estimated replacement cost insurance is permissible for nonprofit groups; only 90 per cent for profit-motivated. Nonprofit construction may be tax-exempt; profit-motivated construction may not be. The period of amortization is set by the FHA and is usually around 40 years.

Loans made with Housing and Home Finance Agency* and through U. S. Department of Agriculture

Section 202 authorizes low-interest, long-term direct loans to assist private, nonprofit corporate sponsors for rental housing and related facilities for the elderly. The purpose is to achieve lower rents than

*Division of Housing for the Elderly, Washington 25, D. C.

are possible under the other programs. Projects under this program must be of economical design and materials because the program is intended to aid those in the lower middle income brackets. Occupancy policies must contain tenant income regulations; they must also extend equal opportunity of occupancy, regardless of race, creed, or national origin.

No founders' fees or life lease contracts or other payments over and above those covering rentals and collateral services may be required of tenants.

The maximum amount of loan is 98 per cent of total development cost. The interest rate of 3⅜ per cent (established in 1961) is subject to redetermination on June 30 of each year for new loans, but the rate at which a loan is made is effective for its full term. Fifty years is maximum maturity.

Legislation has recently been passed to effect a new program of housing for the elderly in rural areas (both farm and non-farm) through the Department of Agriculture. Direct loans will be available for the purchase of individually owned homes and to nonprofit corporations and consumer cooperatives to provide rental housing and related facilities.

State aid program

New York State has what is known as a Limited-Profit Housing Companies Law. "This aids private enterprise to develop housing for the elderly with the help of the State or a municipality, through Article XII of the Public Housing Law of the State of New York. The law grants partial property tax exemption for a period of up to 30 years. It also permits direct state or municipal loans of 90 per cent of cost, for 50 years, at the same interest rate paid by the state or municipality for the money it borrows, plus a proportion of the cost of borrowing.

"The purpose of the law is to encourage private enterprise to invest in such companies to provide housing for families or persons of middle income, including aged persons with such incomes. Banks, foundations, labor unions, employers' organizations, veterans' organizations, and insurance companies, whether alone or in combination, as well as private

builders, are invited to form such corporations and purchase for cash, or receive in exchange for property, the equity securities of such a company. . . .

"In exchange for these advantages, such corporations are limited to a 6 per cent rate of return on equity and are regulated by law and by the State Division of Housing as to the maximum income of tenants (in establishing admission and retention of occupancy rights) and as to rentals, capital, operation, management, etc. The corporation may be a nonprofit cooperative or a private profit-seeking venture.

"A substantial number of projects have been created under this program, including a number with units specially designed for the aging and for the physically handicapped.

"This program has several evident attractions: it can provide lower rentals through 30-year partial local tax exemption; the low interest rate, coupled with a 50-year amortization period, permits lower monthly rentals; the limit of 6 per cent return on stock or income debentures helps assure lower rentals. Low rentals, in turn, help assure full occupancy and sound investment for the sponsor."*

Public Low-Rent Housing

Although these various programs should help provide private housing and group housing for a large segment of the home seekers among our elderly citizens, there are still myriads who simply cannot afford to pay current rents. Unfortunately there are not enough church, labor and fraternal groups equipped to provide partially or wholly subsidized residential facilities for the very low income group. Members of this group must look to publicly aided low-rent housing.

To help cities clear slums, the Housing Act of 1937 makes Federal funds available to local communities in qualifying states to buy land and build public housing to be rented to families of very low income

*"How to Provide Housing Which the Elderly Can Afford," New York State Division of Housing, Dec., 1958.

who are inadequately housed. (A state can qualify for public housing by passing enabling legislation.) The act also provides for annual Federal subsidies to meet deficits in operation which are inevitable because the income from these properties consists of modest rents, the only rents which low-income families can afford to pay. To receive such Federal funds, cities are obligated to waive taxes upon these properties and to accept in lieu of taxes a certain percentage of the rentals paid.

In the past one of the biggest obstacles facing very low-income older persons was the fact that single individuals were not eligible to public housing. Therefore widows and widowers and other single persons of very low incomes were denied admission. To eliminate this injustice, the amendments of 1956 and 1959 permit public housing projects to take low-income single women of 62, men of 65, and disabled persons of 50 or over.

Other provisions of the new amendments authorize construction of new public housing or remodeling of existing public housing projects to provide accommodations especially designed for older people; further, they authorize an additional federal subsidy of $120 per year for each unit for the elderly to help keep local government housing authorities solvent. Public housing authorities are authorized to give preference to elderly applicants and to waive the requirement of the Housing Act that such tenants must come from substandard dwellings.

SECTION III

PLANNING AND CONSTRUCTING THE PROJECT

CHAPTER 10

ACCOMMODATIONS

Man is the Measure of All Things

Architecture

We should aspire in building for the elderly—as in all building—to produce a product which will be, above all else, architecture. Our goal should be a structure that will be a fit and delightful abode for the human spirit as well as a workable shelter for the human body. This is an aesthetic goal.

The human spirit is endlessly responsive to aesthetic considerations in a degree that our culture is still very slow to recognize yet takes into account and acts upon with considerable discrimination, if not full competence. A man may unknowingly make a critical judgment when he prefers one automobile design to another, admires a certain golfer's swing, or has the urge to whistle at one girl and not her companion. A man who prides himself on not knowing which tie to wear with what suit feels perfectly capable of criticizing the dress, hat, or accessories his wife or any other woman wears, and he may smoke a certain cigarette as much because of the design of the package as the taste of the particular blend. These are aesthetic judgments.

When we aspire to produce architecture, we are not setting aside "practical" considerations; we are not adding "unnecessary frills"; we are not thereby upping the cost of the structure. We are rather shifting the attention from what goes into the building to the way in which it is put together. The building materials can be assembled in an infinite number of ways, and the decision to do it one way instead of another will determine whether the construction inspires or depresses, attracts, bores, or repels. We cannot avoid the fact that whatever we build will be a concrete expression to which people will react. We invariably and inevitably have a "feeling" about all buildings, even the ones we don't notice. So it is immensely practical to design for a happy feeling, as well as for durability, workability, and ease of maintenance.

Winston Churchill's oft-quoted statement, "First we shape our buildings and then they shape our lives," characterizes architecture as environment. Architecture may not be the sum of an environment, but it is unquestionably a prime element. In a very concrete and tyrannical sense buildings really do shape our lives. This is true whether one is an intimate user of the building in question or merely a passer-by on the street. Buildings are the clothing for an interior environment and the backdrop for an exterior environment. No amount of talent or inspiration on the part of the architect can make up for poor housekeeping, an inappropriate or hostile neighborhood, an acrimonious atmosphere, ugly furnishings, or inept use of his building inside or out. But no amount of loving care, lavish fittings, gracious deportment, or creative living on the part of the user can substitute for the talent the architect should have brought to his work but didn't. Architecture is not the trimmings of a way of life, but its backbone, and as such it is the deepest, most meaningful expression of a nation's character or an individual's perceptiveness.

Architecture is the art and science which guides the heart and mind of the architect in conceiving a building and governs his hand in designing it. The degree to which he is sensitive to the nuances of the art and attentive to the precepts of the science determines the quality of his product.

To lift thought above the supposedly practical objectives of sound construction, sensible planning, and easily maintained combinations of materials—in other words, to aspire to architectural excellence in what we build — does not mean that we are setting these other, practical considerations aside. Rather it means that in addition we are adding the more durable and precious goal to our requirements, that the resulting building does its part to establish an environment which brings joy, serenity, visual security, and an invigorated outlook on existence. Bo Boustedt speaks eloquently in Section V of this book about the commitment to architecture. Likewise, all who build must care greatly about what they can be doing to and for other people's lives by the act of building. For those building a home for the elderly, one of the principal considerations is the accommodations that this home is going to provide.

Let us define the "accommodations" in an elderly person's home as the living spaces and differentiate them from the service areas. When we speak of the accommodations offered by a hotel, we do not refer to the kitchens, the laundry, or the boiler room, or even to the shops in the arcade off the lobby. We refer to the spaces designed specifically for the use of the guests of the hotel — the lobbies, lounges, terraces, gardens, pools, beaches, dining rooms, party rooms, and private sleeping rooms and suites. The other parts of the hotel exist to serve these guest accommodations.

A private home for an elderly person or couple will also have living space and service space, but the distinction is less sharp. Living space will lap over into the kitchen, perhaps the laundry, and some maintenance areas (lawnmower, etc.). The service area, as such, will be limited to heating and other mechanical equipment, although the kitchen and laundry can shift into this classification in a private home where the work is done by employees. In an apartment house or a congregate home, the definition of accommodations narrows more toward the hotel concept.

The objective of all residence buildings is to provide accommodations — living space — for people, whether as single persons, family groups, social groups, recreation groups, or work groups. Living space needs to be of several varieties to afford diverse types of activities. People need (1) complete personal privacy at times just as they need (2) intimate family activity, and upon occasion (3) varying kinds and sizes of group contact. They also need places to sit and watch things and other people.

Privacy

The individual, whether living alone or in a family group, needs times of complete privacy. This may be obtained in a room of his own. But if he has none, he may need to obtain it by solitary digging in a garden or taking a walk. Accommodation of privacy must extend to bathing and toilet facilities. We do not have the Japanese ability to claim privacy in a group bath or toilet. They do so through their convention that you take no notice of another person bathing or relieving himself, nor does he of you. This is a type of mental seclusion possible only to those who have grown up practicing it.

The principle of privacy can become a fetish in planning. But at the same time, it is often violated in the design of minimum housing and in the planning of group living facilities. The most disturbing affront to the personal dignity of the elderly individual frequently comes at a time when he can least face it, namely, when he is ill. Bathing and toilet planning in infirmaries and nursing homes is more often planned for the convenience of the attendant than for the feelings of the patient.

In housekeeping apartments, the cooking unit is frequently unnecessarily obtrusive. This is a fault in luxury quarters as well as low-income housing. It is most frequent in "efficiency" apartments designed for single people, but it is not uncommon in one- and two-bedroom apartments. In congregate homes, designed to meet the needs of modest-income people, we often find an effort toward economy leads the designer to place the handbowl in the living space where it cannot be screened from the sitting area. These errors in planning for kitchenette and lavatory placement are a violation of the principle of privacy because they expose very personal activities to visitors.

Small groups

Planning for people in groups should strive for the widest possible variety. Friendships are most frequent by two's and three's. Any device which promotes contacts on a person-to-person basis and provides for natural, almost automatic, clustering of two to four people is an admirable one. Opportunities for this kind of contact should be designed into the plans both indoors and out. Alcoves, bays, wide spots in corridors, little paved areas at entrance doors, and small patios, if skillfully located, can serve this purpose. The laundry room for automatic laundry machines in apartment buildings and retirement villages become social gathering places if properly designed.

Provisions for men

It has been said aging is a woman's problem, so many of them seem to outlive the men, but to be successful, the congregate home must make provisions for the men as well as the women. The boy-meets-girl urge is still surprisingly important to the elderly, but with a preponderance of women in congregate homes, the boys need a chance to escape. They should have a club, a billiard room, or a pub that is off limits to the females.

Larger groups

Wherever possible, a design should also accommodate groups of 10 to 12 as well as the big meeting or social event involving 30 to 100 or more. The vitality of self-generated activities among the members of the community is in a degree related to the ease with which a variety of kinds and sizes of activities can be accommodated. Too often, the choice is between a private living-bedroom and the group meeting hall. Too often also, there is no choice of background for an activity. The social hall is also the workshop so that formal, dress-up activities must take place in the same surroundings used for work sessions. The all-

Lounge of Motion Picture Country House, Los Angeles, Calif. Architect: William Pereira.

Kitchen in Chicago Housing Authority Apartments for the Elderly. Architects: Loewenberg and Loewenberg.

purpose kind of room is either too good for ceramics and woodworking or too crude for serving formal teas. We all benefit from a change of scenery.

The sport of watching other people is indulged in by all of us from time to time. The elderly, who have more time at their disposal, frequently make a hobby of it. The house-bound should have as much opportunity for this hobby as possible. Any of us likes a place to eat a meal, do sit-down work chores, read, or play a table game which also provides a view of birds, squirrels, dogs, cats, children, people, or just traffic.

Modus Operandi

It is important to remember sociologist Flora Hatcher's dictum that housing is "a modus operandi for the elderly." The ability of the elderly to "operate" in a residential situation is more directly governed by the physical attributes of the space than that of any other age group except the toddler who must strain to reach a door knob. More at the mercy of his house than someone who is stronger and better coordinated is the person who falls into one of the following categories:

1. One who cannot readily stoop
2. One whose balance is not sure
3. One who does not easily see steps, thresholds, and loose rugs
4. One who does not react instantly when he slips or trips
5. One whose strength is curtailed for getting in and out of a bath tub, getting up out of a chair, cranking a can opener or window operator, lifting or moving furniture for cleaning, opening heavy sash, or reaching up high or down low.
6. One who has difficulty hearing the door bell or telephone.

These personal limitations are not exclusively peculiar to the elderly nor are they universal with them. Some at 80 can climb stairs with ease and even run. (The late King of Sweden regularly played tennis in his 80's.) But taking these limitations into account in unobtrusive ways will not prove a detriment to any residence.

Size is a critical factor in designing for the elderly. Size is so directly related to cost that balancing one against the other to produce accommodations which the elderly can afford and which are not at the same time too cramped becomes a delicate operation. Clearances must be adequate for easy movement in the bathroom. In the kitchen, storage must not be too high, and clearance between cabinets and appliances on opposite walls must allow easy movement and access to lower storage without need to back against a hot oven. If there is eating space in the kitchen, it should not be necessary to move furniture

Glass-enclosed terrace of Actors' Fund Home, Englewood, N. J. Architects: Moon and Iwatsu.

ing for corridors and bath should be provided. Shower stalls present considerably less hazard than bath tubs and are more easily used by many of the handicapped. Shower stalls should have a small seat or stool. Curtain rods in shower stalls or tubs should be able to support 300-lb dead weight. Where a tub is used, the toilet may be placed next to it and used as a seat for soaking the feet in the tub, or as an aid in getting in and out of the tub. If it is properly located, it is as effective and perhaps a little less hazardous than a seat built at the foot of the tub. Tubs and shower stalls should have strong and ample grab bars. The wall or cabinets beside the toilet should be strong enough to hold chrome arm supports which may be installed as they are needed. For appearance's sake, they should certainly be removed when they are not needed.

Laundry facilities on the premises are a great convenience, but if they are not available, a simple device useful to almost anyone is a bracket over the tub or in the shower on which to hang the drip-dry shirts, suits, dresses, and underwear so universally used today.

Wheel chair traffic in congregate homes must be kept in mind. A certain number of private baths—10 to 15 per cent—should be designed for wheel-chair use. Corridors should allow two wheel chairs to pass, and the dining rooms, meeting rooms, and the auditorium or chapel must be able to accept them. A new Catholic home in Connecticut has a wheel chair balcony in its auditorium-chapel with a flat floor and premium view of the platform.

Standards

Most of what has been discussed above should be considered by the architect when designing residences for the elderly, whether they be housekeeping or non-housekeeping, dispersed, proximate or congregate. An exhaustive list of everything everyone has proposed that should be done to solve the detailed problems which the elderly have with houses would fill many pages. A partial one is given in Section V. If they were all observed, the resulting quar-

to reach storage or to get into the refrigerator or oven. Furniture should not have to be moved in living rooms or bedrooms either, especially to do routine cleaning. The bed should have space enough for easy making. A studio bed which must be made up every night is a tiresome makeshift for anyone, but especially for the elderly. All these requirements call for a few more square feet than is customary in economy construction, but the added area makes the residence easier to care for and to live in. All these requirements seem to argue against the usual one-room apartment as suitable for an elderly person. They also leave the average trailer open to grave question.

Light is a critical element to the elderly. Designs which flood rooms with light yet shield the glare of the sky are desirable. Halls, entries, stairs, kitchens, and baths should receive more daylight and artificial light than is customary. Artificial light needs to be abundant and carefully designed to eliminate glare.

Replacing bulbs should be easy; for this purpose pull-down fixtures can be used in certain places.

Stairs give good exercise. It is not mandatory to eliminate all of them. Public Housing people have found that in two-story buildings many oldsters are able to manage the stairs and actually prefer second-floor apartments. A landing in the middle breaks the climb, and a small place to sit down may come in handy if the resident is carrying an armload of packages. Any stairs in group residence should be easy to negotiate with a stretcher (for removing an ill person). Second-floor quarters can be enhanced by the addition of a balcony.

Open fires should be avoided by the elderly. This means electric cooking is best and that auxiliary heat in bathrooms and other rooms should be electric.

The bath, where possible, should lie as near to and on as nearly a straight line as possible from the most used bed. This path should not pass stairs. Night light-

ters would be a kind of padded gymnasium rather than a home.

The important thing for the architect and layman to do is to familiarize himself with the hourly and daily problems of the elderly and to find his own ways of meeting them. Then he must raise his thinking above the problems to seek patterns of architecture which not only handle the basic problems and needs but also do their part to give joy and vigor to the lives of the residents. The architect does this by manipulation of planning, light, color, space, and internal and external relationships so that the resultant dwelling will be as eagerly sought after by the elderly as is a four-bedroom, family-room ranch house by young-marrieds. To repeat, living for old homemakers should look like "living for young homemakers."

We must learn that gadgets are no substitute for a good plan nor are "features" a substitute for a concept. John Ciardi says ". . . the search for values cannot deal in counterfeit coin." The congregate home should have the look of a fine country club or a posh hotel rather than a hospital or a dormitory.

It is apparent today that the so-called aging process is as much psychological as physiological, that it can be arrested and even reversed by the right mental atmosphere, and that treatment is as much moral and psychological as medical. Dramatic results are reported in Michigan hospitals, under the tutelage of Dr. Wilma Donahue, where 75 per cent of the elderly patients were sufficiently improved to be released, and 25 per cent returned to their own homes to live independently. Dr. Donahue reports that many who had been given up to terminal illness were restored to physical and emotional health.

It cannot be claimed that architecture alone can work miracles, but it can be asserted that the atmosphere of an environment is structured by its physical surroundings, and that surroundings of order and beauty make the job of establishing and maintaining a healthy, joyous environment immeasurably easier.

CHAPTER 11

ACTIVITIES

Retirement spells leisure to most of us. But how that leisure is used is of the greatest importance. The spice of life at 65 as at any other age is variety. And the variety of satisfying activities which a living arrangement will permit deserves careful consideration.

Choice of site is important for any category of retirement home. Actual proximity to, or easy public transportation to, churches, libraries, theatres, stores, etc., not to mention the increasingly popular Senior Citizen Centers, not only offers religious, educational, cultural, and recreational activities to the elderly, but provides them with the opportunity for continuing social contacts with people of the larger community.

These opportunities for variety of social experience within proximate or congregate homes must be planned by the architect. He should give the resident as wide a choice as possible for different kinds of activity: group or single; sedentary or active; work or play; physical, mental, or spiritual; cultural or diverting; productive or nonproductive.

Planning activity facilities for proximate housing

Because residents in proximate housing will be occupied to some degree by household chores, facilities need not be as numerous as for those living in congregate homes. For outside sociability, and not too strenuous exercise, consider small garden plots, shuffleboard, and croquet equipment. Outside sitting areas can be planned for intimate groupings. The basic indoor need is a social room large enough to seat twice the number of residents at once, with small tables for cards and other games, record player, and TV set. Storage space for games and records is essential. Marking a shuffleboard court on the floor of the social room might be desirable. Racks for book and magazine exchange should be considered. Such a room should be planned for multiple uses. As well as furnishing a pleasant place for residents to gather

informally, it can be used for religious services, lectures, movies, exhibits, entertaining visiting groups, square dancing, bridge and shuffleboard tournaments. It can also become the meeting place for Golden Age or Senior Citizen groups, and thus increase community ties.

It is very important that a kitchen be planned adjoining the social room, and that it be an adequate kitchen. In one housekeeping residence for the elderly in the Mid-West, the availability of a large enough social room with adequate kitchen led the residents to hire a cateress to prepare one main meal a day, for both good nutrition and desired sociability. This meal is made available at cost to all residents on an optional basis, with reservation required. Responsibility for meal planning is shared by the residents.

A facility which the architect would find popular in either proximate or congregate home is a space in, or a small room adjacent to, the laundry, where several residents can enjoy a game of cards while the automatic machines do the work.

Planning for activities in the congregate home

In the congregate home where meals are served and more or less personal service provided, residents will have far less responsibility and more leisure time. Therefore facilities for a greater variety of activities should be planned. These may include physical, creative, cultural, and remunerative activities and volunteer services in the community.

Physical activities. For outside exercise, consider bowling-on-the-green, fishing on site or off, gardening, and attractive pathways for walking. Benches for occasional resting periods should be provided along the pathways. Shuffleboard, both outdoor and inside, will be found popular. For additional indoor exercise, square dancing is a favorite with elderly people, and records are obtainable for "calls." A large recreation room must be planned for this purpose. (Perhaps in 10 years it will be the twist!)

Creative activities not only give personal satisfaction in achievement, but help to keep the fingers limber. Craft rooms, with adequate storage space for

Douglas Gardens, Jewish Home for the Aged, Miami, Fla. Architects: Smith and Kovach. (Left: sheltered work shop; right: newspaper staff at work.)

materials, can be planned for weaving, ceramics, jewelry making, millinery, dress design, photography, lapidary work, and—especially for the men—wood-carving and making wooden articles with electric tools. (The latter may cause problems. A man of 80 may be perfectly capable of controlled operation of a power tool, while one of fewer years may not. Sometimes the answer is to arrange for the able ones to make use of a tool shop nearby.) It is desirable to find a handicraft teacher to direct creative activities, either on a voluntary or staff basis. The architect may plan a relatively large crafts room where many people may work at different pursuits or enjoy watching what others are doing. Or he may plan smaller rooms for limited activities. Woodworking and tool rooms should be separate.

To assure residents of the home wider community friendships, the architect can plan recreation and hobby rooms of such size and in such location in the

home as to encourage community contemporaries to share them.

Cultural activities facilities for the individual will include a library and reading room, recordings and a player. One Midwest home permits residents to bring pianos from their former homes. These are placed at intersections of hallways in residence wings, with a sofa adjacent, and the old people enjoy playing and singing informally.

Group activities can include religious services, lectures, movies, slides, book reviews, discussion groups of all kinds. A separate chapel may be provided, although an auditorium can double for this purpose. For special interest groups small meeting rooms or lounges will be desirable. A tip received from a resident in a western home suggested that if possible there should be a room which could remain "set up" for movies and slides. In the home where she lives the necessary rearrangement of heavy furniture in the

lounge, setting up and taking down screen and projection table, etc., led to fewer showings of residents' personal travel film than would otherwise be the case. Leadership can be secured from the community, from churches, the American Association of University Women, League of Women Voters, and various service organizations. One suburban Chicago home seeks community contacts for its residents by encouraging them to invite their personal church groups to the home for meetings. A kitchenette is located off the spacious lounge for easy, informal hospitality.

Small tables in informal lounges, ready for card games, checker, chess, scrabble, etc., will encourage mixing. Even visual stimulus promotes activity of the mind, and a simple thing like a goldfish bowl recessed in the wall of the lounge can bring enjoyment. A view of movement on a river or highway will prove a source of entertainment to those whose mobility is limited. One western home has a balcony which overlooks the ball park. A Kentucky home has a porch from which residents can watch the races with binoculars!

Remunerative activities. In its sheltered workshop, Montefiori Home in Cleveland Heights, Ohio, offers residents of the home and their contemporaries from the community an opportunity to do piecework for local industries. Companionship and a chance to earn a little money make this a popular activity. It also promotes community interest in the individual residents of the home. Adjoining the workshop a separate room with cots is provided for an after-lunch rest period for the commuters. One resident who before retirement was a cobbler now has a little room within the home where he repairs shoes for fellow-residents for a limited period each day. Other skills could be similarly utilized if space and equipment were provided.

In the sheltered workshop at Douglas Gardens, Miami, Fla., where the recruitment of piecework from factories and shops is operated on a concession basis, some residents actually earn enough to qualify for Social Security if they are not already covered under the program. The feeling of independence thus engendered is a great boost to their morale.

Volunteer services in the community can be a rewarding activity for residents of a congregate home or for retired people in any living arrangement. Their varied experiences and abilities will be welcomed by many agencies of the Community Chest, as well as churches and service clubs. The sponsors of a home for the elderly would be wise to make community contacts to this end.

Direction of activities

The architect has the responsibility to plan the building so that a wide range of activities can be carried on. The administrator has the responsibility to encourage the use of the building as planned by the architect. The esprit-de-corps of the home reflects the enthusiasm with which the residents actually become involved in satisfying activities. In visiting a generous sampling of fairly new homes in our coun-

Potting room of Rockwood Manor, Spokane, Wash. Architects: Culler-Gale-Martell.

try, it was observed that participation was greatest where resident committees planned their own programs of activity and assumed responsibility for their successful operation. One administrator pointed out that it took skillful direction at the beginning, and much patience, but that now his residents completely manage their activities, and he feels this achievement well worth the effort involved.

Another home achieved resident direction of activities in a different manner. Several months before the project was opened, accepted applicants who lived in the general neighborhood of the home got together and planned alternate activities programs for the first few months of operation. When the home opened, these plans were submitted to the resident body for priority rating. A highly satisfactory program evolved. It includes language classes in French, German and Spanish, Bible study conducted by a dynamic young minister from the nearby city, a current events weekly discussion led by a history professor from the local college, "go-see" group trips in the home's bus to distant points of interest, book reviews by home talent, instruction in painting and ceramics. Local Red Cross people direct volunteer work. This program of great variety offers adventure and excitement.

Obviously, anticipation of the likely interests of those the home will serve will determine space design. The greatest flexibility possible should be the aim of the architect.

CHAPTER 12
BUILDING SERVICES

We will assume that architects are accustomed to dealing with the technical problems of kitchens, laundries, maintenance of buildings and grounds, trash handling, heating, ventilation, air conditioning, electricity, and acoustics. If they encounter problems of this kind they are not versed in, or are called upon to design a building or group which is larger, more complex, or different from that which they are accustomed to, we assume that they know the sources of information they need or how to secure consultants who will assist them with the technicalities involved.

If they engage consultants for the engineering work, for the layout of a kitchen, laundry, infirmary or rehabilitation facility, it is important that they brief the consultants on the geratological considerations and that they make sure the consultants' recommendations are kept in proportion to the budget and scope of the rest of the project.

In general, residence buildings for the elderly present only a few problems in the field of building services which are peculiar or unique. We will endeavor here to point out some items that need to be considered.

Kitchens

In residences for independent living, it would be well to avoid over-mechanization. Gadgets get out of whack, need servicing, and add to the operation cost of the house. A recent newspaper headline quoted an authority to the effect that the monthly service bill of the average family exceeded their doctor bill. For instance, is a garbage grinder necessary to a retired couple who have time to carry out the garbage and perhaps need the exercise?

In any case, an electric range seems a wise choice for safety reasons. A sit-down work space is very desirable; for this, a dining table in the kitchen will suffice. Kitchen storage should be easy to reach, not very high or very low. An old-fashioned pantry closet

might be a good alternative to many little cupboards.

For the design of the central kitchen in a congregate home or the social hall of a retirement village, the architect may wish to consult a specialist.

The details of equipment will vary according to whether the kitchen is operated by employees or by residents themselves. The architect will be responsible for location of the kitchen in the over-all plan so that deliveries and trash removal do not make traffic problems for the rest of the home and will design it so clutter and trash are concealed from the view of living spaces. The comings and goings of trucks, cars, and employees, however, can hold the interest of a people-watcher.

Food storage requirements are changing. Most homes now contract with suppliers for a season's requirements. Deliveries on the contract are made two, three, or five times a week on a flexible, predetermined schedule. Not more than four days' needs are stored at the home.

Food preparation is also reduced because meats are delivered ready trimmed and cut to serving portions and many vegetables arrive cleaned and ready to cook. The use of many frozen vegetables and juices may increase the refrigerator requirements slightly, however.

Some designs scatter small dining rooms throughout a project in order to seek hominess and intimacy. This calls for space in a central kitchen for thermal carts. Scattered kitchens are not usually feasible.

Congregate homes always have a certain number of residents who require special diets. This should be taken into account in the design of the central kitchen and the serving kitchens.

The greatly increased use of paper and other disposable items today speeds certain work and reduces staff. But it also increases the requirements for incinerators or trash removal.

Building maintenance

The owner of a private residence or a unit in a proximate village should make a plan or schedule for maintenance of his building and grounds. He should

include an item in his operating budget to cover this. An architect can be of assistance in making such a plan. Storage is needed for rakes, hoes, fertilizer and the lawn mower if the owner plans to do his own yard work.

A congregate home will have a staff member in charge of a similar plan. As in food buying, many homes have found that a maintenance contract with competent firms for servicing equipment and maintaining buildings and grounds is an economy. Using employees to perform this work may save money on the individual job but cost more in the over-all picture. The architect needs to know what the client's policy will be on this subject, because the program should include central storage of paints and other materials, shops, shelter for mowers, snow removal equipment and the like, as well as lockers and washrooms for employees if the work is not contracted out.

Housekeeping

In the private residence we need storage for the broom, vacuum cleaner, and other cleaning tools. We need storage for sheets, towels, table linen, and blankets. In the elderly person's residence, the rules about good lighting and ease of reaching need to be observed for such storage.

The congregate home will have the same requirements but on a larger scale. Whether linen and cleaning supplies should be kept in a central location or distributed throughout the home is a moot question. The client must answer this question for the architect. It might be a combination of answers. Scrubbing machines and floor waxers might be handled on one basis; brooms and vacuum cleaners on another; linen and paper supplies on yet another. A good administrator will have ideas on this subject, and the architect's ingenuity can be invaluable.

Building specifications should be written with an eye for materials that are easy to keep clean. But these choices should always be made with the resident first in mind and the janitor second. A quick way to make a building look like an institution is to tile the walls, linoleum the floors, and install chrome and vinyl furniture. The janitor would be favored and the resident would be the loser since all sense of a home-like atmosphere would be designed out.

Engineering

Heating the residence for older people is the subject of much discussion. Agreement among a group of people on desirable temperature and ventilation is an unattainable goal. It has been claimed by many that older people require higher temperatures. Perhaps some do. But Public Housing officials and administrators of retirement homes have had satisfactory results with temperatures of 75°F. providing the heating system meets two requirements:

1. That the temperatures be constant around-the-clock.

2. That the design be as draft-free as possible. For this, a good control system is mandatory with careful zoning of the sunny and shaded sides of the building. It means the areas where people will sit for extended periods (at the windows of the living room, dining room, or bed-sitting room) must be carefully blanketed with heat to block cold radiation and cold drafts from glass areas. Double glazing is of great value in such spots. It means also that if forced-air heating is used, high velocities and intermittent flow should be avoided.

The need for air conditioning is much discussed. In many climates there is no question of its desirability. In homes designed for people from 60 to 75, the custom of the area should be a key. For the very elderly, it may not be necessary or desirable. The added cost of construction and operation is to be carefully analyzed before a decision is made.

In individual residences occupied by an elderly couple or single individual, their comings and goings may not be enough to ventilate the house as sufficiently as in a household of active children always running in and out. The very need to doubleglaze and weatherstrip for winter comfort, and for summer economy with air conditioning, makes good ventilation more difficult. Many a kitchen exhaust fan spins ineffectively because the home is constructed too tightly to give it any air to exhaust. A positive source for fresh air and make-up air for exhaust fans is needed.

In the group residence—apartment or congregate home—positive ventilation of corridors is mandatory. This is best accomplished by putting the corridors under slight pressure and allowing air to exhaust through the individual living quarters. The corridor doors may be cut a little short to allow a crack for this purpose or door or wall louvers may be used. If the kitchen and bath have vents to the outside, odors are carried away from the apartment and never intrude into the corridor.

Group dining rooms should be ventilated through the kitchen on the same principle. Meeting rooms need ventilation, of course. The area most in need of careful and thorough ventilation is the infirmary. Poor ventilation in this area is a great detriment. But in all these spaces, ventilation must be as draftless as it is positive.

The statements about lighting of steps, corridors, work areas, yard, walks and driveways made in the chapter on accommodations need to be borne in mind by the architect and his electrical engineer. Lounges, meeting rooms and sitting rooms to be used by the elderly for reading or detail work need brighter light than those for other people.

In many proximate villages and apartments, as well as in congregate homes, it has been found desirable to install a signal system or an intercom system which will allow a person to signal for help. Individuals living alone particularly appreciate this facility. It may connect to a central office or station or it may merely connect with two or three neighbors. Such a system need not be as elaborate as those used in nursing homes and hospitals but should approximate the service found in a hotel (except that in case of a real emergency a dial phone may be too difficult to use). The architect and communications engineer should work closely with the client in thinking through the operation of such a system and design one to meet a given set of needs.

The individual older person living alone in a detached dwelling should devise his own set of communications to be used in case of emergency.

Elevators present some problems in residences for the elderly. Automatic elevators seem acceptable for residents' use, even if some folks are fearful of them. Such people can be assisted and schooled in their use, thereby eliminating the need of an employee. Automatic elevator doors should operate more slowly than usual because of wheel chair riders as well as the slower moving ambulatory. The car itself need not move more slowly. Signal buttons should be placed low enough for easy reach from a wheel chair by a person who is unable to reach up while seated. A hand rail all around is important, and a seat is desirable if it can be provided. Signal buttons and numerals should be large and well lighted. The cab should be ventilated. Both the cab and the elevator lobbies should be well lighted. The lobbies should have a bench, and a table or shelf to rest packages on is desirable. One elevator should be deep enough to accommodate a stretcher.

Much more could be written about building services. A careful study of relevant data in various chapters of this book will assist the architect and layman to develop a basis of thinking which will make for a creative approach to building services in accommodations for the elderly.

CHAPTER 13

STAFF

Many professionals make a distinction between the terms "staff" and "employees." The line is usually drawn between the skilled and unskilled, professionals and nonprofessionals, on the basis of education. For the purpose of this discussion, we are using the term "staff" as a blanket term.

Interrelation of staff and building

The interrelation of staff and building is dynamic. Whoever accepts the role of making a building operate as a home is hampered or assisted in many unseen as well as apparent ways by decisions the architect makes while he is designing, planning, writing specifications, and supervising the construction. Likewise a staff can fail to take advantage of a building, to explore the opportunities it provides. There have been occasions when for one reason or another an administrator has refused to use a building the way it was designed to be used. The more carefully a product is designed, the more intelligently it must be used. We do not employ a surgeon's scalpel to open tin cans.

If the architect's design of a project increases or decreases the number of employees needed to operate the building by only a single person, he is exerting a measurable influence on the operating cost of the project over the years. The experience of one of the authors in designing a new industrial building for an internationally known manufacturer is a case in point. By a careful analysis of the manufacturing process, and particularly of materials handling, the production force was cut in half at the same time the output was doubled.

Even if he does not alter the number of people required to operate the home but makes their job simpler, more orderly and especially, more pleasant, the architect still affects the atmosphere and the esprit-de-corps of the whole establishment. This contribution is of great value because it is communicated to the residents the staff is to serve.

It is of considerable importance for the client and architect to analyze thoroughly all aspects of operation of a building. Their decisions on this subject are reflected directly in the look and the plan of the building. This is an area of discussion where the future administrator of a facility can be of great help. Neither the architect nor the client can divine all the wishes of an as yet unknown administrator because many of these wishes will be based on personal experience.

Determining size of staff

The number of staff required is first indicated, in a general way, when the number of people to be accommodated in the residence is. established and the range of services to be offered is determined. These two factors are reflected throughout the design. A perusal of the tables (Section VI) covering all the projects studied in this book will reveal that there is a direct relation between these two policy decisions and the size of staff. A careful study of the individual projects shown in Section VI will further illuminate the relation between the building plan and these factors: number of residents, services rendered, and resultant number of staff.

The exact number of staff is gradually pinpointed as the operational policy of the home is spelled out and refined. This information is of great importance to those charged with making the proposed operating budget and from it, the proposed schedule of charges. It is of great importance also to the architect.

An apartment house, retirement village, or other proximate form of housekeeping dwellings for elderly people will usually have a small staff, limited in duties to maintenance of buildings and grounds, housekeeping in public spaces and necessary management function of accounting, renting or leasing, and miscellaneous administration. Occasionally such projects will include a restaurant or central dining room. This, at once, increases the staff. It also increases the size of the building. These are costs to be accounted for in the budget and balanced against increased anticipated income.

A congregate home of non-housekeeping units will require staff for food handling, for housekeeping throughout, for organizing an activities program, and probably for dealing with health problems.

It is impossible to give even a rule-of-thumb for the employee-resident ratio because of the number and character of the variables involved. If the number of housekeeping units is increased, the staff changes very gradually. An increase in non-housekeeping units will increase staff in a more direct proportion for maid service, food service, and possibly health service, since non-housekeeping residents are likely to be in the upper age brackets.

On the following page is a check list of staff personnel types that might be needed in a congregate home which is to accommodate 100 or more residents. Not every home will need all these types of workers; some, however, will need additional ones.

Increasing the size of a home may sometimes reduce the resident/staff ratio somewhat and hence the cost per resident. In others it may not reduce it significantly, but the added staff may bring special skills which a smaller home could not provide, and these skills can increase the variety and sophistication of the services offered the resident—an important factor in attracting prospective residents. These added amenities may or may not call for additional building space, depending on their nature, a fact that must be noted by the architect.

Staff requirements

The presence of staff in a home brings a set of requirements independent of the residents' requirements. These requirements have five distinct if not discrete aspects: (1) Staff functioning; (2) staff comfort; (3) staff accommodations; (4) staff organization; (5) staff administration.

1. *Functioning.* Programming and designing the building must proceed from a careful detailing of functions and procedures so that the staff is aided and not hampered in serving the resident.

2. *Comfort.* All areas used by the staff must be designed for creature comfort in terms of light, heat, ventilation, air conditioning, acoustics, elbow room, and atmosphere. Staff tenure and quality of service will reflect the comfort index achieved in the design. Achieving a good comfort index may represent thoughtful consideration as much as expenditure of money.

3. *Accommodations.* Staff must have accommodations in addition to space used in conjunction with the residents. These may include parking, separate entrances, locker rooms, toilets and showers, day room, dining room, meeting room, and even complete living quarters in some cases. Inadequate accommodations may well be reflected in staff efficiency.

4. *Organization.* The way a staff is organized may not affect the amount and kind of space required for staff operation but it can materially affect the location of such spaces; therefore, the client, architect, and administrator need to have a clear idea of staff organization at an early date.

5. *Administration.* Staff administration in terms of policy, control, definition of duties, delegation of authority, cost accounting, and the like is also a significant factor in building planning. It will affect the location of administrative facilities such as offices and equipment. It can affect other elements of design such as amount and location of kitchen storage, housekeeping supplies, maintenance shop, yard equipment. Many times decisions of this nature are made before staff organization and administration are analyzed, with the result that these decisions are incorrect and later regretted.

But first and last, any consideration of staff problems must always be in terms of what staff cost, efficiency, and especially morale means to the resident. The building is conceived, designed and built first for the resident and only secondarily for the staff.

CHAPTER 14

CARE

In planning a residence to serve the total needs of the elderly person, consideration must be given to his health requirements. We have discussed design as a means of minimizing accident hazards and of promoting esthetic satisfaction. We have discussed the relationship of suitable activities to good mental health. Another positive health measure which cannot be overestimated is good nutrition. It is interesting to note that much research is being done today in the field of better nutrition for the elderly.

Preventive medicine starts with the periodic physical checkup to discover incipient troubles and take the proverbial "stitch in time." Serious illnesses often can be detected in an early stage and corrective programs initiated. "Hardening of the arteries is not a necessary accompaniment of old age. Deterioration of the nervous system can often be delayed," according to Dr. Edward L. Bortz, past president of the American Medical Association. Santa Cruz County, Calif., has experienced a tremendous reduction in cost to the taxpayer since inaugurating their program of periodic health examination for all recipients of state aid for the aged (California Report).

At some time, however, sooner or later, for longer or shorter periods, the elderly person may have need for special nursing care or hospitalization, and any planning for his well being would be remiss without taking this potential need into account. After 75 the incidence of infirmities rises.

Categories of care

The basic needs for health care of the elderly are the same as of any other segment of our population. They include access to (1) examination, diagnosis, and treatment; (2) a general hospital for care of acute illness or surgery; (3) nursing care; (4) special treatment by oculist, dentist, podiatrist, psychiatrist;

Fenced patio outside sheltered care section of Kenny Presbyterian Home, Seattle, Wash. Architects: Durham, Anderson & Freed.

(5) rehabilitation services; and (6) protective care for senility.

How will these basic needs be met? Does the architect have a responsibility? The sponsor? The individual elderly person himself? The answer is clearly yes—*all* of them. The degree of responsibility varies in different situations.

Care in dispersed living situations

For those living in independent situations, the choice of site would be as important as the architect's design. It is always difficult to project ourselves five, ten, fifteen years hence and to realize that we will have waning physical strength and endurance. Therefore the size of the lot is important. And its actual proximity to health facilities—or to easy transportation to them—is equally important. The day will surely come when it will not be desirable to drive. The individual and the architect must consider these points in planning the independent dwelling.

Care in proximate residences

Sponsors of proximate residences often do not assume any responsibility for the residents' health. But they could at least be sure residents have thought through the problem. Sponsor's choice of site should bear in mind the need of the residents for convenient access to health facilities.

The architect may plan some sort of system for the resident to summon aid in emergency. It may be a buzz, a bell, a light, or a combination of signals. Cedar Apartments, a public housing project in Natick, Mass., has an emergency system by which switches in the apartment activate both light and electric door opener. A number of projects studied have fire detection and reporting devices.

A simple infirmary may be and often is incorporated in the proximate project, where a nurse can give care during short term illness or disability. The relative desirable size seems to be one bed to 15 or 20 residents. Such an infirmary need consist only of patient rooms, nurse station for records and intercom system, kitchenette, and utility rooms. For patient rooms in such an infirmary, most authorities recommend two-bed units, with a minimum of singles, believing that companionship at time of confinement is a stimulant to recovery. Others, however, feel a person wants privacy especially during illness and therefore recommend only single rooms. The resident patient would provide his own physician.

Care in congregate homes

The resident of the congregate home chooses to live there, among other reasons, because it offers freedom from responsibilities and a sense of security. Often he will choose a particular home because of the quality and extent of health services provided.

Swedish architect Bo Boustedt does not include infirmaries in his homes for the elderly. Beds of special design, which do not resemble hospital beds but are adaptable for sickroom care, are furnished in all rooms. There is always on the staff a nurse competent to care for temporary illness in the individual room under the direction of a physician. For other illness the resident is transferred to the local hospital, which reserves a certain percentage of beds for care of the elderly. Mr. Boustedt feels the presence of an infirmary spoils the home atmosphere and can provide at best only mediocre medical care. His homes are relatively small, caring for a maximum of fifty to seventy persons.

In our country, however, it is customary for the congregate home to provide a nursing unit. In addition to short term care, it may offer nursing service for convalescence from a hospitalized condition, or for chronic disease for long periods. "Health protection is one of the most important advantages which a congregate home has over an individual's private home," comments Robert L. Durham, architect, Seattle, Wash., planning a retirement home in the Northwest. "Many people have no comprehension of the changes in care which can be required. Those who enter at 62 are most active.... Fifteen years later many of them may need actual feeding and dressing care.... In our new home the monthly payment will include complete health care through a group medical plan, without any strings attached."

The nursing unit in a congregate home will have patient rooms, doctor's office(s) and examining rooms, nurse station, intercom system, kitchen and utility rooms, the latter including storage for wheelchairs, walkers, etc. Any schematic arrangement of the unit should have the joint planning of doctor, *nurse,* and architect. The nursing unit may or may not include diagnostic and rehabilitation facilities.

Dr. Stanley Simon, Director of Drake Memorial Hospital, Cincinnati, Ohio, advises use of community diagnostic facilities by the congregate home if at all possible. If provided within the home, he points out, rooms must be planned for x-ray equipment, film development and viewing, fluoroscope, etc., all of which adds greatly to the cost of the project. Equipment is very expensive, repairs are costly, and obsolescence is a factor to be considered. Most of all, he says, competent staff is very difficult, often impossible, to obtain, whereas if an arrangement is made at the beginning to use community facilities, good medical care can be provided and a continuation of qualified staff assured, often at a greatly reduced cost. Obviously the size of the project and its proximity to adequate community facilities must be the deciding factors. Under all circumstances, the local medical society should be consulted on this problem early in the planning stage.

Facilities for rehabilitation, on the other hand, may be desirable on site. Wonderful results have been obtained with early treatment following accidents, strokes, certain surgical procedures and circulatory afflictions to help the patient regain stability, coordination, mobility, and strength. Any program of rehabilitation requires the services of trained psycho-, physio-, and occupational therapists. Such people are today in short supply, but the recognized need and increasing demand for their services is stimulating more training programs. In some large cities therapists are available on a shared basis.

Syllabus of Rehabilitation Methods and Techniques (Stratford Press, Cleveland, 1962) by Beth H. Fowles details training methods. Dr. Mieczyslaw Peszcynski,

Chief of the Department of Physical Medicine and Rehabilitation, Highland View Hospital, Cleveland, advises: "The so-called rehabilitation nursing training should include gait training, transfer techniques, grooming and dressing techniques, bathroom activities, and in many instances homemaking activities for the following four groups of disabilities: strokes, fractured hips, arthritides, and amputations."

Because most congregate homes will have relatively few cases requiring rehabilitation follow-up after discharge from a hospital, he says, arrangements can be improvised for their care either in their own rooms or in the corridor. "A medium-sized congregate home may need a small gym . . . but for any long range planning it would be wise to have the area as flexible as possible and in a section where the adjoining rooms can be easily incorporated, and when not needed the space can be as easily converted into living quarters. Experience in rehabilitation has shown that such flexibility is necessary because of changing patterns in medical care."

One feature of the congregate home's nursing unit deserves special mention. This is the bath. If possible both tub and shower should be provided. The tub is desirable particularly for the patient who needs heat for arthritic joints, a sitz bath, etc. For the ambulatory patient the shower provides great satisfaction, especially when he can use it independently. The tub room should have a door wide enough to admit a patient bed. The tub may be raised, and a hydrolift installed to transfer patient from bed to tub, or a standard height tub may be used and the adjacent floor area made adjustable, up and down, for the attendant's convenience. The shower stall should admit a wheelchair and have controls at the seated position. The patient simply sits in the shower seat or in his wheelchair for his shower. Cork seats are warmer. Nurses say it is easier to wash the patient's head in the shower.

The accepted national average ratio of nursing unit beds to resident population of church-operated congregate homes has been one to three. However, with the new emphasis on positive health measures,

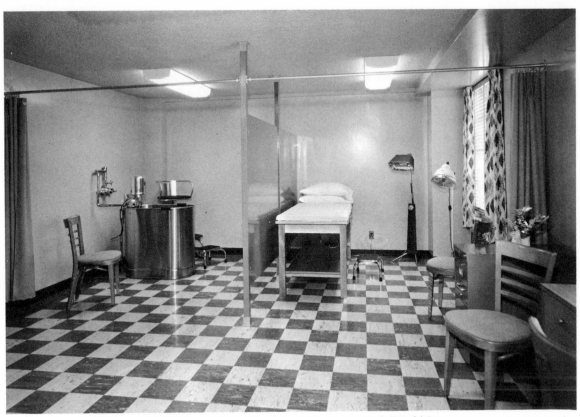

Rehabilitation area of Carroll Manor, Hyattsville, Md. Architect: E. Philip Schrier.

including better nutrition, periodical physical check-ups, but most of all programs of stimulating activities, both physical and mental, an encouraging change is taking place. Kingsley Manor, Los Angeles, the oldest of the homes under Methodist Pacific Homes management, is an outstanding example. Fifty of their 423 residents are over 90 years of age. In their nursing unit of sixty beds, seldom is more than one patient bedfast. A new solarium in the medical unit has a piano and television. Patients are taken in their wheel chairs, walkers, etc., and enjoy special programs prepared for them, including community singing. There is an incentive to get well, and to stay well. They hate to be missing anything. Such efforts, generally adopted, could eventually alter proportionate needs for nursing unit beds. And with the increasing

number of younger applicants for residents in modern retirement homes, such statistics will be further influenced.

Some congregate homes plan nursing units large enough to serve the community as well as their own residents. For the sponsors of homes with this goal, the following statistics may be of help:

Based on 1950 Census figures, some 2 million people in the United States (apart from mentally ill and tuberculosis patients) suffer from chronic illness so seriously that they require long-term care. Of this number one-half to two-thirds receive care in their own homes, but the remainder, more than 750,000, must have care in some type of institutional facility. On this basis it is estimated that five beds per thousand population are required for such care. It is further estimated that 67 per cent of those needing such care are above 65 years of age.* Thus if your city has a population of 100,000, 500 beds could be used for chronic-disease patients, and 67 per cent of 500, or 335 beds, would serve the elderly people of your community so afflicted.

The problem of senility

"Modern medicine does wonderful things, but sometimes it keeps the body alive longer than the mind." The problem of the confused elderly resident requires special planning. He may only be disoriented, forgetful, unable to accept responsibility for his own care. He may be noisy and a nuisance to other residents. Or he may become even a safety risk to himself and to others and require protective care. Some administration policies provide for the transfer of such residents to special institutions. Other homes make provision for the care of these unfortunate people within the project. Occasionally a separate wing is constructed with special soundproofing, restraining devices on windows and doors, and even on beds if needed. Walled gardens and special dining rooms are desirable.

Insurance

Health insurance is needed to help meet today's high cost of medical care. Coverage insuring against hospital expense, surgical expense, and regular medical expense is available through many sources. The best known programs are Blue Cross, covering hospital services, and its companion, Blue Shield, covering physicians' services. These are nation-wide, set up on regional or state bases, sponsored by local hospitals and physicians. Although contracts vary in different areas, the programs enjoy reciprocity in operation. Most people enroll for group coverage while employed and maintain group coverage or convert to individual coverage and billing after retirement.

Insurance companies and independent groups also offer health insurance coverage, the costs and con-

*Edna Nicholson, *Planning New Institutional Facilities for Long-Term Care,* Putnam, New York, 1956.

ditions varying widely. Some 60 insurance companies by the end of 1960 were offering substandard health insurance protection, providing coverage to persons who cannot meet normal health requirements. A total of 165 insurance companies issued health protection to persons in the 65-and-over age category.

To meet costs of catastrophic or prolonged illness or injury, major medical insurance is available. The major medical policy may include a deductible provision such as is common in automobile insurance. It may offer co-insurance, whereby the insured assumes a certain percentage of the risk and the carrier the balance: perhaps 25 per cent borne by the insured and 75 per cent by the insurance company. Federal employees are now offered optional programs for major medical coverage by insurance companies, Blue Cross and Blue Shield. Such programs are increasingly available to the public as well, through insurance companies, nonprofit service plans, and independent groups. The number of insurance companies writing major medical expense insurance totaled 186 in 1960, representing a growth of 114 per cent from 1953.

Thus health insurance is undergoing constant change in order to meet the public's need for greater and more varied protection against the costs of its health care.

Those elderly who choose to live independently and those living in proximate arrangements will be responsible for carrying their own health insurance. Whether or not the resident in a congregate home needs to maintain his health insurance in force depends upon individual home decision. Some homes furnish nursing care, and often physicians' services, within facilities on site, but the resident must meet the costs of both doctor and hospital for acute conditions requiring hospitalization. In such homes the resident maintains his own health policy to meet such an emergency. In other homes, the management assumes all responsibility and the resident need not maintain health insurance personally. The amount of the monthly fee usually reflects the variation in health service furnished.

CHAPTER 15

SUPPLEMENTAL

COMMUNITY SERVICES

Today many communities have a number of services available to help elderly people in time of need and generally to brighten their lives. But all communities do not have all services. Sometimes the services that are available overlap each other; again, there is often not adequate communication between the sponsors of the services and consequently poor or no coordination.

It is important for anyone contemplating building for the elderly to determine what services will be needed, to inventory the community to find what is available, and to organize to make full use of them. A further step would be to stimulate the development of needed services not now available, and to effect the coordination of existing and needed services to do a unified and total job. The Council on Aging (where one exists), Community Welfare Council, or Community Chest is a good focal point for coordination.

We shall briefly describe some of these services.

Health clinics

Most city health departments, some county health departments, and many hospital outpatient departments operate clinics for diagnosis and treatment of various health problems. Such clinics constitute a public service intended for those unable to pay a private physician. They serve people of all ages.

Mental hygiene clinics

Mental hygiene clinics are today being established in increasing numbers but have not begun to even scratch the surface of existing need. Here the citizen (of any age) may obtain help on many types of personal problems. In recent years, because of the general acceptance of the interdependent relationship between emotional stability and religious faith, many clergymen have been trained in counseling procedures in this field and are prepared to help the individual needing assistance.

Geriatric clinics

Geriatric clinics are being set up in some progressive communities by city or county health departments, sometimes through the initiative of citizen groups, to help older people maintain maximum health. Periodic checks are made and advice given on dietary and other health problems. Proper referrals are made for special treatment as indicated, either to the private doctor or the public clinic. Elderly people are encouraged at the geriatric clinic to report problems as they arise, for early attention often avoids serious conditions.

The Toledo, Ohio, "Well Oldster Conference" has attracted attention for its effort to find a definition of normal health—or "how well is well" after a person reaches 65. This is a five-year project. Because the number of over-65 citizens has already reached 11 per cent of the city's population, there is a possibility that the employed people will have an overwhelming burden of sick and infirm to support unless something is done to keep them well, active and productive. How to keep them well is a major problem, but the big question is to know just what constitutes normal health in a person this age. Therefore this effort.*

Transportation to clinics

The American Red Cross in many large cities furnishes emergency transportation to and from clinics for health appointments. For information, contact your local Red Cross office.

Loan closets

The American Red Cross and the Visiting Nurse Association frequently have supplies of sickroom equipment which may be borrowed, such as hospital beds, crutches, wheelchairs, canes, walkers, and even occasionally a hydraulic lift. It seems highly desirable to have such facilities available from a central source.

*Ohio State Medical Journal, December 1961.

Usually the Red Cross keeps an inventory, lends without charge, and delivers via its motor service.

Home medical care

This is still in the experimental stage, but is attracting most favorable attention. It is a team effort by doctor, nurse, therapist and social worker to care for the patient in the home when hospitalization is not necessary. Chronic disease patients often can be managed satisfactorily at much less cost under such a program. It is applicable also to the care of patients convalescing from hospitalization for an acute condition. Follow-up care and rehabilitation procedures can be continued as long as indicated, without need for a lengthy stay in the hospital. Charges are based on ability to pay.

Visiting Nurse Association

The most generally available home health service is that of the Visiting Nurse Association. (It is reported, however, that only about half of the million completely homebound cases in our country are receiving professional nursing service.) This organization is usually operated under the Community Chest or under the city or county health department. On request, a nurse will be sent into a home to bathe a patient, change dressings, and under the direction of a physician administer medication or perform other desired professional nursing service. Visits are made according to the need of the patient, and charges are based on the cost involved and the ability to pay. This service is used by people in all economic brackets. It is available by phoning the Visiting Nurse Association to make the necessary arrangements.

Meals-on-wheels

A service related to health is the Meals-on-Wheels program. Through it a balanced meal is provided daily to the elderly person who may not be eating properly. He or she may find it difficult to prepare suitable meals, or may be just lonely and emotionally upset and therefore lacking in appetite. The meal is prepared to meet individual nutritional requirements,

sometimes in the diet kitchen of a hospital, often in a church kitchen by volunteer workers. It is transported to the home of the recipient in an insulated container especially designed for the purpose. Often a second meal, cold, will be included, to which the recipient may add a hot beverage for supper. The cost to the older person receiving it varies, depending upon the subsidy available and the individual's ability to pay. Sometimes it is as little as fifty cents, sometimes considerably more, for the two meals. This service is performed by a volunteer group in the community. Potential customers are reported by social worker, visiting nurse, physician, clergyman, or other interested person recognizing or suspecting nutritional need in the older person. The fact that a fee is charged, however small, makes the older person more willing to accept the service.

Homemakers' services

This program furnishes help to the elderly person in his home at an hourly rate. It may include cleaning, cooking, laundry, shopping, etc. Family Service Departments of Community Chest organizations or of the Catholic, Jewish or Protestant Social Service Agencies which sponsor the service agree that if more of it could be made available, institutional care at far greater cost often could be avoided. Reports indicate that today only about 3000 families have the benefit of homemaker services in our country, and these include people of all ages. When an elderly person living alone suffers a minor illness or accident, he just cannot manage for the time being. He is therefore frequently placed in a nursing home, or even a hospital, just because there is no other place available. All he really needs is a hand with his household chores for the period of temporary disability. Payment for this service is based upon time involved and ability to pay.

Apropos of the same basic problem, but reporting a different approach to its solution, is a press release from the *Manchester Guardian*. The story relates that high school pupils regularly run errands and do odd household jobs for elderly people resident in a project near Doncaster, England. Some ninety students have volunteered for this service. The girls visit the older people at lunchtime, write down in a book any jobs that need doing. A squad of boys takes care of the heavy work and the girls assume the lighter tasks after school hours. School officials cooperate with the management of the project.

In our country, church groups often assume responsibility for meeting such temporary needs on a voluntary basis. Women's "circles" see an elderly couple, or single person, through a crisis by sharing among their group the various home duties of the oldster during the period of disability. Young people's groups in our churches frequently "adopt" a grandfather or grandmother of their congregation, and not only send birthday cards and gifts and plan occasional treats, but also check for need of special help and supply it.

Friendly visitor service

Under the direction of a Community Chest agency or a church or private social or service group, individual volunteers assume the responsibility to call regularly upon certain elderly persons and perform whatever services appear to be needed. These may include writing a letter, providing transportation to a clinic or to some desired activity, doing an errand, helping with mending, or just—as the name of the service implies—being a friendly visitor. The whole effort is to make the older person know that *someone cares* about his welfare. Some communities have well organized groups performing this service with regularity and continuity.

Senior Citizen Centers

Senior Citizen Centers or Golden Age Clubs are inclusive membership groups which have sprung up like Topsy all across the country in recent years. They may be sponsored by Community Chest organizations, local governments, churches, social or service groups. The purpose is to provide a rendezvous for older people—a place to meet contemporaries, share experiences, and have fun together. In larger cities the Recreation Commission often provides trained leadership for activities programs. As morale boosters for many elderly people, such facilities may well be classified as health-related services.

In fact at one Ohio city's Senior Citizen Centers, weekly health talks are an important part of the regular program. One of the most popular talks was that of a chiropodist on the proper care of the feet. Out of the general interest aroused by the health talks has come the sponsorship of such projects as TB tests of the members, conducted at the centers by the local Anti-Tuberculosis League, clinics for diabetic detection during National Diabetes Week, clinics for cancer detection, and auditory testing of members by the Hearing and Speech Society.

Many large cities have mobile auditory testing units, as do most state health departments, and smaller cities and villages frequently can borrow this equipment to meet their needs. It is very desirable to have the auditory program at the Senior Center where older people are among friends and everyone is doing it. This is far more successful than to try to get them to a clinic. No one wants to confess that he is having a hearing difficulty, even though he knows he should be doing something about it. But when it is a program item, and everyone is being tested, then it is easy to go along with the crowd.

The same is true for faulty vision. Cataracts are frequent among the elderly, and diagnosis and proper referral for treatment are important. The Goodwill Industries Rehabilitation Centers in many communities operate sightsaving clinics available to those who are unable to pay.

Many service clubs, notably Rotary, Kiwanis, Lions, Optimists, etc., elect as their philanthropic project the provision of dentures for elderly people, sightsaving programs, and other special services. More people may be served when the approach is made through the Senior Citizen Centers.

Outlets for marketing handicraft

Marketing products of elderly citizens is a valuable community service. Management is often undertaken by church groups or service organizations in cooperation with local merchants who give space for the effort. It greatly encourages the elderly to find that people want and will buy what they make.

Library service

In many cities a shut-in may call the public library and someone will pick out a book and deliver it. Also bookmobiles often go to Senior Centers at regular intervals for the convenience of the older people.

Volunteer bureau for retired adults

In the vanguard in this field is a project initiated by the Philadelphia section of the National Council of Jewish Women in cooperation with the Council on Volunteers of Health and Welfare, Inc. The bureau provides an "exchange" where retired adults may register their skills and abilities for volunteer service, and where agencies may record their needs. A preliminary survey showed that various "jobs" are available for older volunteers and that the agencies would welcome their services. The sponsor organization will interview, set standards, and collate material.

The Community Health Services and Facilities Act of 1961

This act includes among its many provisions an expanded program of matching grants to states for developing new and improved out-of-hospital health and related health services for the chronically ill and aged, and means of making these services known to the public. Programs envisioned would include those discussed in this chapter—nursing care of the sick at home, homemaker services, home medical care, rehabilitative and social services. They also would include "information and referral services to assist patients in getting to the right type of facility or service, education and training, and diagnostic or screening activities for the early detection of disease at a time when treatment can be most effective in preventing complications and disability."

It is to be hoped that the implementation of this legislation will arouse even more widespread interest and cooperation.

CHAPTER 16

CONSTRUCTING THE PROJECT

On any given project let us assume the following set of circumstances:

1. The architect has been selected and engaged
2. An attorney has been engaged
3. The site has been secured
4. Surveys and borings have been made
5. Deed restrictions and zoning present no problems
6. The architectural program has been written
7. Budgets have been set
8. The architect is ready to prepare preliminary designs.

At this point or even before, a preliminary schedule should be prepared which would establish tentative dates for:

1. Acceptance of preliminary designs
2. Completion of working drawings and specifications
3. Bidding
4. Signing of contracts
5. Starting construction
6. Completion of construction
7. Delivery of furniture and special equipment
8. Moving into the building.

This schedule is useful for several reasons. It gives a preliminary account of when a number of things must be done:

1. Selection of building materials and equipment
2. Engagement of consultants
3. Selection of bidders
4. Completion of financing arrangements
5. Making money available for payment to architects, consultants, contractors, equipment and furniture suppliers
6. Selection of manager or administrator
7. Hiring of staff
8. Inauguration of promotion.

All the major decisions to be made and actions to be taken by the owner should be clearly understood at this time. The architect should begin to prepare his preliminary design.

Preliminary drawings

When presented, the preliminary design should be studied very carefully by the owner (individual or committee), and he should be certain he understands the drawings and their implication. These drawings represent the essential concept, the very heart and soul, of the project. Development and refinement of the basic parti (scheme) must be completed at this stage. All significant decisions are to be embodied in these drawings; upon acceptance, they will clearly reflect the quality and thoroughness of thinking given the project by the owner/architect team. Future changes should be minor or unnecessary. In fact, changes made later on, except in minor detail, indicate lack of study or understanding at this critical basic stage. To forestall such changes, the architect may have to prepare a progressive series of three or four preliminary drawings, each of which comes a step closer to the final idea for the building as more and more details fall into place. Occasionally, the first design is completely satisfactory. It would be ideal if the future administrator of a home could sit in on the process.

Acceptance of the preliminary drawings by the owner as a basis for preparation of working drawings is his legal approval of the design and the estimated cost which should accompany it. At this point, the owner and the architect should agree on any consultants to be engaged and how they are to be paid. The architect is not required to pay for consultants on work for which he may receive no fee, for instance, draperies and carpets, or perhaps landscape design. He is often reimbursed for the work of kitchen layout or hospital equipment consultants.

Working drawings

The next step is the preparation of working drawings. The owner may or may not wish to concern himself with the detail selection of materials and equipment and the solution to problems of site drainage and the like. If he does, he should be helped to do so in an orderly fashion by the architect. The owner should deal with one person on the architect's staff. If the owner is a committee or board, they should appoint one person to deal with the architect's staff. This might be the future administrator if he is available. This person must take care not to slow the work by delaying or changing decisions.

There are many details to be worked out that are in the owner's province and that will find their solution in his concept of how the building will be used. One of these details is the use of keys on a project, for example, the kind and number of master keys to be provided. On a larger project, any one of the following may have keys which pass more than one door but not all doors: the residents, the maid, the kitchen help, the dietitian, the maintenance engineer, nurses, the office staff. Someone naturally holds a grand master which passes all doors.

Bidding procedure

Bidding procedure should be established and a list of bidders prepared before the working drawings and specifications are completed. It is quite unwise to allow anyone to bid on a project whom the architect or owner would not trust with the work. As bidding is a costly procedure to the bidder, it is unethical to allow a dubious candidate to expend his money on it. His bid may be a source of contention if it should happen to be low.

Bidding instructions sometimes direct bidders to submit alternate bids on substitute materials or construction techniques. There should be as few of these alternates as possible. A large number of them may affect the reliability of the bids submitted. They indicate an architect who is not sure of his costs or an owner who either can't make up his mind or has an appetite for more than his purse will cover. Alternates, if taken, should be confined to items which will make a major difference in cost. It should be remembered that some alternates may mean a change in working drawings, and the owner should be prepared to pay the architect for the changes in the drawings if the alternate is accepted. Often acceptance of such alternates puts the architect to additional work that will increase his production costs at the same time the alternates are reducing his fee. Bid analysis becomes more complex if there are alternates to accept or reject, and the writing of construction contracts may be more complicated. Unnecessary alternates should be avoided for this reason if for no other. Signing of contracts may be delayed four or five weeks by the need to come to a decision on alternates, make the necessary changes in the drawings and specifications, and write a construction contract to cover these changes.

Contracts

Contracts are the province of lawyers. Many lawyers, however, do not possess sufficient knowledge of construction procedures and practices to equip them to write a contract between owner and contractor from scratch. In particular, they may not be conversant with certain special conditions which need to be covered. Every project is special, and no blanket form can cover them all. But attorneys will find many models available, and the architect should bring his detailed knowledge of the project to the assistance of the owner's attorney. He may even prepare a first draft of all the special conditions to be covered. He knows building trade practices, payment customs, insurance coverage requirements in the area, whereas the attorney understands the legal in's and out's of liens and owner-contractor legal commitments.

The correct person to sign contracts must be determined. Legal requirements vary in respect to boards, corporations, churches, orders, etc. The attorney will settle this matter. When the contract is signed, the team has gained a third member, and a three-way deal can become a source of trouble if the lines of command are not clearly drawn. Upon occasion the owner may be a board, the architect a firm, and the contractor a corporation. This three-

party team may actually be composed of 10 to 15 principals, not to mention subordinates. The need for lines of command is most obvious in such cases.

In brief, the architect is the owner's agent and expert, and the owner must deal with the contractor through his architect. This means he does not even deal through the architect's inspector on the job, except with the architect's specific consent in each individual case. Likewise the contractor must use this same line of command to conduct business. He does not deal with the owner except through the architect. Neither the owner nor the architect gives any information or decisions to sub-contractors or workmen on the job except through the contractor. Abiding by these simple rules insures a business-like handling of all communications and avoids the misunderstandings possible in a complex operation. It would be valuable at this point to review the "chain of command" discussion and diagram found at the beginning of Chap. 7.

No changes in the work should be made by anyone without a written order prepared by the architect showing the contractor's charges or credits for the change and signed by the owner.

Scheduling

After the contract has been signed, a new schedule should be made which will tell the owner more precisely when he will need various sums of money, when certain decisions on furnishings and equipment must be made, when promotion should be stepped up, when staff should be hired, when furniture may be delivered, and when the building is expected to be ready to occupy. This schedule involves complex calculations based on the delivery time of certain key items of structure and equipment. An interlocking of responsibilities of the members of the team is necessary to make the schedule work, and these responsibilities should be spelled out and given target dates. Poor weather, strikes, and nonavailability of workmen in certain trades may upset the schedule. It should therefore be adjusted and reissued from time to time.

Payments

One responsibility of the owner is to make payments on schedule, but only as certified by the architect. Laxity in financial dealings can make a job situation go sour. When the architect issues his certificate for the final payment, it signifies that he has evidence (which usually accompanies his certificate) that all bills have been paid by the contractor and that he is satisfied the building is completed in full compliance with the drawings and specifications.

After the final payment is made, the contractor and his subcontractors, as well as manufacturers of many pieces of equipment, usually give guarantees on their workmanship and materials for stated periods of a year or more. The architect, of course, as a professional man makes no guarantee of the building or other people's performance. He renders a professional service, and he has a professional responsibility to the owner akin to the responsibility a lawyer or physician has to a client.

Occupancy

The owner who tries to occupy a building in advance of its substantial completion makes a mistake. The psychological atmosphere in a residence for the elderly is particularly bad if the friction of completing the building is added to the problems of new residents' acclimatizing themselves to a strange new home while a new staff is also undergoing a shakedown period. For this reason, residents should not be moved in before the building is completed, and arrivals should be limited to one or two per day at the very most. A slower pace of filling the residence is even better. Among other things, the building itself is a new, complex creature whose full nature, idiosyncrasies, and maladjustments are not fully known to anyone. It takes a full turn of the seasons to get a heating or air-conditioning system in balance, and all the other equipment demands patience and understanding if one is to discover its capabilities and to learn how to operate it at top efficiency.

CHAPTER 17

CHOOSING THE

ADMINISTRATOR

One of the greatest responsibilities of the sponsors of a home for the elderly is to select an administrator. They should acquire one as soon as possible.

Administrator for the proximate home

The administrator of the proximate home has less direct responsibility for the residents than has the administrator of the congregate home. He will be the business manager and as such collect the rents and direct the maintenance of the property. But he can do much more. If he has a sincere interest in the well-being of the residents, that interest will motivate and direct his observation of and concern for their individual behavior. An important effort will be to see that they become acquainted with each other. To this end he could help them initiate group activities. Another very important service he could render would be to become carefully informed about all community services available and where they can be procured. He would thus be prepared for emergency need. Keeping a bulletin board on which are posted current community attractions would be appreciated by the residents. The services of the proximate home administrator can be as varied and as numerous as his imagination is fertile and his willingness to serve is sincere.

Administrator for the congregate home

The charm of the setting and the beauty of the structure are of tremendous importance in establishing the atmosphere of a congregate home. The space within the walls is the reality of the building and the use for which the space was designed is its reason for being. But whether these spaces are used as they were intended by the architect, and how well, determines the quality of living experienced by those who wish to call it home. The administrator has a moral obligation to see that the building is used as it was designed to be used and that the residents are encouraged to take advantage of the opportunities it offers.

When the architect steps out, the administrator is the key figure. It is he who makes the wheels go round, who sets the tone for the home. Depending on his abilities, and no less his attitudes and his personality, there will either be irritation, discord, indifference and apathy among the residents, or harmony and increasingly close friendships; either a deadly dull existence or a stimulating interest in "what's new today?"

What qualifications should the sponsors seek in an administrator? Ideally he should have had training in institutional management of both personnel and funds. He should have an understanding of the health needs of older people, what constitutes good nutrition, suitable exercise, adequate rest. He should recognize the relationship of satisfying activities to good mental health of the individual and the esprit de corps of the group. Of greater importance is the image which the administrator holds of the resident. For this will communicate itself to the resident body and the staff and will affect the atmosphere of the home and its entire operation.

If he looks upon the residents merely as inmates of an institution with whose custodial care he is entrusted, rules and regulations will be the paramount emphasis and efficiency the goal of management. But warmth may be entirely lacking. We are reminded of Albert Einstein's words: "Perfection of tools and confusion of aims characterize our times." If he considers the residents as children under his paternal protection, everything may be minutely planned for them to the last detail, but individual initiative may wither and die and a spirit of frustration prevail. If his attitude is patronizing, the residents will soon sense and resent it, and he will never secure their confidence and cooperation.

But if he has a genuine respect for and a sincere interest in the welfare and happiness of the residents as individual people and as fellow members of the home family, he will make an effort to understand each of them, to know their background and experience to the extent of learning what makes them tick. The wise, resourceful administrator of one congregate home says he tells his "family" to drop in for a chat whenever his door is open, and it is seldom closed. He is glad to talk with them, to get to know them personally, even if they are often repetitious and reminiscent. He says he finds them opening up freely after a short time, and he can always learn something of value from each of them. Thus he gains their confidence and friendship, and if a problem should arise he knows they will come to him without hesitation. Such an administrator will earn the respect and affection of the residents and a genuine friendly, homey atmosphere will be evident in all relationships of the home: between him and the residents, between them and the employees, and even more important, among the residents themselves.

A building is for the resident, not for the management, the cook or the janitor. Regimentation has no place in a home for older people. Of course there must be order and basic regulations, but flexibility of rules makes for a homelike atmosphere. Freedom to sit where they like in the dining room, with different people at each meal if they prefer, or a plan to effect periodic interchange of table companions should some be shy, may be a small matter but very important in its desirable consequences. If there can be a spread of time for service of meals, rather than one specific hour when everyone must be in his place at the table, this too is greatly appreciated. Mealtime should be a happy, friendly experience for residents of any home. But communication is denied the hard-of-hearing if he must face strong light from windows. It prevents his reading the lips of his table companions, a necessary factor in his conversation. The good administrator will be alert to this situation.

A good administrator will strive to create in the residents a feeling of personal responsibility for an atmosphere of hospitality and friendship, and for achieving maximum participation in program activities.

In a certain western home a group of residents cornered one of the authors and asked that she not comment to anyone about their administrator. Surprised, the author expressed a very favorable impression of the executive. "That's the trouble," they replied. "We like him so well we don't want anyone else to try to take him away from us."

The administrator and public relations

The administrator can be most effective in establishing good public relations. To promote community understanding and acceptance of the new home, it is most helpful for him to speak before local organizations of all kinds. By offering talks on neighborhood facilities for better community life and by showing film of existing projects in Europe as well as in this country, not to mention film of the local home under construction, the administrator (and Board members) of First Community Village, Columbus, Ohio, have aroused wide citizen interest and enthusiasm in their project. This may well lead to close community ties for the future residents of the home. And it affords the administrator the opportunity to learn who does what, information which may be most helpful to him later on in securing desired program leadership and opportunities for community service for home residents.

Training programs for administrators

The Federal Government is cooperating with universities in developing courses to train managers of housing facilities for older people. Preliminary plans call for setting up a two-year postgraduate course to be open to persons planning to go into senior housing management. Emphasis will be placed on the principles of administration, personnel and human relations, and gerontology. An internship in a senior housing center is planned as part of the course. It is hoped that several universities will be offering such courses by the fall of 1963. (For current information, write to Special Staff on Aging, Department of Health, Education, and Welfare, Washington 25, D. C.)

CHAPTER 18

ADMINISTRATIVE POLICIES

Administrative policies involved in the operation of a home for the elderly—either proximate or congregate—include financial policies as well as policies concerning admission, services, house rules, and operational jurisdiction. They also govern promotion of the home and all contract documents.

Financial policies

Financial policies determine the solvency of a project. If management contemplates financing a home largely through the founders' fee method, it will anticipate a continuous source of this income over the years as units are resold following the death of residents. How large should the entrance payment be? Mr. Willard E. Stanton, Director of Wesley Gardens, Des Moines, Wash., points out that ordinary life expectancy figures will not hold for residents in a well run retirement home. Such residents live longer for three reasons: better balanced diet; nursing service before an illness becomes serious; and generally better health because of the feeling of security. Because mortality rates will therefore be lowered, Mr. Stanton advises it will take seven to ten years of operation before the turnover reaches 7 per cent per year. He therefore recommends that the sponsor set the entrance fee sufficiently high to meet 55 per cent of the costs of the project.

As we mentioned in Chap. 9, sponsors of a home must check state laws to determine how property tax exemption is established and maintained. They must also check with the regional office of the Internal Revenue Service for specific requirements for income tax exemption on founders' fees, life occupancy fees, or by whatever name entrance payments are called. Basically the requirement is that the nonprofit motive of the sponsor be established and that a certain amount of charitable work be done.

The Board must decide how much charity work it will carry and how it will be financed. Some churches have unallocated funds which can be used to underwrite fees partially or wholly for desirable residents with limited means. Some organizations solicit substantial contributions to a special fund to cover charitable work from the outset of operation, either as reduced admission fees or reduced monthly fees, or both, in order to make firm the qualification for tax exemption. Whatever policy is decided upon should of course be put on record, but need not be made public.

Calling the entrance payment a "founder's *gift*" (with no provision for refund) may effect tax saving for both institution and resident in some states. The home is not required to report a gift as income, and the resident may deduct the amount as a contribution to a nonprofit organization.

The Reverend Mr. Robert Netting, Cincinnati, says sometimes the management of a home finds it possible and financially profitable to assume title to residence property owned by an applicant. The procedure often proves more advantageous than if the applicant sells the property himself to realize funds for entrance payment, because Management may then sell the property at a possibly higher interest rate on the mortgage it negotiates than it could have earned from investing proceeds of sale by applicant. Also the applicant may profit because he will not have to pay a capital gains tax if he transfers the property to the home, a nonprofit organization.

Since it is necessary to show nonprofit status annually to maintain tax exempt status, homes should make use of allowable deductions for depreciation of equipment and furnishings which will someday need replacement.

What will be the monthly fee and what will it cover? Will there be an escalator clause to permit management to increase the monthly fee to meet the cost-of-living index? (Of 37 homes furnishing information on this important question, 29 have escalator clauses, two have such clauses applying to all residents except those who have prepaid on a life-care

basis, and six do not change the monthly fee after the contract is signed.)

If prepayment of a lump sum for life care, actuarily computed, is considered as an optional method for paying fees, both entrance and monthly, the contracts of some homes include a clause granting the home the right to abrogate the original contract if the resident outlives his expectancy. This permits the home to write a new contract to cover the resident's care, but also permits application for state aid to help underwrite the costs.

Admission

Admission policies fix limitations, if any, on the age, sex, race, faith, or group affiliation of the applicants. Any requirements concerning the state of applicant's health should be agreed upon. Must he be ambulatory and in good general health, or will he be acceptable if he needs nursing care on entrance?

The Admissions Committee is of course highly important to the success of the project. Sponsors have an image of what they expect of the home—the atmosphere they wish created, the service they hope it can render. So it is important to evaluate each applicant in terms of how the home can meet his particular needs and how he will affect the desired tone of the home. This takes time, patience, insight, firmness, and a real love of people. Although for a large home it becomes practically a full-time voluntary job, those who undertake it find it most rewarding.

Service

All services to be provided should be clearly defined. Will the entrance fee entitle the resident to life occupancy of room, suite, apartment, or cottage? What furnishings will be included—carpeting, draperies, linens, furniture, etc.? What items must or may the resident furnish?

Will the monthly fee cover meals? How many? What about special diets? Will laundry be furnished by the home, and if so, is it linen laundry only or personal as well? Will this be done on the premises or contracted? Will laundry facilities be available for

resident use? Will there be daily, weekly, or less frequent maid service? What recreational facilities will be provided, both outside and inside?

And what about health services? Will nursing care be available in an infirmary or nursing unit? Will this be for temporary illness only, or will it cover convalescent conditions and long-term chronic illness? Will there be an extra charge for infirmary care or will the cost be included in the monthly fee? Will routine physical examination be provided? Will there be treatment facilities for dentist, oculist, podiatrist? If hospitalization is required, who will pay the hospital bill and the doctor? Must the resident maintain in force his own health insurance to meet this potential need, or will the home offer him group insurance?

If senility develops, will the home accommodate the resident in special quarters? In such case will the resident be expected to relinquish his room or apartment? If the home is not equipped for this type of care, may the management elect to relocate the resident in a suitable institution, or will it be the responsibility of the resident's family to make other arrangements for his care?

House rules

House rules may cover such matters as dining room hours, seating arrangements, conditions under which residents may have guests, tipping or gifts to employees, etc. In case of extended absence will the resident be entitled to a refund? What about the use of alcohol? (In congregate homes studied, 49 reported regulation as follows: prohibited, 25; discouraged, 4; restricted, 3; unrestricted, 17.)

Operational jurisdiction

Placing of responsibility for staff employment and regulation and for purchasing and handling of supplies should be agreed upon and made clearly a matter of record. In the case of a cooperative home for elderly people, it is essential that an executive committee handle details of administration. Without this arrangement it can be difficult to reach decisions.

Promotion

Promotion is a continuous process from the inception of the project to its formal dedication, and long after. The original survey to determine the need arouses a basic interest in a large number of people. News releases from time to time reporting the progress of different phases of the work of the building committee will advance that interest. Interviews with different committee members, with the architect, and with the administrator can be featured in press articles or on radio or TV to keep the project in public focus. A model of the project placed in a prominent window will also draw attention.

One sponsor ran a large advertisement in a local newspaper announcing the completion of plans for a project, showing perspectives of the buildings, stating costs, and incorporating a mail-in blank asking for an interview with the Admissions Committee. Applications poured in.

An interesting promotion device was most successful in the Northwest. A special small concrete structure was erected on a corner of the site of a new home under construction at a street intersection where many people passed daily. This structure was scaled to represent a dwelling unit in the new home. Its attractive furnishings could easily be viewed through the windows. Where to get information about costs and admission requirements was posted on the building. This attracted much attention and many applications. The home was completely sold out before it opened, and it has had a waiting list ever since.

Promotion literature can be distributed through churches, Senior Citizen Centers, doctors' offices, beauty parlors, barber shops, etc. Young people will be interested for their parents, and of course the elderly for themselves. Promotion literature and material generally includes the following:

1. Flyer—An inexpensive piece, intended for wide distribution, containing highlights on WHAT, WHERE, and FOR WHOM, the entrance fee range, and the monthly fee. A tear-off form may be incorporated to mail to the administrator requesting a brochure.

2. Brochure—This is the information pamphlet with full details, as attractive as budget and talent will permit. It should state location and size of the project and give photographs or perspectives of the buildings. A city map is desirable. It should describe in detail types of accommodations available, giving cost of each and showing floor plans if possible. Advantages, opportunities, and activities should be detailed fully. Charges and services should be clearly stated. An application-for-admission form should be included.

3. A chatty news letter—This is published by some larger homes during construction, giving details of progress, etc.

4. A set of color slides—These are made from the architect's drawings and especially prepared data on costs and are for use in public talks.

Documents

1. The application for admission—This form usually assures applicant that information submitted will be kept confidential. Data and information requested may include: (a) personal data: age (birth date), citizenship, church membership or preference, occupation, interests (it may request a photograph); (b) references; (c) names of relatives or close friends to contact in emergency; (d) sufficient data to establish applicant's credit (social security, investments, pension etc.); (e) priority choice of accommodation; and (f) desired date of entrance and explanation of business affairs which might affect this, that is, selling house, etc. (Note: application need not be too detailed or personal. Interview will afford opportunity for careful evaluation.)

2. Medical certificates—These are usually (a) furnished by applicant's physician and submitted with application, and (b) filled out by the home's physician after examination of applicant.

3. Contract—This should be a form carefully drawn up by an attorney, or approved by one. Basically it should establish that the home accepts the application and agrees to furnish certain accommodations and services, stating for what period, and that the applicant agrees to pay certain fees for such accommodations and services, stating in what manner. A period of probation may be established. Provisions should be stated for procedure in case applicant becomes senile. Procedure should be defined for disposition of applicant's property at death. Conditions governing cancellation of contract should be stated. Liabilities should be defined.

CHAPTER 19

BUDGETS

At an early stage of the planning, an economic analysis of the proposed project should be made and three budgets should be prepared. The budgets are: (1) the income budget, (2) the operating budget, and (3) the construction budget.

The entrepreneur or committee building a group project needs a careful and thorough market survey to establish the income level of residents available and the range of charges they can and will pay. (See Chap. 6 for a discussion of market surveys.) This does not mean that the project must be pegged for the largest segment of the market disclosed. But if the project is to appeal to those wanting luxury accommodations, the owner must have evidence of an ample reservoir of such people to draw upon.

Building is a deep psychological experience with romantic overtones, and it is common for the dream to expand as it begins to take concrete form. Seldom does a project shrink in size or cost in the process.

Income budget

The income budget, out of which a home is to be operated, takes account of all sources of expected income. It must be carefully analyzed in terms of the economic status of the individual or group to occupy the home. Optimism must be kept in bounds, and the budget projections must be factual and realistic.

The income budget will normally include the following items, among others:

1. Entrance fees

2. Monthly fees for room, food, and standard services

3. Fees for special services like nursing, medical treatment, therapy, beauty salon, etc.

4. Subsidies from charitable sources to cover part or all of the monthly fees of certain residents

5. Gifts and bequests (conjectural, but usual)

6. Special rents for garage space, apartments, and the like.

Estimates of real income are usually based on a 90 to 95 per cent occupancy.

Operating budget

The operating budget should cover the normal monthly and yearly operating costs of the project (individual house or group home) after the first year or two of occupancy. During the first year or two, expenses may exceed those normal after the home is in good operating order. There are many reasons for this. There are unforeseen, miscellaneous items of furniture, equipment, and utensils needed or wanted to implement recreation programs; to complete furnishings or landscaping; or to make some detail operation go more smoothly. The site and building may demand minor adjustments; moving in entails costs not usually budgeted; operation costs may be higher during the initial shakedown. Each of these items is usually minor, but sometimes they add up to a tidy sum. The period during which a congregate home is filling with residents, and the expenses continue as usual before the income builds up to a full flow, is a period of financial stress for many projects.

The operating budget may be broken down in many ways but will include the following items:

1. Salaries, plus payroll taxes, hospitalization, retirement fund payments

2. Administration costs and supplies

3. Legal and accounting fees

4. Public relations, advertising, publicity, printing, postage

5. Licenses and memberships

6. Housekeeping costs and supplies

7. Laundry

8. Food

9. Health fees, costs, and supplies

10. Costs of supplies and other expenses for program, crafts, and activities

11. Utilities: telephone, water, fuel, electricity

12. Expense accounts and allowances

13. Travel and gasoline, etc.

14. Outside hospital fees

15. Contract services: laboratory, X-ray, sterilizing, elevator, air conditioning, septic tank, window cleaning, exterminator, etc.

16. Taxes

17. Debt service

18. Insurance: fire and wind, liability, malpractice

19. Replacement reserve: furniture, equipment, utensils, dinnerware, flatware, linens, etc.

20. Maintenance of building, grounds, furnishings, equipment, cars, trucks, etc.

21. Depreciation of building, furniture, equipment

22. Funerals

Supplies are regularly needed for: office, housekeeper, janitor, dining room, kitchen, laundry, infirmary, health, recreation, therapy, crafts, buildings, grounds, and religious services.

Equipment types are: office addressing, duplicating machines; household cleaning, scrubbing, polishing machines; laundry machines; kitchen equipment and utensils; dining room; infirmary; laboratory; therapy department; recreation department; building and grounds maintenance; carpentry and paint shop.

Construction budget

The construction budget should reflect the total financial plan of investment for land, construction, site improvement, landscaping, furnishings, equipment, builders' fees, architects' fees, and auxiliary costs, such as real estate fees, financing charges, taxes, legal fees, and interest during construction.

The construction budget will include the following items:

1. Legal and accounting fees

2. Real estate fees

3. Architect's fees

4. Landscape architect's fees

5. Consultants' fees (interior design, kitchen design, infirmary and therapy design, elderly housing expert)

6. Financing costs

7. Permits, surveys, test borings

8. Construction loan interest

9. Utility connection fees (water and gas taps, etc.)
10. Land
11. Building
12. Equipment
13. Furnishings
14. Site improvements, clearing, demolishing

For a group project of proximate or congregate kind, we must add corporation organization costs, advertising promotion, personnel costs during construction (such as the manager's salary if he is hired before the project is complete). We must also add carrying charges on the mortgage, and personnel and operating costs in excess of income at the beginning stage until the project is fully occupied.

The total of the construction budget will be covered by a combination of a mortgage, cash on hand, or gifts of various sorts. Gifts may include land, materials, services, equipment, furnishings, landscape materials or, best of all, money. Whatever is not covered by cash on hand or gifts must be included in the mortgage, and payments on the interest and principal must be represented in the debt service item in the operating budget.

Reconciling the various budgets

These three budgets must be reconciled with each other. The mortgage costs are fitted into the operating budget and the operating budget is balanced against expected income.

The debt service item in the operating budget must equal the mortgage payments or be upped to meet them, perhaps by revising the income budget. Otherwise the elements of the construction budget must be reduced so that mortgage payments will fall within the allotment for debt service and so that both will conform to the projections of anticipated income.

A study of preliminary budgets will make clear how initial organizing and construction costs can affect the monthly charges to be met over the years. Therefore, the budget parts must be adjusted several times at the outset to assure that they are mutually feasible. They should be thoroughly reviewed periodically and especially just before the major expenditures are started.

A number of items, not normally considered in building project financing, can be of considerable importance to a group undertaking elderly housing. Some of these are:

1. Tax-exempt status
2. Life expectancy projections
3. Health expectancy projections
4. Cost of moving in
5. Cost of putting the project in operation
6. Cost of first year's operation over income
7. Founder's fee and entrance fee figures
8. Size of the project
9. Transportation
10. Operating cushion
11. Entrance fee refunds
12. Fallacy of too low salary scale in eleemosynary homes
13. Employees' retirement fund
14. Charity budget for assistance to certain residents

There are still other items that will come to light as the planning progresses.

Certain devices are used by fraternal and eleemosynary groups to balance unusual expenses of establishing a retirement home. These need careful analysis in terms of their tax status, their psychological effect on admissions, and their effect on operations of the home. Founder's fees or entrance fees need most careful scrutiny by a tax consultant. One home which handled founder's fees unwisely was bankrupted when the Federal Bureau of Internal Revenue declared such fees regular income and taxed them accordingly. Signing over all personal possessions by a new resident of a home is not the popular custom it used to be, and such a stipulation can keep prospective residents hesitating or scare them away. There are right and wrong ways to receive such property under current tax laws. The whole concept is open to much rethinking both by sponsors and residents.

Tax-exempt status, where anticipated, must be carefully defined, legally established, and watchfully guarded. The administrator of a home should be concerned about the tax-exempt status of other homes in the vicinity and state because bad practices in this respect in one home can bring about conditions inimical to other homes in the same jurisdiction. Finally, minor gifts of memorial nature such as furniture and equipment must be accepted as a memorial of duration commensurate with the value or service life of the gift. Thus a gift of a building should probably have an acknowledged duration of 50 years whereas memorial plaques for room furniture and the like should be considered to have a life of five years, or ten at the most. Otherwise, a group residence can become the repository of an accretion of memorials in perpetuity which eventually ossify the entire atmosphere of the home.

SECTION V • HOW HOMES FOR THE AGED MAY BE DE-INSTITUTIONALIZED

by Bo Boustedt, Architect SAR, Kungalv, Sweden

(All homes illustrated were designed by the author.)

Very early in Swedish history the community began providing social services to its citizens. Hospitals and a certain amount of support of the aged, for example, were a responsibility of society as early as the Middle Ages. Consequently, the principle that society has an obligation to care for the sick and for the old has had a long tradition in Sweden. To build homes for the aged is an important part of our social nature.

Sweden is a nation with a strong democratic tradition. In any culture it is the task of the architect both to reflect and to improve the society in which he lives and works. In a democracy, I believe, it is the duty of the architect to foster and protect respect for individuality and dignity—even in an institution. It is a difficult problem to find solutions that will provide protection for individuality and yet allow efficient management of institutional problems.

Many older people can live in apartments or in detached or semi-detached housing. Homes for the aged, on the other hand, are built for pensioners who cannot live by themselves in apartments or dwellings. Such homes are needed by a rather limited number of pensioners—an average of only 5 to 10 per cent of the people over seventy. These older citizens, while requiring some physical care in the form of housekeeping and meal preparation, are neither bedridden, requiring hospital-type care, nor mentally deficient, requiring custodial care. In the average small city of 50,000 population, they would amount to some 500 oldsters.

Homes for these people are built and run by the local governments, who receive some support from the national government for construction costs. The tenants also contribute to the costs of the homes with their old-age pensions. The total number of homes for the aged built since 1947 when the new principles were accepted by the Parliament is 650, and another 100 homes will be built in 1962. All local governments are trying to meet the need of homes for the aged as soon as possible.

I would like to underline how necessary it is that *all* types of care for the aged function fully at the

1

same time. Lack of hospital beds, for example, will result in having to care for sick people in homes for the aged rather than in hospitals. Lack of apartments for old people will also overload homes for the aged, which, of course, represent a more expensive form of care than apartment or family home help.

Homes for the aged, of course, are a sort of institution, and so a most important part of the design problem is to avoid the impression of an institution and to create real homes. I would like to quote Dr. Ali Berggren of the Swedish National Social Welfare Board: "We look upon aging as a normal phase of human life, and we fight against such uncritical, unrealistic, passive, and dangerous attitudes toward old persons that imply that everyone of them *must* be sick and senile." This is our basis for designing homes for the aged.

For me, the problem of the milieu or environment is the most important and most stimulating part of designing these homes for the aged. The right milieu is built up by many different things, all the way from the fundamental elements to the smallest details. By means of the following pictures and text I will try to illustrate some factors of special significance.

We primarily build small homes for 50 to 70 occupants where residents can continue to live in the locale in which they have spent their earlier years. We have found this size of home the most economically sound.

1. *Adaption to site*—The first problem is adaption to site. We adapt the exterior design details to fit the characteristics of the architecture of the region as much as possible while still striving for new forms.

We make an effort to have the homes fit in with the family houses in the neighborhood. This makes the home familiar to the resident and esthetically satisfying to the community.

We have continually modified the floor plans to give as much privacy as possible within the home while at the same time breaking facade areas into continually smaller units. This is contrary to the trend of most contemporary architecture, but it is a desirable approach to make homes for the aged belong to the ordinary residential neighborhood.

Closeness to a village center or a view over a square or a much frequented road is more valuable than a beautiful view in a quiet, removed location.

2. *Approach*—A friendly house-like approach to the home is important for a good first impression every time the resident returns home. Sheltered log-

gias, terraces, and yards easy to reach and with different orientations stimulate and facilitate outdoor life.

3. *Small units*—Since pensioners come more and more from dwindled households, they should not be forced to live in a great collective. The home must be broken down into small units of five to seven rooms, each with its own entrance, living room, coffee-kitchen, dining room, etc. The staggered house is a way to get a minor scale. At the gables are separated entrances and small living rooms.

The small unit must be developed in a manner which retains convenient traffic patterns for the staff. This is accomplished through several general types of floor plans.

4. *Entrance halls* — Inside the home, departures from institutional patterns should become immediately apparent. I design small entrance halls to establish a sense of welcoming intimacy.

The entrance must be given immediate contact with furnished spaces. It should have an interesting outlook on the living room. When one enters, the view into the living room combined with dining room should give a positive and stimulating first impression of the home.

5. *Living rooms*—The main living room is at the entrance. It is often connected with one of the dining rooms. The two rooms are separated by a movable curtain wall but can be combined for use as an assembly hall. The rule of thumb in planning the combinations is to provide enough space to seat twice as many people as there are residents. Since these halls are used only a few times a year, it is very important to be able to reduce them to more intimate, specialized rooms the remainder of the time.

2

2 3

4 5

5.

The second type of living room is the *dagrum,* or small unit living room. These living rooms and sitting-groups are spread all over the home, varying both in location and in character. They are the size of a small family living room and usually contain a fireplace. The furniture is designed specifically for the needs of the elderly.

6. *Corridors*—One of the major problems of the humanization of institutions is the design of the corridor. The long, dark, antiseptic hall, lined with rows of doors and facing a dead end, is one of the distinguishing signs of the institution. To get away from this situation, we have developed several solutions:

a. The goal is to create short and well-lighted corridors with visual contacts with furnished spaces; the staggered plan helps this.

b. Varying the width of the corridor breaks the monotony and can provide supplemental living space.

c. Having furnished rooms always in the viewline helps give a homelike atmosphere.

d. Visual and physical contact with outdoor areas removes sterility.

e. Recessing doors in niches varies the corridor width and conceals the number of doors.

f. Both structural and decorative materials are chosen that will underline the non-institutional character of the home.

7. *Pensioners' rooms*—Because the residents use their individual rooms as private sitting rooms, they need privacy and as much usable floor space as is economically feasible. The rooms must be comfortable and familiar and not have too much of a bedroom character.

Placement of the lavatory and a specially designed and pre-built closet unit in the vestibule leaves the remainder of the room free for flexible furniture arrangement. This closet also provides space for outdoor clothing.

The floor plan permits lengthwise placement of the bed on the inside wall. The bed is designed to eliminate the bedroom appearance while still functioning as a hospital bed. Other furniture may belong either

5

6

to the resident or to the home, at the discretion of the resident.

Each room has a large window, and the rooms are oriented toward receiving maximum sunlight. Absence of double rooms makes it possible completely to avoid special sickrooms. For married couples, two single rooms are also used as bedroom/sitting room suites.

8. *Dining room and coffee-kitchen*—I use small dining rooms for a maximum of twelve tenants (with tables for four) in open contact with the coffee-kitchen. The food is served from wagons with the character of a piece of furniture. The wagon is equipped with heater, drawers for cutlery, table-service (clean and soiled), linen, trays, etc.

Since the kitchen is the heart of home life, especially for women, a home-size kitchen is provided in the units, and here every pensioner has a locker for his or her supplies. The residents can chat over a cup of freshly brewed coffee as they did in their own homes.

9. *Hobby rooms*—Men and women alike are used to working and producing usable products. They can continue such occupations in the hobby workroom. Their products can then be sold in the little shop, and the profits will provide additional spending money as well as giving a sense of pride to the creator.

6

6

In conclusion, I would like to state that different segments of our population need different types of housing just as they did when they were younger. Every day we will analyze another element of the problem, solve it, and wonder why the solution did not occur to us before. But we will reach acceptable solutions only so long as we remember that the first principle of the architect of homes for the aged must be to preserve human dignity and to provide a milieu where a life with interest and meaning can be continued.

7

7

8

8

SECTION VI • EXHIBIT OF PROJECTS

The following data has been furnished by architects and administrators of the various projects described. The authors do not assume responsibility for its accuracy.

CONGREGATE HOUSING: TABLE 1

Explanation of symbols describing health facilities—*Future*; Care: *Infirmary*; *Nursing Unit*; *Hospital*; Treatment: *Diagnosis*; *Special* (dentist, oculist, podiatrist, psychiatrist); Therapy (*physio-*, *psycho-*, *occupational*); Age figures: *Admission average*; *Average now*; *Spread* of ages. Data on projects supplied by architects and sponsors.

Name of project	Capacity	Total cost	Cost per sq. ft.	Cost per cu. ft.	Year bid	Health facilities			Ages of residents		
						No. beds	Care	Treatment	Adm.	Av.	Spread
Actors' Fund of America Retirement Home	40	$723,500	$23.20	—	1958	2	I	T	—	—	—
American Lutheran	65	$583,000	$17.70	$1.72	—	100(F)	—	—	—	—	—
Appelman Jewish	112	$678,000	$13.56	$1.21	1949	80	N	D,S,T	70	80	65-98
Baptist Home and Center	118 (86)	$502,875	$17.30	—	1959	50	N	—	77	80	67-93
Baptist Village	112	$1,250,000	$15.50	$1.20	57/59	14	I	D,T	72	76	65-86
Bayview Manor	296	$3,600,000	$18.25	$1.66	1959	28	N	T	74	76	60-91
Crestview Club Apartments	210	$1,785,000	$18.52	—	1959	6	I	—	75	76	60-92
Good Samaritan	106	$200,000	$20.80	$1.90	1959	31	N	S,T	79	83	70-97
Harold Haaland's Home	68	$647,000	$17.93	$1.45	1961	—	—	—	—	—	—
Hillcrest Homes	137	$2,007,800	$15.50	—	1961	12	N	T	—	—	—
Houston Jewish	100	$850,000	$22.82	$2.08	54/58	17	N	D,S,T	76	79	65-96
Lutheran Senior City	286	$2,380,284	$17.07	—	1962	24	N	S,T	—	—	—
Norse Home	140	$1,200,000	$12.00	$1.20	1955	54	I	—	75	79	69-98
Presbyterian Homes	44	$400,000	$14.30	$1.14	1954	4	N	T	—	84	—
Rest Haven	69	$490,000	$19.17	$1.93	1954	(Contract with hospital on site)			—	80	70-97
Rockwood Manor	300	$3,130,000	$15.12	$1.60	1960	30	N	—	—	74	60-92
Rogue Valley Manor	340	$5,206,000	$20.25	$1.82	1959	40	N	D,T	—	70	57-89
St. James House	47	$425,000	$15.53	—	1959	10	I	T	78	79	61-98
St. Mary's Memorial	20	$273,855	$22.80	$1.54	1955	2	I	—	77	78	66-92
The Sequoias	334	$3,304,971	$18.01	$1.96	1960	4	I	(Contract with hospital)	—	73	62-88
Wesley Palms	350	$5,500,000	—	—	1961	6	I	(Management hospital)	—	70	58-92
Wesley Gardens	250	$2,372,268	$15.95	$1.70	1956	56	N	T	74	79	60-98
Wesley Terrace	283	$3,488,711	$17.01	$1.62	1960	21	I	T	73	—	—
Winebrenner Haven	52	$501,542	$16.57	—	1958	6	N	T	81	81	70-96

CONGREGATE HOUSING: TABLE 2

Explanation of symbols: Parking spaces: Resident; Institution; Visitor; Staff allocation: Administration; Health; Food; Maid; Laundry; Building and grounds maintenance; part-time staff shown in parentheses. Data on projects supplied by architects and sponsors.

Name of project	Capacity	Parking spaces			Extent of health services	Staff allocation						Fees	
		R	I	V		A	H	F	M	L	B	Entrance	Monthly
Actors' Fund of America Retirement Home	40	Ample			Minimum	2	1	3	6	—	3	None	None
American Lutheran	65	15	5	10	Minimum	1	7	3	—	—	—	None	$130-135
Appelman Jewish	112				Complete	3	50	15	10	5	3	—	As able
Baptist Home and Center	118	40 total			Limited	3	26	11	8	2	2	$500-5,000	$75
Baptist Village	112	30	20	10	Limited	3(1)	2(1)	3	3(1)	—	1(1)	As able	$150
Bayview Manor	296	60		24	Limited	9(1)	10(5)	17(15)	4	—	3(5)	$8,750-19,250	$112 and up
Crestview Club Apartments	210	35		40	Limited	6(4)	3(5)	11(8)	11	—	5	$7,000-37,000	$150
Good Samaritan	106	Lot			Complete	4	18	8(2)	8(6)	—	4	None	$150
Harold Haaland's Home	68	20	10	20	Limited	15 total						As able	$100-120
Hillcrest Homes	137	56		12	Limited	6	4	8	4	—	3	$6,800-32,500	$125 and up
Houston Jewish	100	36 total			Limited	3	(4)	7	9	2	2	None-$5,000	None-$275
Lutheran Senior City	286	240 total			Limited	6	21	20	11	5	4	One month's fee	$160-200
Norse Home	140	10	10	St	Minimum	2	1	1	—	—	1	$6,000-7,000	$107-145
Presbyterian Homes	44	Ample			Limited	15 total						$750	$125 and 140
Rest Haven	69	—	—	18	Limited	2(1)	27(4)	15(3)	7(2)	—	1(1)	None	$150
Rockwood Manor	300	40 garage and lot			Limited	6	8	15(5)	8	—	5(1)	$7,500	$120 and up
Rogue Valley Manor	340	56	—	14	Limited	9	15	34	10	4	17	$8,500-30,000	$110
St. James House	47	30	—	—	Limited	1	1	2	2	—	1	None	$100-225
St. Mary's Memorial	20	2	1	3	Minimum	1(1)	1(3)	4(1)	1	(1)	(1)	$500	$100-135
The Sequoias	334	120	50	50	Complete	8	3	27	14	—	6	$10,500-32,000	$185-255
Wesley Palms	350	186 total			Complete (90% hosp.)	100 total (est.)						$7,500-27,500	$200
Wesley Gardens	250	50	60	—	Limited	3(1)	7(6)	26(20)	5	3	4(1)	$7,000-17,000	$110
Wesley Terrace	283	59	18	70	Minimum	3(2)	7(2)	26(21)	6	3	3(1)	$8,000-19,000	$110
Winebrenner Haven	52	3	5	20	Limited	2	4(3)	4(3)	1(1)	1	—	None	$153-220

CONGREGATE HOUSING

ACTORS' FUND OF AMERICA RETIREMENT HOME
(Englewood, N. J.; completed 1961)

Sponsor: The Actors' Fund of America, N. Y., N. Y.
Architects: Moon & Iwatsu, A.I.A., Englewood, N. J.
Consultants: Dwight Engineering Assoc., mechanical; R. Joseph Raymond & Son, kitchen
Site: Part of estate in old residential area, middle-income, slightly integrated; approximately ½ mile to churches, stores; near public transportation
Capacity: 40 (64 possible, if necessary)
People served: Men and women 70 and over who have spent most of their lives in the theatre; ambulatory, good general health; Caucasian, interfaith
Buildings: One two-story and seven one-story structures with 32 nonhousekeeping units, designed for possible double occupancy
Health facilities: Two-bed infirmary, care for temporary illness; doctor's office, examining room; physio-, occupational therapy
Auxiliary facilities: Dining rooms (resident, 50; staff, 4; employees, 10); laundry facilities; library (312 sq ft); recreation (1,100 sq ft); shuffleboard; two social rooms with kitchenettes (12 each); auditorium-lounge (1,040 sq ft); outdoor croquet, greenhouses (orchids)
Service facilities: Central kitchen; maintenance shop; resident storage; parking spaces (unlimited)
Staff: Total: 15 (Administration, 2; health, 1; food, 3; maid, 6; maintenance, 3)
Charges and services: No charges; charitable institution; guests chosen through various theatrical organizations
Construction: Total building area, 31,000 sq ft; building materials: stud frame, 2-story section steel and concrete (exterior: walls—brick; sash—aluminum; roofs—asphalt shingle; terraces—flagstone, brick; walks—concrete; interior: walls—plaster; floors—asphalt tile, carpet; ceilings—acoustic plaster; partitions—stud, plaster; trim—metal, wood; bathrooms—Kalistron walls, tile); heating, cooling: hot water and chilled water; fuel: gas
Site development: Blacktop driveway; landscaping: trees, lawn, fountain, lily pool
Cost (1958): Total site development, buildings, built-in equipment, fees, but not furnishings: $723,500; cost per square foot: $23.20; furnishings, $70,000; health, $3500
Financing: Endowment; contributions (every Broadway show running ten weeks has one benefit Sunday performance for this Home)
Architect says: "To solve the myriad of problems presented, the architects spent considerable time researching designs, plans and latest thinking in existing . . . homes, both here and abroad. They drew heavily on those which have been evolving in Sweden. . . . The Actors' Fund Home is equipped and designed to meet every need and care of the older person, yet with an atmosphere that is club-like, gracious, and intimate. The overall spaciousness, delightful furnishings, memorabilia with which the guests are surrounded, the charming gardens in which they can stroll, while chatting of the past with companions who shared their former world, all add up to happy, leisurely living."

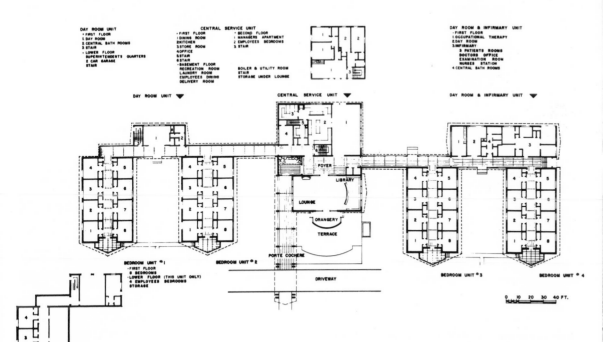

DAY ROOM UNIT
· FIRST FLOOR
1. DAY ROOM
2. CENTRAL BATH ROOMS
3. STAIR
· LOWER FLOOR
SUPERINTENDENTS QUARTERS
2 CAR GARAGE
STAIR

CENTRAL SERVICE UNIT
· FIRST FLOOR
1. DINING ROOM
2. KITCHEN
3. STORE ROOM
4. OFFICE
5. STAIR
6. STAIR
· BASEMENT FLOOR
RECREATION ROOM
LAUNDRY ROOM
EMPLOYEES DINING
DELIVERY ROOM

· SECOND FLOOR
1. MANAGERS APARTMENT
2. EMPLOYEES BEDROOMS
3. STAIR

BOILER & UTILITY ROOM
STAIR
STORAGE UNDER LOUNGE

DAY ROOM & INFIRMARY UNIT
· FIRST FLOOR
1. OCCUPATIONAL THERAPY
2. DAY ROOM
3. INFIRMARY
3 PATIENTS ROOMS
DOCTORS OFFICE
EXAMINATION ROOM
NURSES STATION
4 CENTRAL BATH ROOMS

DAY ROOM UNIT ▼   CENTRAL SERVICE UNIT ▼   DAY ROOM & INFIRMARY UNIT ▼

FOYER

LIBRARY

LOUNGE

ORANGERY

TERRACE

PORTE COCHERE

DRIVEWAY

BEDROOM UNIT #1
· FIRST FLOOR
8 BEDROOMS
· LOWER FLOOR (THIS UNIT ONLY)
4 EMPLOYEES BEDROOMS
STORAGE

BEDROOM UNIT #2

BEDROOM UNIT #3   BEDROOM UNIT #4

0 10 20 30 40 FT.

CONGREGATE HOUSING

AMERICAN LUTHERAN HOMES, INC., RETIREMENT HOME
(Fargo, N. D.; anticipated completion 1963)

Sponsor: American Lutheran Homes, Inc.
Architects: Foss & Co., A.I.A., Moorhead, Minn.
Site: One-half acre plot in old residential section of large homes; near commercial area, churches, public transportation
Capacity: 65
People served: Men and women 65 and over; interdenominational (Lutheran preferred); ambulatory, in good health
Buildings: One 6-story structure with 55 non-housekeeping units (45 singles; 10 doubles)
Health facilities: Short term illness cared for in resident's room; sponsor will build 100-bed nursing home on adjoining site
Auxiliary facilities: Five dining rooms, one on each of five resident floors, serving 13 residents each (one staff); resident kitchenette each floor with individual locked compartments for

snack supplies; automatic laundry each floor; central lounge—living room—chapel; five lounges, 256 sq ft, with balcony, one on each floor; crafts room
Service facilities: Central kitchen; central laundry (in future nursing home); resident storage, 15 sq ft each; 30 parking spaces (resident, 15; staff, 5; visitors, 10)
Staff: Estimated total: 12
Charges and services: No entrance fee; monthly fee of $130–$135 covers room, meals, maid
Construction: Total building area: 32,750 sq ft, 337,000 cu ft; building materials (exterior: walls—4" brick, 4" LWC block, 1" styrofoam; sash—aluminum; roofs—concrete lift slab; walks—concrete slab on grade; interior: walls—metal stud, metal lath, plaster, prefinished wood paneling; floors—carpeting; ceilings—

plaster, exposed concrete lift slab; partitions—metal studs with plaster; trim—hollow metal); Heating: hot water; fuel: oil
Site development: Concrete terraces; hyperbolic paraboloid canopy shelter
Cost (estimated): Total, including site development, but not furnishings: $583,000; construction, including mechanical, electrical, and elevators: $533,000; cost per sq ft: $17.70; cost per cu ft: $1.72; kitchen equipment: $15,000; furnishings: $49,000
Financing: HHFA Insured Loan, 98 per cent; balance, cash on hand
Architect says: Purpose is "to provide an adequate, comfortable home for the elderly in a manner which will eliminate the institutional feeling."

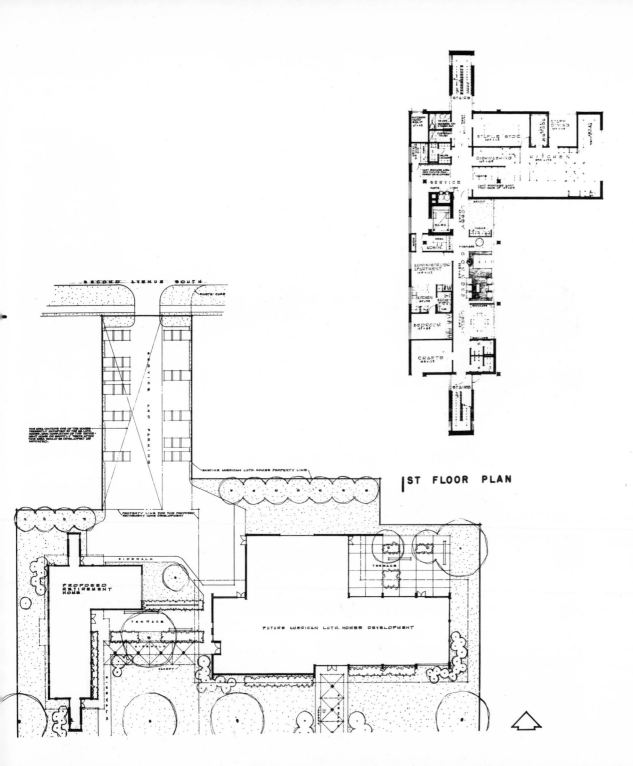

1ST FLOOR PLAN

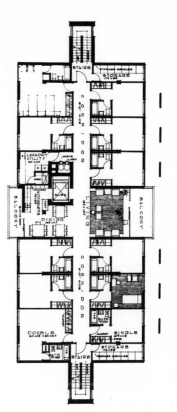

2ND, 3RD, 4TH, 5TH & 6TH FLOOR PLANS

CONGREGATE HOUSING

APPELMAN HOME FOR THE JEWISH AGED
(Kansas City, Mo.; completed 1950)

Sponsor: Jewish Federation & Council, Kansas City, Mo.
Architects: Kivett & Myers & McCallum, A.I.A., Kansas City, Mo.
Consultants: Landscape architect: A. L. Thomas; interior design: Kivett & Myers & McCallum; engineer: Erwin Pfuhl; mechanical engineer: William L. Cassell
Site: 16½-acre plot in gently rolling, wooded middle-class residential area; near stores, public transportation
Capacity: 112 plus infirmary for 80 (future, 200)
People served: White Jewish men and women, 65 and over, all income levels; ambulatory and chronically ill (except contagious); current ages 65 to 98, average 80
Buildings: One multi-story structure with 55 two-bed non-housekeeping rooms and 2 singles
Health facilities: Nursing unit: 8 beds for temporary illness, 58 beds for chronic illness, 14 beds for sheltered care; treatment: dentist, oculist, podiatrist; rehabilitation: physio- and occupational therapy; diagnostic: e.k.g., b.m.r.; contract with local medical center for acute and surgical care
Auxiliary facilities: Dining rooms (residents' main, 80; infirmary, 10; two staff, 20 and 30); synagogue; library; large living room (multiple uses); four lounges (two 308 sq ft; two 350 sq ft); crafts room; tool shop; barber shop; beauty parlor; outdoor: croquet, horseshoes, flower beds
Service facilities: Central kitchen; central laundry; maintenance shop; storage (resident, 5 sq ft each; institutional); 25 parking spaces (institution, 11; visitors, 14)
Staff: Total: 89 (Administration, 3; health, 50 [3 shifts]; food, 15; housekeeping, 10; laundry, 5; maintenance, grounds and building, 3; counseling, 1; barber and beauty, 2)
Charges and services: No entrance fee; monthly fee, dependent upon ability to pay, covers meals, maid, laundry, complete health care, including hospitalization and surgery
Construction: Total building area: 50,000 sq ft, 557,000 cu ft; building materials: concrete frame (exterior: walls—brick and limestone; sash—aluminum; roofs—flat built-up; terraces—quarry tile; walks—concrete; interior: walls—concrete; floors—asphalt tile; ceilings—plaster; partitions—plaster and concrete block; trim—wood; bathrooms—ceramic tile; kitchen walls—glazed tile); heating: hot water; cooling: multizone air conditioning first floor; fuel: natural gas (oil standby)
Site development: Bituminous driveway; landscaping
Cost (1949): Total, including site development, fees, and construction, but not land or furnishings: $678,000; cost per sq ft: $13.56; cost per cu ft: $1.21; kitchen equipment: $14,600; furnishings, $20,725
Financing: Contributions
Architect says: "For those who must live their remaining years in a home of this nature, it is essential that an illusion of home life be recreated. Every effort has been made to give to residents the feeling of 'being at home' in congenial informality and, at the same time, through the use of a contemporary design and functional planning, to provide every necessary facility to administer the finest physical care and social services."

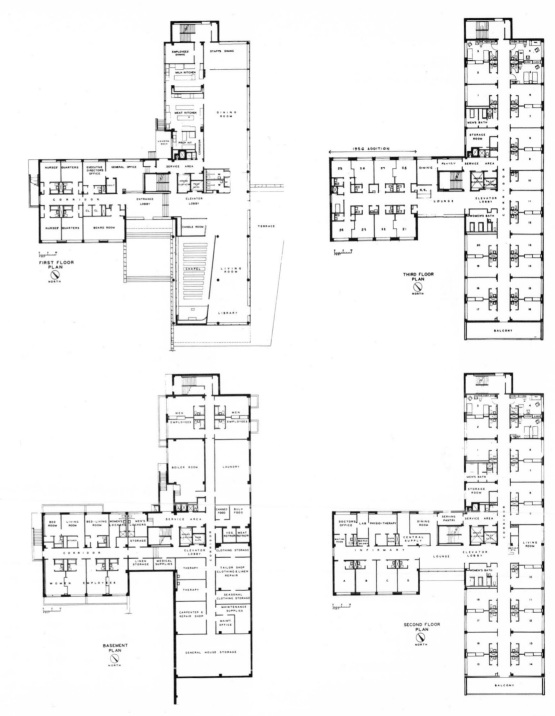

FIRST FLOOR PLAN

NURSES QUARTERS · EXECUTIVE DIRECTORS OFFICE · GENERAL OFFICE · SERVICE AREA

CORRIDOR · ENTRANCE LOBBY · ELEVATOR LOBBY

NURSES QUARTERS · BOARD ROOM · CANDLE ROOM · TERRACE

CHAPEL · LIVING ROOM · LIBRARY

EMPLOYEES DINING · STAFF'S DINING

MILK KITCHEN

MEAT KITCHEN · DINING ROOM

LOADING DOCK · PREP KIT.

THIRD FLOOR PLAN

1956 ADDITION

MEN'S BATH · STORAGE ROOM

DINING · PANTRY · SERVICE AREA

LOUNGE · ELEVATOR LOBBY

WOMEN'S BATH

BALCONY

BASEMENT PLAN

MEN EMPLOYEES · MEN EMPLOYEES

BOILER ROOM · LAUNDRY

BED ROOM · LIVING ROOM · BED-LIVING ROOM · WOMEN'S LOCKERS · MEN'S LOCKERS · SERVICE AREA · CANNED FOOD · BULK FOOD

STORAGE · VEG. MEAT REFRIG. REFRIG.

CORRIDOR · ELEVATOR LOBBY · CLOTHING STORAGE

WOMEN EMPLOYEES · LINEN STORAGE · MEDICAL SUPPLIES · THERAPY · TAILOR SHOP CLOTHING & LINEN REPAIR

THERAPY · SEASONAL CLOTHING STORAGE

CARPENTER & REPAIR SHOP · MAINTENANCE SUPPLIES

MAINT. OFFICE

GENERAL HOUSE STORAGE

SECOND FLOOR PLAN

MEN'S BATH · STORAGE ROOM

DOCTORS OFFICE · LAB · PHYSIO-THERAPY · DINING ROOM · SERVING PANTRY · SERVICE AREA

WAITING ROOM · CENTRAL SUPPLY · DARK ROOM · LOUNGE · ELEVATOR LOBBY · LIVING ROOM

INFIRMARY

A · B · C · D · WOMEN'S BATH

BALCONY

CONGREGATE HOUSING

BAPTIST HOME AND CENTER
(Cincinnati, Ohio; completed 1960)

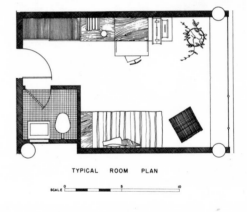

TYPICAL ROOM PLAN

SCALE

Sponsor: Board of Trustees of Cooperating Baptist Churches
Architects: Woodie Garber & Associates, A.I.A., Cincinnati, Ohio
Site: 17⅔ wooded acres, both level and rolling, in white, upper-middle-class residential area; near stores, churches, public transportation
Capacity: 68 in residence; 50 in nursing center (expansion planned to 104 residents, 100 nursing)
People served: Men and women, 65 and over, all income levels; interdenominational (priority to Baptists); current ages 67 to 93, average 79.7; admission average, 76.7
Buildings: One two-story old mansion for administration and 24 residents; four-story addition to mansion (two stories, 18 residents each; two stories, nursing unit, 25 beds each); two conventional houses on site: total eight singles; total, 56 singles, six doubles
Health facilities: 50-bed nursing center (one- and two-bed rooms with lavatory, baths shared, ceiling intercom); nursing care for temporary and chronic illness, convalescence; open also to community; resident rooms have two-way voice communication and call system
Auxiliary facilities: Dining rooms (resident, 100; employees', 26); chapel-auditorium (72); library space; five lounges, snack kitchenettes; gift shop; beauty parlor; outdoor: croquet, individual gardening
Service facilities: Central kitchen; central laundry; maintenance shop; parking spaces (40)
Staff: Total: 52 (Administration, 3; health, 26 [3 shifts]; food, 11; maid, 8; laundry, 2 [linen sent out]; maintenance, 2)
Charges and services: Entrance fee of $500 to $5,000; monthly fee of $75 covers meals, maid, laundry, nursing care (except doctor and drugs); nursing care available to community with charges on individual basis
Construction (relates to addition to mansion): Total building area: 29,039 sq ft; building materials: reinforced concrete frame, steel over dining room (exterior: walls—brick and glass; sash—aluminum; roofs—built-up asphalt and gravel; walks—concrete; interior: walls—brick and plaster, walnut screen between dining room and waiting lounge; floors—vinyl asbestos tile; ceilings—sprayed acoustic; partitions—metal stud and plaster; trim—steel door frames; bathrooms—glazed tile); heating: hot water; fuel: gas
Site development: Blacktop driveway
Cost (addition only, 1959): Total building costs, including site development, buildings and built-in equipment, but not furnishings and not fees: $502,875.50; cost per sq ft: $17.30
Financing: Contributions and $300,000 worth of bonds sold to constituency

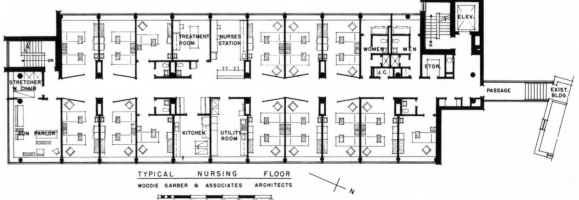

TYPICAL NURSING FLOOR
WOODIE GARBER & ASSOCIATES ARCHITECTS

CONGREGATE HOUSING

BAPTIST VILLAGE
(Waycross, Ga.; completed 1962)

Sponsor: Georgia Baptist Convention
Architects: Stevens & Wilkinson, A.I.A., Atlanta, Ga.
Consultants: Landscape architect: Edward L. Daugherty, Atlanta; interior design, Jane Kidder, New York
Site: 546 flat acres, 25 miles north of Florida line and 50 miles from Atlantic Ocean; white neighborhood; 3 miles to city limits, stores, churches, public transportation (project transportation)
Capacity: 112 (1962); plus 14-bed infirmary (planned, 300 plus 56-bed nursing unit)
People served: White men and women, 65 and over; ambulatory, good health on admission; interfaith; current ages, 65 to 86; average age, 76; admission average, 72
Buildings: Five one-story buildings, including administration, with 88 single units, 12 doubles, all nonhousekeeping (grouped in clusters for 28 people; covered walkways between buildings)
Health facilities: 14-bed infirmary (planned: to 56 beds, for long-term and sheltered care, diagnostic, rehabilitation); arrangement with Waycross doctors
Auxiliary facilities: Dining rooms (resident, 150; infirmary, 14; employee, 26); chapel (planned, 150); library (one each cluster); day-room-lounge (one each cluster); crafts (planned, 50); tool shop (1,200 sq ft); beauty shop (2 chairs); guest rooms (each cluster); recreation room (planned); outdoor: shuffleboard, croquet, gardening, fishing, walking lanes
Service facilities: Central kitchen; central laundry; storage (resident, 25 sq ft in unit; institution, two areas, each 720 sq ft); 60 parking spaces (resident, 30; visitors, 20; institution, 10)
Staff (part-time in parentheses): Total: 12 (5). Administration, 3 (1); health, 2 (2); food, 3; maid, 3 (1); maintenance, 1 (1)
Charges and services: Founders' gift, based on ability to pay; monthly fee of $150 (some residents assisted by Baptist Benevolent Fund) covers meals, weekly maid, linen laundry; charges for infirmary care: $3.00 for double room and $5.00 for single per day, plus costs of doctor, medicines
Construction: Total building area: 66,000 sq ft, 900,000 cu ft; building materials: steel, wood frame (exterior: walls—brick, solid masonry; sash—aluminum; roofs—built-up; terraces—brick; walks—concrete; covering over walks—wood; interior: walls—plaster; floors—carpet, concrete; ceilings—plaster; partitions—steel, wood stud, plaster; trim—wood; bathrooms—tile); heating and cooling: first unit, hot and chilled water; second unit, electric resistance heating, individual air conditioning units; fuel: electricity
Site development: Sewage treatment: modern disposal plant; water supply: deep well; asphalt driveway, some gravel; landscaping: natural trees, planted shrubbery
Cost (1957, 1959): Total, including site development, buildings, built-in equipment, fees, but not furnishings: $1,250,000; cost per sq ft: $15.50; cost per cu ft: $1.20; furnishings: $125,000
Financing: Endowment; $600,000 to be borrowed from House & Home Finance Agency to increase from 56 to 112 beds

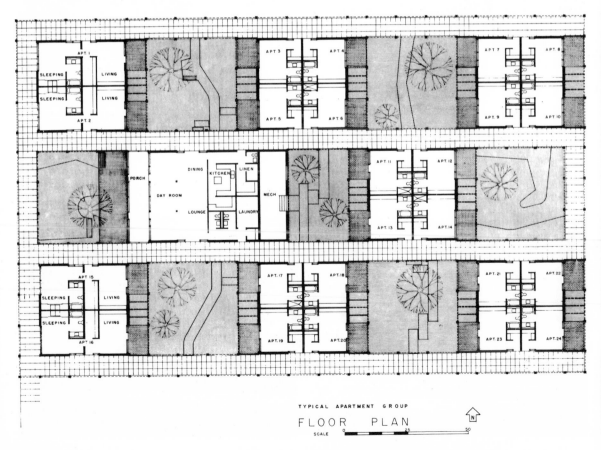

TYPICAL APARTMENT GROUP

FLOOR PLAN

SCALE 0   25   50

CONGREGATE HOUSING

BAYVIEW MANOR
(Seattle, Wash.; completed 1960)

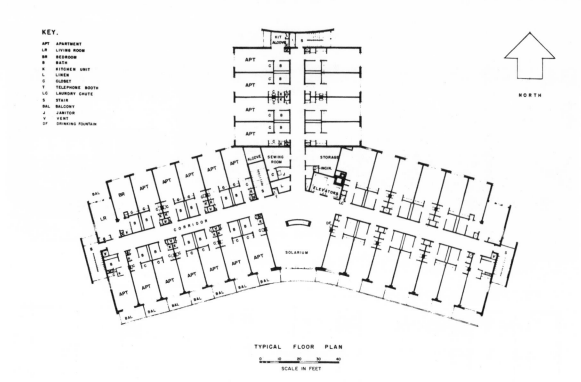

TYPICAL FLOOR PLAN

0 10 20 30 40
SCALE IN FEET

Sponsor: Seattle First Methodist Home Inc., Seattle, Wash.
Architects: John Graham and Company, A.I.A., Seattle and New York
Financing and promotion: Craftsmaster Inc., Seattle, Wash.
Site: Double city block, 2 acres, overlooking Puget Sound; near churches, shops; 10 minutes from center of city; public transportation at door
Capacity: 237
People served: Men and women, 62 and over, upper-middle income level; interdenominational, interracial (34 per cent Methodist; remainder, all faiths); current ages, 60 to 91; average age, 76; admission average, 74
Buildings: One 10-story building (with basement) including 261 units divided into 128 singles, 50 doubles, 34 1½ units (non-housekeeping; all with electric kitchenettes)
Health facilities: 28-bed nursing unit (facilities for expansion to 46 beds); care for temporary illness, convalescence, chronic disease; rehabilitation therapy; incoming residents may be bed patients and then assigned residence unit when recovered (fees on individual basis)
Auxiliary facilities: Dining rooms (main, 230; small, 30; guest, on roof, with kitchen, 16; infirmary, 24); library; chapel-auditorium; social room; 11 lounges (first floor approximately 1,500 sq ft, others 400 sq ft each); solarium on roof with panoramic view; automatic laundries each floor; craft shop, woodworking shop; outdoor: croquet, garden plots, shuffleboard on roof
Service facilities: Central kitchen; resident storage rooms; maintenance shop; 92 parking spaces: 68 resident, in basement, 24 guest, on site
Staff: Total: 80 full-time and part-time
Charges and services: Entrance fee of $8,750 to $19,250; monthly fee of $112 per individual in single unit covers meals, maid, linen laundry, limited health service
Construction: Total building area: 197,000 sq ft, 2,100,000 cu ft; building materials: reinforced concrete frame (exterior: walls—architectural concrete, brick veneer, cast stone; sash—aluminum; roofs—built-up asphalt felt, gravel; terraces—exposed aggregate concrete; walks—concrete, flagstone; interior: walls—plaster on foam plastic insulation; floors—carpet; ceilings—plaster, acoustical tile; partitions—metal studs, gypsum lath, plaster; trim—metal; bathrooms—sheet vinyl, ceramic tile); heating: hot water; cooling: central chilled water; fuel: interruptible natural gas, heavy fuel oil
Site development: Asphaltic concrete driveway; landscaping: Pacific Northwest type planting, exterior patio, fountain
Cost (1960): Total building cost, including land (donated), site development, fees, but not furnishings: $3,600,000; cost per sq ft: $18.25; cost per cu ft: $1.66; kitchen equipment: $40,500; health facilities: $25,000; furnishings: $35,000
Financing: Contributions; FHA insured loan

CONGREGATE HOUSING

BAYVIEW MANOR—*Continued*
(Seattle, Wash.; completed 1960)

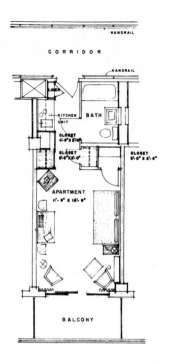

CORRIDOR

HANDRAIL

HANDRAIL

LINEN

KITCHEN UNIT

BATH

CLOSET 4'-0" X 2'-0"

CLOSET 2'-6" X 2'-0"

CLOSET 5'-0" X 2'-0"

APARTMENT 11'-6" X 18'-0"

BALCONY

CORRIDOR

HANDRAIL

HANDRAIL

LINEN

CLOSET 4'-0" X 2'-0"

DINING

KITCHEN UNIT

BATH

CLOSET 4'-0" X 2'-0"

DRESSING

CLOSET 3'-3" X 2'-0"

LIVING ROOM 11'-6" X 18'-0"

BEDROOM 11'-6" X 16'-0"

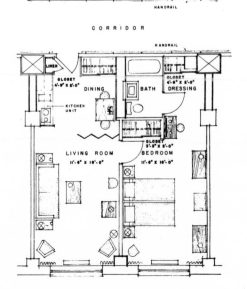

89

CRESTVIEW CLUB APARTMENTS
(Sylvania, Ohio; completed 1960)

Sponsor: Flower Hospital (Methodist related)
Architects: Samborn, Steketee, Otis and Evans, Toledo, Ohio
Capacity: 200
People served: Men and women, 60 and over, middle income; executives, professional persons, teachers; retired people of all occupations; current ages, 60 to 92; average, 76; admission average, 75
Buildings: One six-story building with 171 apartment units (55 single studios; 72 single studios with kitchenette; 12 double studios; 32 two-room doubles with kitchenette)
Health facilities: Six-bed nursing unit, 24-hour R.N.; periodic physical examinations by resident physician; comprehensive hospitalization plan
Auxiliary facilities: Dining rooms (main, 1; private, 5; staff, 1); library; lounges (first floor lounge approximately 1,300 sq ft; solarium with kitchenette each floor); auditorium-chapel; recreation: stage, shuffleboard; crafts room; sewing room; laundry facilities; beauty, barber; outdoor: putting green, individual gardens
Service facilities: Central kitchen; central laundry; resident storage; parking spaces: 35 resident garages, lot for visitors, staff
Staff for total occupancy (part-time in parentheses): Total: 37 (19). Administration, 6 (4); health, 3 (5); food, 11 (8); maids, 11; maintenance, grounds, building, 5; barber, beauty shop, 1 (1); counseling, (1)
Charges and services: Entrance fee of $7,000 to $37,000; monthly fee of $150 (basic) for single occupancy covers meals, maid, linen laundry, limited health services
Construction: Total building area: 95,740 sq ft; building materials: frame, steel columns, void lift slabs (exterior: walls—brick, porcelain, enamel; sash—aluminum; roofs—four-ply T. & A.; terraces—walks, concrete; interior: walls—metal stud plaster; floors—carpet on concrete; ceilings—concrete, suspended plaster; partitions—concrete block, metal studs, plaster; trim—metal; bathrooms—glazed tile, plaster); heating: hot water; fuel: natural gas
Site development: Bituminous-topped driveway; landscaping features: duck and fish pond, putting green
Cost (1958): Total building cost, including land, site development, fees, but not furnishings: $1,785,000; cost per sq ft: $18.52; kitchen equipment: $35,000; health: $17,000; furnishings: $86,000
Financing: Contributions; Flower Hospital; Methodist Conference; FHA loan
Special feature: Guarantee of care: reserve funds will be used to provide care for those whose resources have been depleted through causes beyond their control, and for care of selected indigent people who are worthy but have insufficient resources for retirement at Crestview. However, if depletion of funds is caused by member's own act, Crestview reserves right to cancel life lease on such terms as it deems equitable.

COMMONS

A | BED RM | D | D | LIV. RM | BED RM | A | A | A | ELEV | | MECH EQUIP | A | A | A | BED RM | LIV. RM | LIV RM | BED RM | A
ELEV

STAFF DINING | DW

C | KIT | B | KIT | KIT | B | B | B | KIT | KIT | B | B | MAID | TRASH | B | KIT | B | B | KIT | KIT | B | B | KIT | KIT | B | C

MAIL BOX
VISITOR COATS
SUNDRIES

KITCHEN

SERVING

BIRD CAGE

COMMONS

A | BED RM | D | D | LIV. RM | BED RM | A | A | A | ELEV | | MECH EQUIP | DINING

ELEV

LOUNGE | PATIO

C | KIT | B | B | B | KIT | KIT | B | B | MAID | STORAGE | TRASH

BED RM | LIV. RM | LIV. RM | D | D

PLANTER

OFFICE | DESK | PBX | MAIL

OFFICE

TYPICAL FLOOR PLAN

FIRST FLOOR PLAN
CRESTVIEW OF OHIO

N
GRAPHIC SCALE

SAMBORN, STEKETEE & ASSOC. OTIS & EVANS
ENGINEERS & ARCHITECTS   TOLEDO, OHIO

CONGREGATE HOUSING

GOOD SAMARITAN HOME FOR THE AGED
(St. Louis, Mo.; completed 1959)

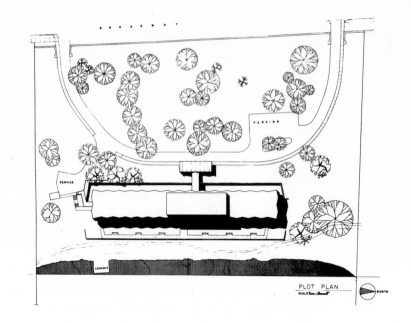

PLOT PLAN

Sponsor: The Board of Trustees of The Good Samaritan Hospital, Inc. (affiliated with The United Church of Christ)

Architects: Manske & Dieckmann, A.I.A., St. Louis; Hellmuth, Obata & Kassabaum, A.I.A., St. Louis

Site: Seven acres in residential area overlooking Mississippi; approximately 4 miles to downtown; close to stores; public transportation at site

Capacity: 106 plus 31 in nursing unit (planned, 75 in second building; 50-100 in third)

People served: Men and women, 70 and over; good general health on admission; interracial; interfaith (priority to members of United Church of Christ); current ages, 70 to 97; average age, 83; average on admission, 79

Buildings: One four-story building (86 single units; 10 double units)

Health facilities: 31-bed nursing unit; protected care; podiatrist; occupational therapy planned; dentist on call; oculist nearby; diagnostic center at nearby hospital

Auxiliary facilities: Dining rooms (resident, 120; staff, 25); resident snack kitchen each floor; resident laundry each wing; library; chapel-auditorium; large social room; small meeting rooms; lounges (one large on entrance floor, seven on residence floors, each 540 sq ft); crafts; occupational therapy unit; beauty parlor, barber shop; outdoor: croquet, gardening, Hurl-O-Dart, bowling-on-green

Service facilities: Central kitchen; diet kitchen in nursing unit; central laundry; resident storage, own unit and penthouse

Staff (part-time in parentheses): Total: 40 (19). Administration, 4; health, 18 (1); food, 8 (2); maid and laundry, 8 (6); maintenance, 4; counseling, (2); barber, 1; beauty shop, (8) (for permanents only)

Charges and services: Entrance fee varies for three categories: (1) life resident: calculated lump sum, bearing 4 per cent, balance refundable; (2) resident: according to ability; (3) guest: pay-as-you-go (not encouraged); monthly fee of $150 covers meals, maid, laundry, complete medical care

Construction: Total building area: 58,600 sq ft, 649,000 cu ft; building materials: reinforced concrete frame (exterior: walls—brick, aluminum curtain wall; sash—aluminum; roofs—tar, gravel; terraces, walks—concrete; interior: walls—plaster; floors—asphalt, vinyl tile; ceilings—plaster; partitions—steel stud, plaster; bathrooms—ceramic tile); heating and cooling: fan units, circulating hot and cold water; fuel: gas

Site development: Building on site of old estate overlooking river; fine mature trees; minimum new material

Cost (1959): Total, including land, site development, fees, equipment: $1,050,000; cost per sq ft: $20.80; cost per cu ft: $1.90; furnishings: approximately $200,000

Financing: Minimum endowment; contributions of churches and individuals applied to expenses; building fund campaign; legacies

Special feature: A professionally trained social worker has been employed to counsel applicants whose names have been placed on the waiting list.

CONGREGATE HOUSING

GOOD SAMARITAN HOME FOR THE AGED
(St. Louis, Mo.; completed 1959)
—Continued

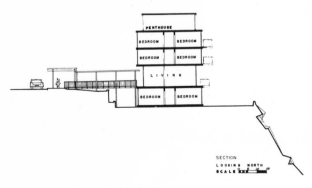

SECTION
LOOKING NORTH
SCALE

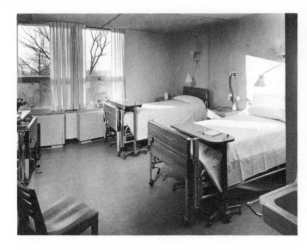

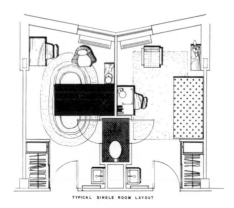

TYPICAL SINGLE ROOM LAYOUT

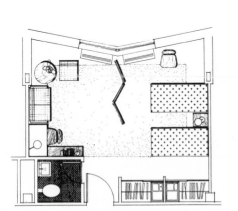

TYPICAL DOUBLE ROOM LAYOUT

CONGREGATE HOUSING

THE HAROLD S. HAALAND'S HOME
(Rugby, N. D.; completed 1962)

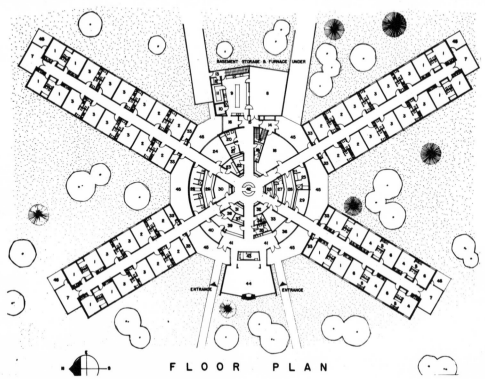

Sponsor: Good Samaritan Hospital Assoc.
Architects: Foss & Co., A.I.A., Moorhead, Minn.
Site: Approximately 4½ acres on edge of city in residential area; near churches and stores
Capacity: 68
People served: Men and women 62 and over; ambulatory
Buildings: One building with 52 units: 16 doubles, 36 singles (four doubles have living room, bedroom, kitchen and bath; 12 doubles have lavatory only; 16 singles have bath; 20 lavatory only)
Health facilities: Intercom system from nurse station to all rooms, private and communal
Auxiliary facilities: Dining room, equipped for formal service, cafeteria, or informal eating; living room-lounge-chapel; library; crafts room; laundry with automatic washers and dryers; barber shop-beauty parlor
Service facilities: Central kitchen; central laundry; maintenance shop; storage (resident, 15 sq ft each; institution, 900 sq ft); 50 offstreet parking spaces (20 resident, 20 visitor, 10 staff)
Staff: Estimated total: 15
Charges and services: No entrance fee; monthly fee of $100-120, according to ability to pay
Construction: Total building area: 35,432 sq ft, 438,023 cu ft; building materials: (exterior: walls—face brick veneer on metal studs, blanket insulation; sash—aluminum windowall, awning and casement sash; roofs—precast concrete deck; walks—concrete slabs on grade; interior: walls—metal studs, plaster, face brick; floors—vinyl asbestos, ceramic tile; ceilings—painted precast concrete slabs, plaster; trim—hollow-metal door frames); heating: hot water; fuel: oil
Site development: Underground telephone, electric service; concrete patios; landscaping, privacy areas
Cost (1961): Total, including land, fees, site development, but not furnishings: $647,000; construction only, including mechanical, electrical, elevator: $599,750; site development, roads, landscaping: $11,750; cost per sq ft, $17.93; cost per cu ft, $1.45; kitchen equipment, $15,000; laundry, $10,000; furnishings, $45,000
Financing: Endowment ($100,000 gift from Mr. Harold S. Haaland); contributions; FHA Insured Loan ($500,000)
Architect says: Purpose "to provide a livable, comfortable residential surrounding with all rooms close to central facilities, and to provide ease of control and administration"

FLOOR PLAN

CONGREGATE HOUSING

HILLCREST HOMES
(Bozeman, Mont.; anticipated completion 1963)

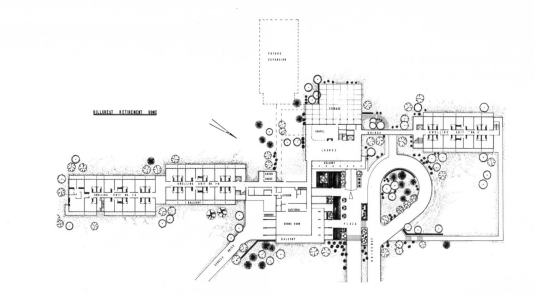

Sponsor: Montana Conference, The Methodist Church, and Bozeman Deaconess Hospital
Architects: O. Berg, Jr. & Associates, A.I.A., Bozeman, Mont.
Landscape Architect: Lawrence C. Gerkins
Consultant Engineers: Mechanical, Roy Prussing; electrical, Alex Drapes
Site: 21 rolling acres on edge of business district with panoramic mountain view; near future church and shopping area; transportation by home or taxi
Capacity: 137 plus 12-bed nursing unit (planned cottages for couples as needed)
People served: Retired men and women; no restriction age, health; interracial, interfaith; charity cases (deserving persons with religious background) limited to available resources
Buildings: Two multistory, multiunit buildings with 79 apartments for singles; 29 apartments for couples (some with kitchenette)
Health facilities: 12-bed nursing unit; sheltered care in future construction; physio- and occupational therapy; complete hospital facilities at Deaconess Hospital
Auxiliary facilities: Dining rooms (two resident, 135 and 60; infirmary, planned); lounge-auditorium-chapel (2,560 sq ft); other lounges (1,200, 672, 880 sq ft); library; laundry facilities; crafts, tool rooms; recreation (shuffleboard, billiards, etc.); beauty parlor; shops (gifts, drugs, etc., in future); outdoor: garden terrace games, shuffleboard, croquet, bowling-on-green, horseshoes, fishing, individual gardens
Service facilities: Central kitchen; central laundry (future); maintenance shop; storage (institutional, resident); 118 parking spaces (garages for residents, 56; outside spaces for visitors and residents, 50; staff, 12)
Staff (part-time in parentheses): Total: 17 (2). Administration, 1 (1); health, 6; food, 7; maid, 2; maintenance, 1 (1)
Charges and services: Entrance fee of $6,800 to $32,500 (may be paid at 1 per cent per month); monthly fee of $125 (higher if special care needed) covers meals, maid, linen, laundry (nursing service covered under different arrangements)
Construction: Total building area: 101,000 sq ft; building materials: reinforced concrete frame, steel joists, (exterior: walls—masonry; sash—wood with thermopane; roofs—20-year built-up, wood shingles; terraces, walks—concrete; interior: walls—masonry; floors—concrete with carpet; ceilings—sheetrock, acoustical tile; partitions—masonry; trim—wood; bathrooms—ceramic tile); heating and cooling: hot water, air conditioning; fuel: gas
Site development: "Lagoon" sewage treatment; asphalt cement driveway; landscaping: lawn, evergreens, deciduous trees
Cost (estimated 1961): Total, including land, site development, fees, but not furnishings: $2,007,800; cost per sq ft (building only): $15.50; kitchen equipment: $30,000; furnishings: $30,000
Financing: FHA Insured Loan (#231 program); endowment and contributions for charity cases
Special features: Exceptional historical and cultural advantages in community; home of Montana State College; center dude ranch and mountain resort area; adjacent to national parks and forest reserves; long-range program for meeting needs of people of retirement age, including new general hospital, nursing home and possibly a medical center

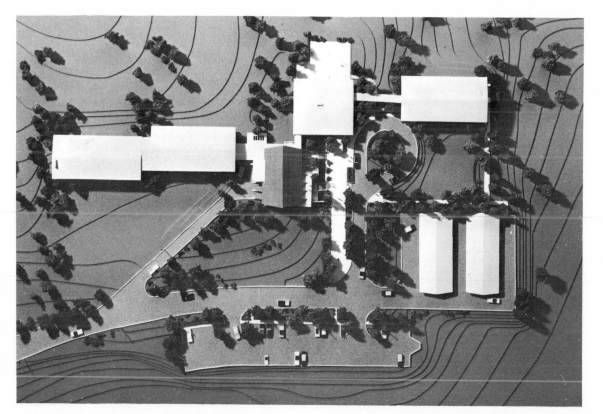

CONGREGATE HOUSING

HILLCREST HOMES—*Continued*
(Bozeman, Mont.; anticipated completion 1963)

APARTMENT UNIT #1

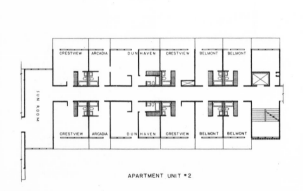

APARTMENT UNIT #2

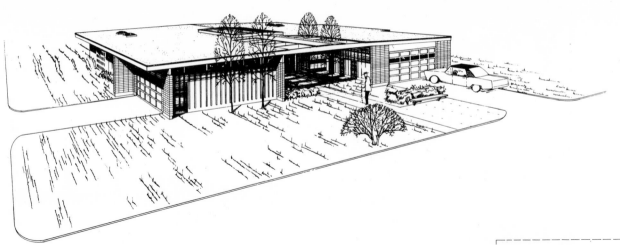

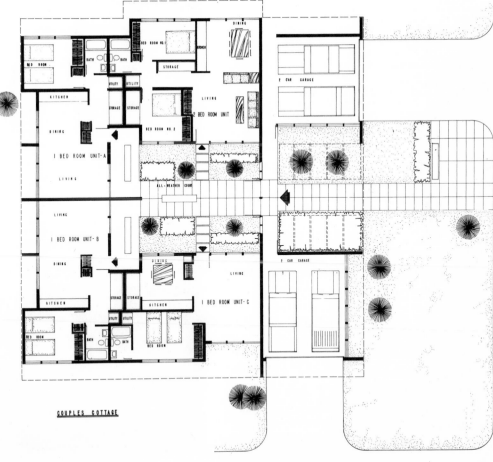

COUPLES COTTAGE

CONGREGATE HOUSING

HOUSTON JEWISH HOME FOR THE AGED
(Houston, Tex.; completed 1960)

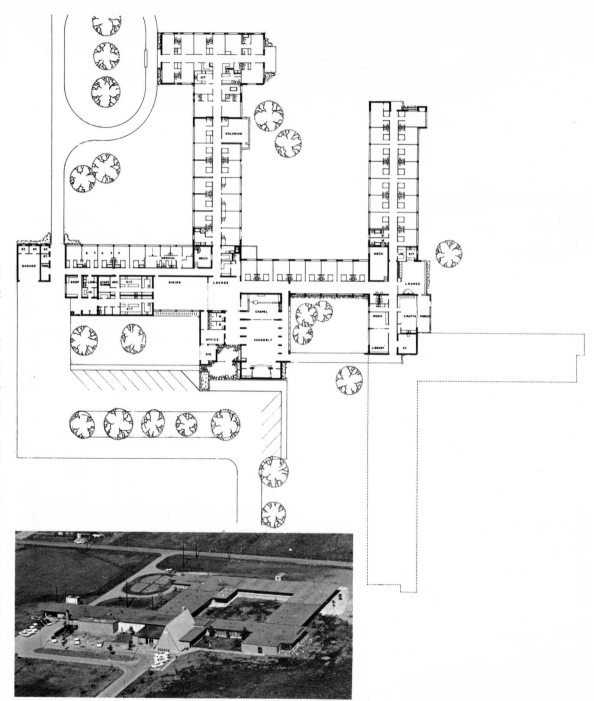

Sponsor: Houston Jewish Community Council
Architects: First unit: Lenard Gabert—Joseph Krakower, A.I.A. Associated Architects, Houston; second and third units: Lenard Gabert, A.I.A., and Associates, Houston
Consultants: I.A. Naman Mechanical and Electrical Consulting Engineers
Site: Sufficient suburban acreage for expansion; near stores, public transportation
Capacity: 75 (eventually 100)
People served: Jewish men and women, 65 and over; priority to financially needy; current ages, 65 to 96; average, 79; admission average, 76
Buildings: One-story main building with central facilities and 28 single rooms, three doubles; residence wing with 16 singles, four doubles (all rooms have private lavatories, shared baths); nursing unit
Health facilities: 17-bed nursing unit (protected care unit planned); clinic: diagnostic, rehabilitation equipment; special treatment: dentist, chiropodist; regular services of physician, psychiatrist
Auxiliary facilities: Dining rooms (resident, staff, nursing unit); chapel-auditorium; candle-lighting room; library; music room; lounges (two solariums, kitchenettes; staff); automatic laundry; crafts room; beauty parlor; barber shop
Service facilities: Two kitchens; central laundry; parking: total 36 spaces
Staff (part-time in parentheses): Total: 23 (7). Administration, 3; health, (4); food, 7; maid, 9; laundry, 2; maintenance, 2; counseling—chaplain, psychiatric, (2); barber, beauty shop, (1); volunteers, Council Jewish Women
Charges and services: Fees contingent upon ability to pay; entrance fee: none to $5,000; monthly fee to $275 covers meals, maid, laundry, complete medical care except surgery
Construction: Total building area: 39,744 sq ft; building materials: steel frame (exterior: walls—masonry; sash—aluminum, awnings; roofs—built-up roof on steel deck and insulated board with corrugated cement asbestos over chapel and auditorium; terraces, walks—concrete; interior: walls—plaster; floors—wood, rubber, asbestos or vinyl tile; bathrooms—ceramic tile); heating: hot water; cooling, chilled water; fuel: electric, gas
Site development: Well water
Cost (three units, '54, '56, '60): Total, including land, site development, fees, but not furnishings: $850,000; cost per sq ft: $22.82; cost per cu ft: $2.08; kitchen equipment: $20,000; health: $10,000; furnishings: $50,000
Financing: Contributions and private loan
Special feature: Aged members of the community may come to the home to participate in activities

CONGREGATE HOUSING

LUTHERAN SENIOR CITY
(Columbus, Ohio; anticipated completion, fall 1963)

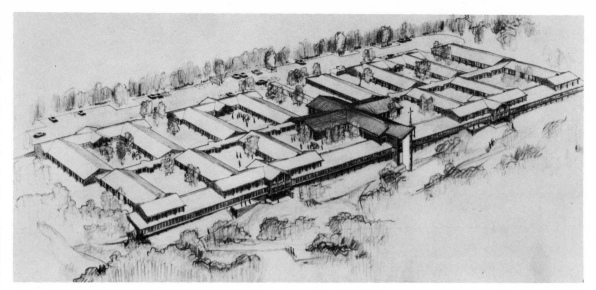

Sponsor: The Lutheran Welfare League of Central Ohio, Columbus, Ohio
Architects: Tibbals, Crumley, Musson, A.I.A., Columbus, Ohio
Site: 20 acres on a high bluff with meadow and stream below; suburban neighborhood near churches, stores, public transportation
Capacity: 286 plus 22-bed nursing unit
People served: Men and women, 60 and over; ambulatory, handicapped, needing nursing care; interfaith (Lutherans preferred); interracial
Buildings: One single-story structure (243 single, 10 double non-housekeeping units)
Health facilities: 22-bed nursing unit; sheltered care; treatment: dentist, oculist, podiatrist; rehabilitation: physio- and occupational therapy; social worker
Auxiliary facilities: Dining rooms (resident, capacity 280; staff, 24); chapel (flexible size to 4560 sq ft); library; two auditoriums (capacity 50, 100); two social rooms (capacity 50, 100); seven lounges (each 1,008 sq ft); resident laundry facilities; two craft rooms (capacity 50 each); two recreation rooms (capacity 100 each; shuffleboard, billiards); shop (gifts, candy); beauty parlor (3); barber shop (2); outdoor: shuffleboard, croquet, bowling-on-green, gardening, greenhouse, fishing, horseshoes, amphitheatre
Service facilities: Central kitchen; central laundry; maintenance shop; storage (institution: four areas, 368 sq ft each; one area, 936 sq ft; one area, 672 sq ft; residents: 8 sq ft each); parking spaces: total 240
Staff: Administration, 6; health, 21; food, 20; maid, 11; laundry, 5; building and grounds maintenance, 4; counseling, 1; beauty operator, 1; barber, 1; volunteer vacation help
Charges and services: Entrance fee: one month's fee; monthly fee of $160 to $200 covers meals, maid, laundry, limited health services
Construction: Total building area: 139,424 sq ft; building materials: frame, wood trusses, timber arches (exterior: walls—masonry, brick, block; sash—aluminum, sliding; roofs—asphalt shingle; terraces—lawn; walks—concrete; interior: walls—block and drywall on studs; floors—concrete with asphalt tile; ceilings—dry wall; partitions—dry wall; trim—metal door frames, mahogany doors, birch trim; bathrooms—tile); heating: hot water; fuel: gas
Site development: Asphalt driveway construction
Estimated cost (year bid, 1962): Total, site development, buildings, built-in equipment, fees, but not furnishings: $2,380,284; cost per sq ft, $17.07
Financing: FHA insured loan (No. 231); furnishings and equipment to be underwritten by corporation churches
Architect says: "This project has a plan like a town. In the center is the core of the town life with space for administration and community socializing, dining, recreation, creative and cultural activities. The services are located here too—the kitchen, barber shop, beauty shop, housekeeping center, laundry, etc. Rooms in this core open onto terraces for group gatherings, with a broad view of the creek and the city of Columbus. From this town core a main street leads out north and south through several neighborhoods. Each neighborhood is built around its own court, and each is broken down internally into three families of 10 to 12 residents who have their own living room and kitchenette. Many rooms open into the courts. Others have a view over the stream to the west. A stroll down the main street presents an ever-changing view of the landscaped courts. Along the way are furnished stopping places where sitters may watch the passers-by. There is a suburb too, on the lower level over the brow of the hill, where couples and the more able-bodied will live. Like a medieval village, the chapel is the center of the core and climaxes the design.

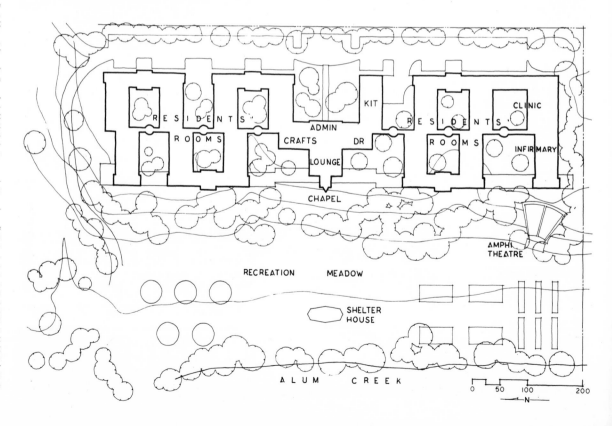

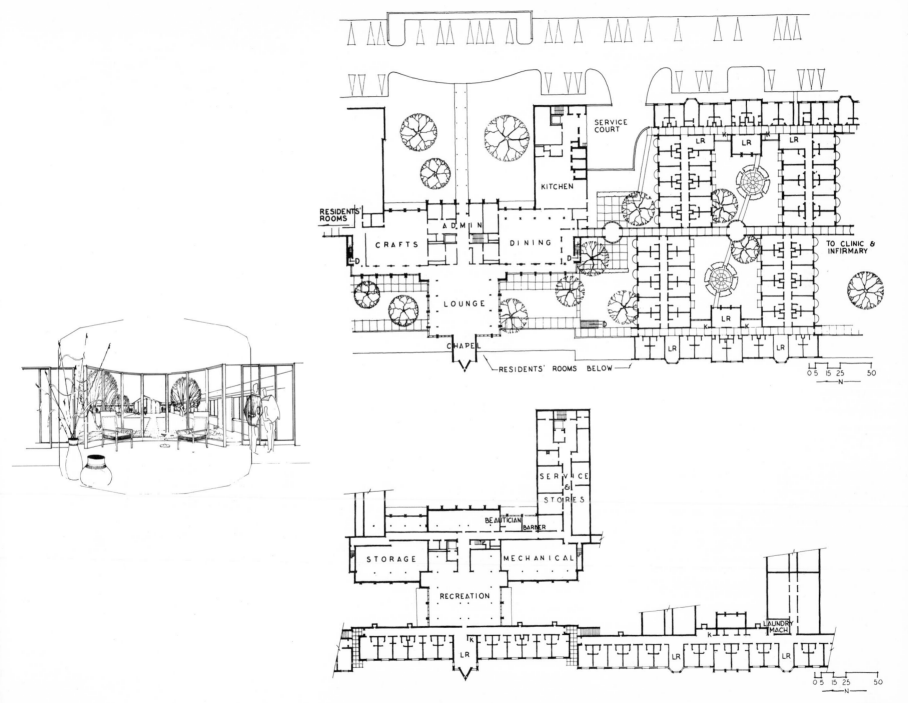

RESIDENTS'
ROOMS

CRAFTS

ADMIN

DINING

SERVICE
COURT

KITCHEN

LR   LR   LR

TO CLINIC &
INFIRMARY

LOUNGE

LR

CHAPEL

RESIDENTS' ROOMS BELOW

LR   LR

0 5 15 25   50
N

SERVICE
&
STORES

BEAUTICIAN BARBER

STORAGE

MECHANICAL

RECREATION

LR

LR

K

LAUNDRY
MACH

LR   LR

0 5 15 25   50
N

CONGREGATE HOUSING

LUTHERAN SENIOR CITY—*Continued*
(Columbus, O.; anticipated completion, fall 1963)

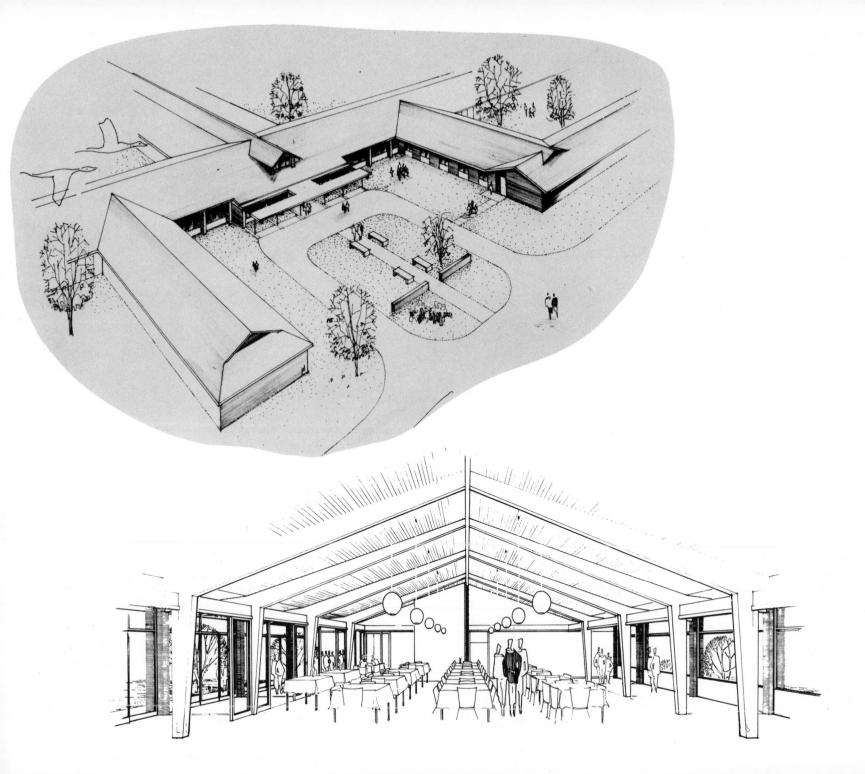

CONGREGATE HOUSING

NORSE HOME
(Seattle, Wash.; completed 1957)

Sponsor: The Norse Home, Inc., Seattle, Wash.
Architect: Edward Mahlum, A. I. A., Seattle, Wash.
Landscape architect: Sigurd Holm
Engineers: Peter H. Hostmark, structural; Dewitt C. Griffin, mechanical and electrical
Site: ¾ acre overlooking Puget Sound, sloping 20 ft in 170; above average residential neighborhood near churches, stores; public transportation at site
Capacity: 135, plus 54-bed infirmary
People served: Men and women, 60 and over; ambulatory on entrance; interracial; interfaith; current ages, 69 to 98; average, 79; admission average, 75
Buildings: One multi-story building with 130 nonhousekeeping units (120 singles; 10 doubles)
Health facilities: 54-bed infirmary with minimum nursing care; resident chooses, pays doctor
Auxiliary facilities: Dining rooms (one resident, 160; one staff); kitchenette each floor; automatic laundry each floor; three libraries; chapel-auditorium-reception (3,200 sq ft, 200); two lounges each floor (400 sq ft, 30 each); hobby room (20); fourteen recreation rooms (30 each); tool shop, woodworking (10); beauty parlor, barber shop; outdoor: croquet, bowling-on-green, gardening
Service facilities: Central kitchen; resident storage (156 lockers, 128 cu ft); 20 parking spaces (resident, 10; institution, 10; visitors, on street)
Staff (part-time in parentheses): Total: 46 (24). Administration, 2; health, 1; food, 1; maintenance, 1; counseling, 1; beauty, 1; barber, (1)
Charges and services: Entrance fee of $6,000 to $7,000; monthly fee of $107 to $145 covers meals, linen-laundry, minimum health care
Construction: Total building area: 100,000 sq ft, 1,000,000 cu ft; building materials: concrete frame, plate slabs (exterior: walls—architectural concrete; sash—aluminum, gold anodized; roofs—built-up; terraces, walks—concrete; other—sand stone; interior: walls—steel studs, plaster; floors—asphalt tile, carpet; ceilings—concrete, plaster, acoustical tile; trim—metal; bathrooms—ceramic tile; other—kitchen, freezers, quarry tile floor, ceramic walls); heating: sunrad radiator units; ventilating: in lounges and dining rooms; fuel: oil
Cost (1955-1956): Total, including site development, buildings, built-in equipment, fees, but not land or furnishings: $1,200,000; cost per sq ft: $12.00; cost per cu ft: $1.20; furnishings: $100,000
Financing: Founders' fees; FHA insured loan
Architect says: Effort was "to create a friendly building, fit for a king, at very low cost, utilizing all possible efficiency in planning structure and plumbing and utilities, leaving as much money as possible for the fine finishes and the esthetic touches. Utilizing the site to the nth degree . . . with a most magnificent view towards the west of Puget Sound and the Olympic Mountains beyond . . . and to the east the marvelous Woodland Park and the Cascade Mountains beyond. I had one real hope in this design . . . to create a building with an atmosphere where your mother, and mine, could be most happy. . . . To me architecture is not an end . . . it is another servant of mankind . . . culturally as well as physically, spiritually, emotionally, and most of all—humbly."

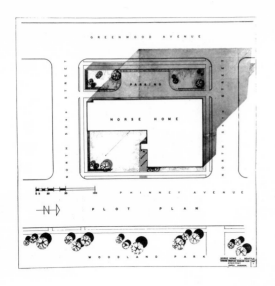

GREENWOOD AVENUE

PARKING

NORSE HOME

NORTH 55th STREET

NORTH 56th STREET

PHINNEY AVENUE

PLOT PLAN

WOODLAND PARK

NORSE HOME — SEATTLE
EDWARD KREISLER DUNLAP, A.I.A.
ARCHITECT
SEATTLE, WASHINGTON

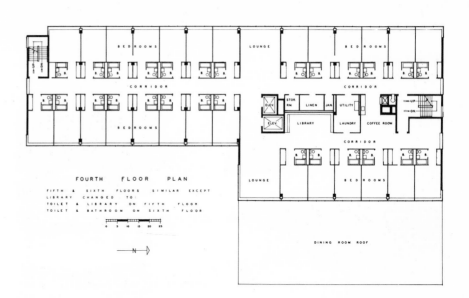

BEDROOMS   LOUNGE   BEDROOMS

CORRIDOR   CORRIDOR

BEDROOMS

ELEV.   STOR. RM.   LINEN   JAN.   UTILITY
ELEV.   LIBRARY   LAUNDRY   COFFEE ROOM

CORRIDOR

LOUNGE   BEDROOMS

FOURTH FLOOR PLAN

FIFTH & SIXTH FLOORS SIMILAR EXCEPT
LIBRARY CHANGED TO:
TOILET & LIBRARY ON FIFTH FLOOR
TOILET & BATHROOM ON SIXTH FLOOR

DINING ROOM ROOF

PARKING AREA

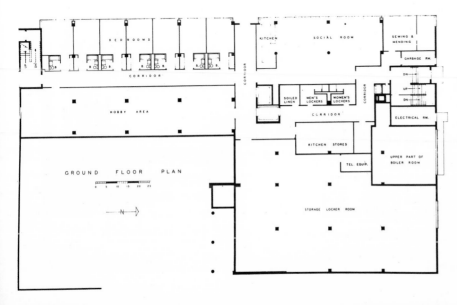

BEDROOMS

CORRIDOR

HOBBY AREA

GROUND FLOOR PLAN

KITCHEN   SOCIAL ROOM   SEWING & MENDING
GARBAGE RM.

SOILED LINEN   MEN'S LOCKERS   WOMEN'S LOCKERS

CORRIDOR

KITCHEN STORES   ELECTRICAL RM.

TEL. EQUIP.   UPPER PART OF BOILER ROOM

STORAGE LOCKER ROOM

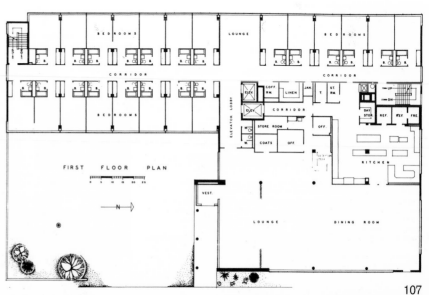

BEDROOMS   LOUNGE   BEDROOMS

CORRIDOR   CORRIDOR

BEDROOMS

ELEVATOR LOBBY

ELEV.   COFF. RM.   LINEN   JAN.   T. RM.   UP   DN.   DAY STOR.   REF.   REF.   FRE.
ELEV.   CORRIDOR

STORE ROOM   OFF.
W.   COATS   OFF.

KITCHEN

FIRST FLOOR PLAN

VEST.

LOUNGE   DINING ROOM

107

CONGREGATE HOUSING

PRESBYTERIAN HOMES
(Arden Hills, Minn. Completed 1955)

Sponsor: Presbyterian Homes, Inc., Minneapolis, Minn.
Architects: Armstrong & Schlichting, A.I.A., Minneapolis
Site: Hilly site on lake; suburban neighborhood; 4 to 5 miles to churches; transportation furnished; near stores, public transportation
Capacity: 44 plus four-bed nursing unit; planned, 60
People served: White men and women, 65 and over; ambulatory; Presbyterian; average age, 84
Buildings: One one-floor (40 single nonhousekeeping units; two doubles)
Health facilities: Four-bed nursing unit for temporary or long-term illness; occupational therapy
Auxiliary facilities: Dining room (50); laundry facilities; chapel; library; auditorium (75); three lounges; recreation room (50): shuffleboard; crafts room; beauty parlor; outdoor: croquet, gardening, fishing
Service facilities: Central kitchen; central laundry; resident storage; ample parking spaces
Staff: Total, 15
Charges and services: Entrance fee, $750; monthly fee of $125 and $140 covers meals, maid, linen laundry, limited health services
Construction: Total building area, 24,600 sq ft; 305,800 cu ft; building materials: brick frame (exterior: walls—masonry, brick; sash—double hung; interior: walls—brick and plaster; floors—mastic tile on cement; ceilings — acoustical; bathroms — tile walls); heating: steam; fuel: oil
Site development: Well water
Cost: Total site development, buildings, built-in equipment, fees, but not land or furnishings: $400,000; cost per sq ft: $14.40; cost per cu ft: $1.14
Financing: Contributions and private loan

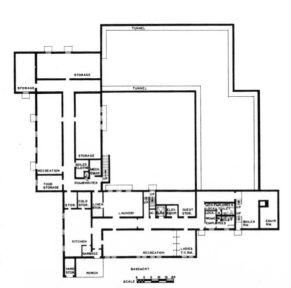

BASEMENT

FIRST FLOOR

CONGREGATE HOUSING

REST HAVEN
(Independence, Mo.; completed 1956)

Sponsor: Reorganized Church of Jesus Christ of Latter Day Saints
Architects: Dane D. Morgan & Associates, Burlington, Iowa
Engineers: Beling Engineering Consultants, Moline, Ill.
Site: 4 acres in good neighborhood; near churches, stores, public transportation
Capacity: 83 (69 in new building; 14 in conventional house on site)
People served: White men and women, 70 and over; members of sponsoring church; current ages, 70 to 97; average age, 80
Buildings: One two-story building with 34 double nonhousekeeping rooms; one existing conventional house with seven double rooms
Health facilities: Long-term nursing care to residents in rooms as needed; two-bed unit for protected care; arrangement with hospital across street for other care
Auxiliary facilities: Dining room (50); chapel (1,750 sq ft); auditorium (1,800 sq ft, 100); library (288 sq ft); three lounges (2,700, 576, 1,000 sq ft); two social rooms (40 each); hobbycrafts room (20); two recreation rooms; outdoor: croquet, individual gardening
Service facilities: Central kitchen; central laundry; maintenance building; parking spaces (visitors, 18)
Staff (part-time in parentheses): Total: 52 (15). Administration, 2 (1); health, 27 (4); food, 15 (3); maid and laundry, 7 (2); maintenance, 1 (1); counseling (2); barber, (1); beauty, (1)
Charges and services: No entrance fee; monthly fee of $150 covers meals, laundry, complete health care except surgery
Construction: Total building area, approximately 22,708 sq ft, 225,278 cu ft; building materials: steel frame exterior: (walls—brick; sash—aluminum; roofs—composition; walks—concrete; interior: walls—brick and plaster; floors—concrete, tile; ceilings—plaster, acoustical plaster; trim—wood; bathrooms—tile) heating: steam; fuel: gas, oil
Site development: Concrete driveway; large terrace at front; landscaping: shrubs, flowers, trees
Cost (1954): Total, including site development, buildings, built-in equipment, fees, but not land or furnishings: $490,000; cost per sq ft; $19.17; cost per cu ft: $1.93; furnishings: approximately $55,000
Financing: Contributions
Architect says: "Basic design was toward an ultimate cross shape, which would be most economical to operate and give the best control and at same time create a homelike atmosphere. In reality and for practicality and economy, the result is an institution, but in appearance and in feeling, it is a home. . . . It is wise to design more than just a few rooms to accommodate wheel chairs."

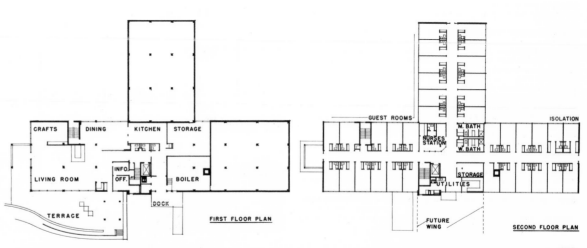

CONGREGATE HOUSING

ROCKWOOD MANOR
(Spokane, Wash.; completed 1960)

Sponsor: Spokane Methodist Homes, Inc.
Architects: Culler, Gale, Martell, Norrie & Davis, A.I.A., Spokane
Consultants: L. Keith Hellstrom, landscape architect; Lyle Marque & Associates, mechanical engineers; Joseph M. Doyle, electrical engineer
Site: 32-acre wooded, rocky area, outskirts of city, mountain-view; near shopping; public transportation at site
Capacity: 300 plus 30-bed nursing unit (planned: second multi-story structure and cottage development)
People served: Men and women, 60 and over, retired; ambulatory, good health at admission; interfaith; current ages, 60 to 92; average age, 74
Buildings: One seven-story building with 250 nonhousekeeping units, approximately half with kitchenettes (200 singles; 50 doubles; adjacent singles can be converted into two-room suite, second bath becoming a kitchenette)
Health facilities: 30-bed nursing unit with 15 two-bed rooms; clinic; future unit for sheltered care
Auxiliary facilities: Dining rooms (resident, 300; nursing unit, 40; employee, 25); chapel-auditorium (500); library (approx. 600 sq ft); lounges (one adjacent entrance lobby; one each floor at elevators, one small at end of each wing); large game room; utility room each floor (laundry, kitchenette); recreation (5,000 sq ft); small crafts rooms, woodworking shop (8 power tools); green thumb room; roof deck; beauty shop (2 chairs); outdoor: planned miniature golf course; horseshoes; shuffleboard; individual gardens; picnic area; beverage, ice cream dispensers near game rooms; guest rooms available; intercommunication system
Service facilities: Central kitchen; laundry station; maintenance shop; resident storage (105 cu ft; extra should resident become long-term patient in nursing unit); parking (40 garages, resident; lot for visitors, institution); fire detection system, sprinklers in storage area
Staff: Total: 58 full-time; 10 part-time
Charges and services: Entrance fee of $7,000 to $18,750; monthly fee of $120 covers meals, weekly maid, telephone, linen laundry, limited health care (10 days each month, noncumulative, in nursing unit without charge; current charge thereafter)
Construction: Total building area: 187,340 sq ft, 1,686,000 cu ft; building materials: reinforced concrete frame (exterior: walls—metal window wall; sash—aluminum, glare reducing glass; roofs—built-up; terraces, walks—concrete; interior: floors—carpet, vinyl tile, concrete; ceilings—plaster; bathrooms—ceramic tile); heating: hot water; cooling: chilled water; fuel: gas
Site development: Small lake on site
Cost (1960): Total, including land, fees, site development, but not furnishings: $3,130,000; construction only: $2,833,000; site development: $50,000; cost per sq ft: $15.12; cost per cu ft: $1.60; furnishings: $50,000; draperies: $120,000
Financing: FHA insured loan
Architect says: "We were endeavoring to provide comfortable, friendly, congenial surroundings—a simple building, yet one which would function efficiently. This building was conceived as a simple block dominating the highest part of a rocky, densely wooded, unspoiled area, with an inspiring view. We endeavored to integrate our construction with its environment so the existing natural beauty might be preserved. Local stone from the site and excavation was used in construction, creating a continuity between site and building."

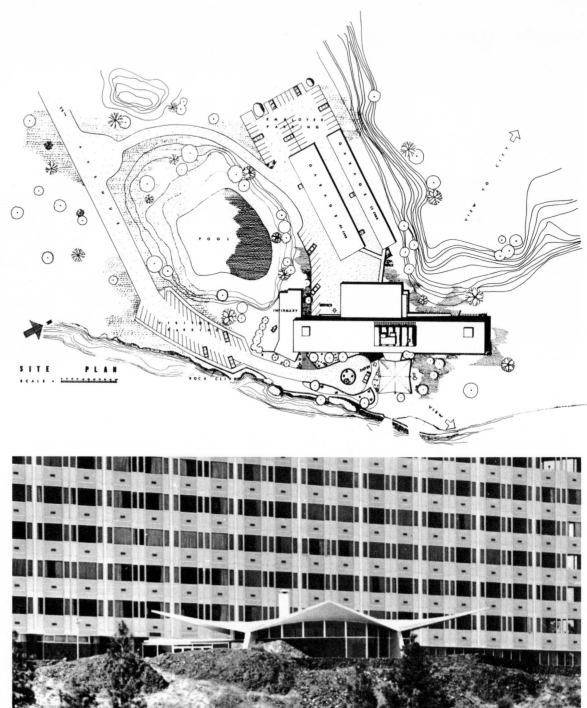

SITE PLAN
SCALE

ROCKWOOD MANOR —*Continued*
(Spokane, Wash.; completed 1960)

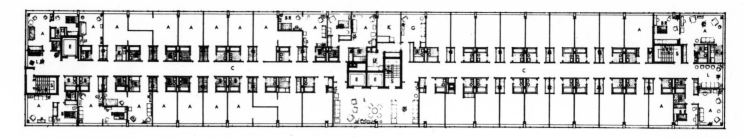

TYPICAL APARTMENT FLOOR
SECOND   THRU   SEVENTH
SCALE

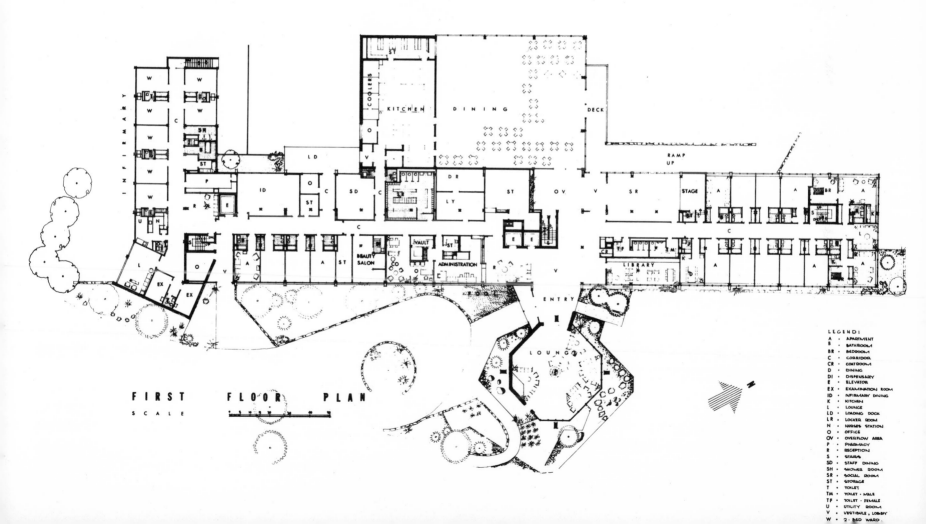

FIRST   FLOOR   PLAN
SCALE

CONGREGATE HOUSING

ROGUE VALLEY MANOR
(Medford, Ore.; completed 1961)

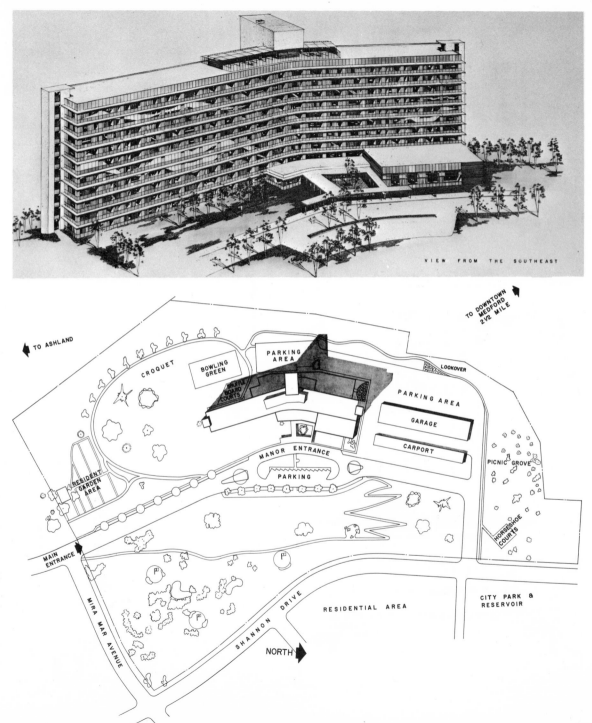

VIEW FROM THE SOUTHEAST

Sponsor: Methodist, Episcopal, and Presbyterian Churches
Architect: John W. Maloney, A.I.A., Seattle, Wash.
Site: 17 acres in center of Rogue River Valley; suburban, high-class residential neighborhood; near churches; 2½ miles to stores; free bus to downtown seven times daily
Capacity: 414 plus 40-bed nursing unit
People served: White men and women, 65 and over; ambulatory; interfaith; current ages, 57 to 89; average age, 70
Buildings: One 10-story building with 126 single units, 144 doubles (227 have kitchenettes)
Health facilities: 40-bed nursing unit, including two beds for sheltered care; clinic: diagnostic, x-ray, e.k.g.; physiotherapy completely equipped; pharmacy
Auxiliary facilities: Dining rooms (resident, 4,176 sq ft, 260; resident smoking, 26; nursing unit, 30; employee, 30); chapel (513 sq ft, 42); auditorium (3,344 sq ft, 425); library (660 sq ft); social room (4,416 sq ft); nine lounges (main, 1,674 sq ft; each floor, 435 sq ft; employee, 390 sq ft; two crafts rooms (783, 360 sq ft); recreation; outdoor: shuffleboard, croquet, bowling-on-green, horseshoes, putting green, flowerbeds (greenhouse planned); laundries; gift shop; barber, beauty shop
Service facilities: Central kitchen (2,772 sq ft); central laundry (1,080 sq ft); linen storage (540 sq ft); parking spaces (resident, 36 in garage, 26 in carport, 56 open; visitors, 14; institution, 16)
Staff: Total: 89. Administration, 9; health, 15; food, 34; maid, 10; laundry, 4; maintenance, 17
Charges and services: Entrance fee of $8,500 to $30,000; monthly fee of $110 covers meals, maid, linen laundry, all health services except hospitalization and surgery
Construction: Total building area of 256,634 sq ft, 2,857,000 cu ft; building materials: reinforced concrete frame (exterior: walls—porcelain enameled steel panels, brick veneer, window wall; sash—aluminum (steel, boiler room); roofs—20-year bonded tar, gravel; terraces, concrete sun decks, roof, nursing unit walks—concrete, asphalt; interior: walls—reinforced concrete; floors—carpet, vinyl, vinyl asbestos, asphalt, slate; ceilings—acoustical tile, plaster, painted; partitions—concrete block, structural clay tile, gypsum, plaster; trim—metal; bathrooms—ceramic tile; other—oak paneling in lobby, lounge, chapel); heating and cooling: induction units in apartments, corridors, nursing areas, lounges and low-pressure recirculating ceiling diffusers in public rooms; fuel: oil; diesel generating emergency power supply
Site development: Asphaltic concrete driveway; landscaping, natural and cultivated
Cost (1959): Total, including site development, buildings, built-in equipment, fees, but not furnishings: $5,206,000; cost per sq ft: $20.25; cost per cu ft: $1.82
Financing: Private loan and membership fees

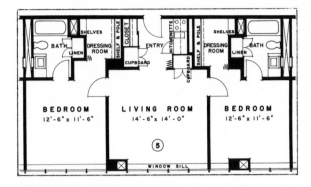

BATH · LINEN · DRESSING ROOM · SHELVES · SHELF & POLE · CLOSET · KITCHENETTE · ENTRY · SHELF & POLE · DRESSING ROOM · LINEN · SHELVES · BATH

CUPBOARD · CUPBOARD

| BEDROOM
12'-6" x 11'-6" | LIVING ROOM
14'-6" x 14'-0" | BEDROOM
12'-6" x 11'-6" |

(5)

WINDOW SILL

VIEW OF MAIN ENTRANCE

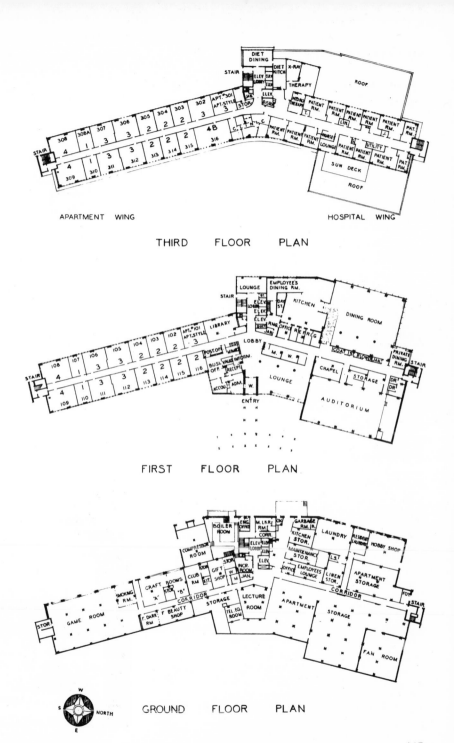

APARTMENT WING   HOSPITAL WING

THIRD   FLOOR   PLAN

FIRST   FLOOR   PLAN

GROUND   FLOOR   PLAN

CONGREGATE HOUSING

ST. JAMES HOUSE
(Baytown, Tex.; completed 1960)

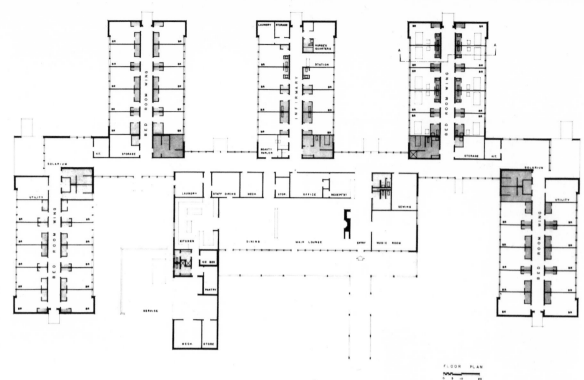

FLOOR PLAN

Sponsor: Episcopal Diocese of Texas
Architects: Cameron Fairchild & Associates, A.I.A., Houston
Site: Seven acres in wooded, residential area 25 miles from Houston
Capacity: 48 plus 10-bed infirmary, (planned, 100)
People served: Men and women, 65 and over; ambulatory; interfaith; current ages, 61 to 98; average age, 79; admission average, 78
Buildings: One-story building with 48 single bedrooms, each with private lavatory and toilet, shared bath
Health facilities: 10-room infirmary; limited therapy
Auxiliary facilities: Dining room (100); library-temporary chapel; solariums at end of each wing (group occupational therapy); craft rooms; two game rooms, kitchenettes; two corridor lounges; two open porches, front veranda; outdoor: flower beds, perimeter walks
Service facilities: Central kitchen; resident storage (20 sq ft each); parking (total, 30 spaces)
Staff (part-time employees in parentheses): Total: 17 (2). Administration, 1 (1); health, 6; food, 7; maid, 2; maintenance, 1 (1)
Charges and services: No entrance fee; monthly fee (3 groups, evenly divided: $100-$125; $125-$150; $150-200 or $225) covers meals, maid, minimum health care
Construction: Total building area: 27,600 sq ft; building materials: steel frame (exterior: walls—cavity brick; sash—aluminum; walks—concrete; interior: walls—masonry, solid plaster; ceilings—acoustical plaster, gypsum plaster; partitions—plaster; bathrooms—glazed tile); heating, cooling: hot, chilled water; fuel: gas
Cost (1959): Total cost, construction only: $425,000; cost per sq ft: $15.53 (building, fees, but not site development, land); kitchen equipment: $11,200
Financing: FHA insured loan
Special features: Occupational therapy provided in two large solariums at ends of two residential wings so flow of traffic will encourage interest and participation
Architect says: "Beyond the basic considerations of safety, convenience and easy maintenance, our design concept has been to provide an interesting and colorful residential atmosphere as suitable background for companionship, hobbies, and program.
"We find that elderly people accept colorful and nonprosaic surroundings readily. They are cheerful and outgoing, as though they were on a cruise.
"We have aimed to give them security, both physical and financial, plus congenial companions, an opportunity for privacy and an optional program, and to place all of this in the proper architectural setting."

CONGREGATE HOUSING

ST. MARY'S MEMORIAL HOME
(Glendale, Ohio; completed 1957)

Sponsor: Society of the Transfiguration (Episcopal), Glendale, Ohio
Architects: Cellarius & Hilmer, A.I.A., Cincinnati
Landscape architect: Henry Fletcher Kenney, Cincinnati
Site: 1.1 acres, part of large site of sponsor, sloping, heavily wooded; residential village, 10 miles north of Cincinnati; 1 mile to churches (Episcopal chapel adjacent), stores, public transportation
Capacity: 20 plus two-bed infirmary
People served: White, Episcopal women only, 64 and over; ambulatory, financially able; current ages, 66 to 92; average age, 78; admission average, 77
Buildings: One two-story building with 20 nonhousekeeping single units (140 sq ft each) with lavatory; toilets shared by two units; baths shared by all
Health facilities: Two-bed infirmary
Auxiliary facilities: Dining room (400 sq ft, 28); chapel, separate building on site; living room (350 sq ft); reading room—TV (196 sq ft); snack kitchenette
Service facilities: Central kitchen; central laundry; resident storage (361 sq ft); 6 parking spaces (resident, 2; visitors, 3; institution, 1)
Staff (part-time in parentheses): Total: 7 (9). Administration, (1) (some volunteers); health, 1 (3); food, 4 (1); maid, 1 (2); maintenance, (1); counseling, (1)
Charges and services: Entrance fee of $500; monthly fee of $100 to $135 covers meals, maid, laundry, limited health care
Construction: Total building area: 11,000 sq ft, 163,200 cu ft; building materials: concrete frame (exterior: walls—face brick, cinder block; sash—steel, casement; roofs—gabled, slate; terraces—flagstone; interior: walls—plaster, masonry; floors—concrete; ceilings—lath, plaster; trim—metal buck, wood; bathrooms —ceramic tile); heating: hot water; fuel: gas
Site development: Blacktop driveway; landscaping: flagstone terraces, patio
Cost (1955): Total, including site development, buildings, built-in equipment, fees, but not furnishings: $273,855; cost per sq ft: $22.80 (less fees, landscaping); cost per cu ft: $1.54 (less fees, landscaping); kitchen equipment: $7,673; furnishings: $18,000
Financing: Private loan for construction; trust fund; self suppor

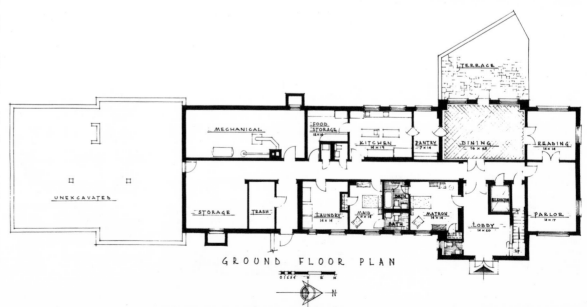

GROUND FLOOR PLAN

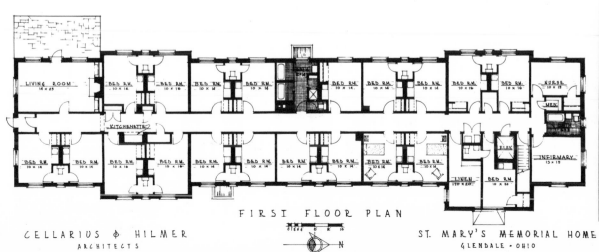

FIRST FLOOR PLAN

CELLARIUS & HILMER
ARCHITECTS
CINCINNATI, OHIO

ST. MARY'S MEMORIAL HOME
GLENDALE · OHIO

CONGREGATE HOUSING

"THE SEQUOIAS"
(Portola Valley, Calif.; completed 1961)

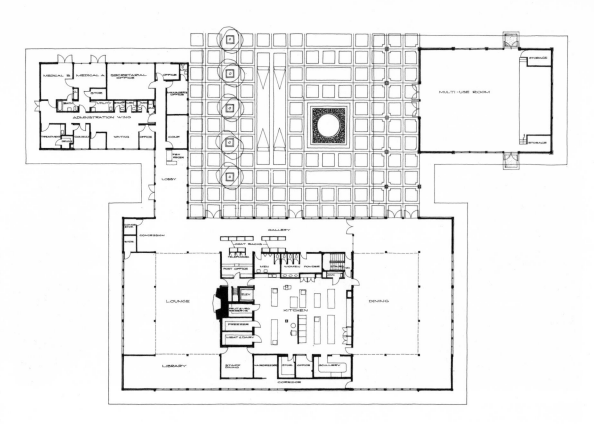

Sponsor: Northern California Presbyterian Homes, Inc.
Architects: Skidmore, Owings & Merrill, San Francisco
Consultants: Sasaki, Walker and Associates, landscape architects
Site: 43 acres in rolling, wooded mountain foothills; 2 miles to village, 7 miles to City of Palo Alto; free transportation provided by management
Capacity: 315 plus four-bed infirmary
People served: Men and women 60 and over, middle and upper income; reasonably good health; interfaith
Buildings: 24 one-story buildings with 228 nonhousekeeping apartments (106 doubles with kitchenettes; 122 singles)
Health facilities: Four-bed infirmary; 24-hour registered nurse; contract with Palo Alto Clinic for complete care
Auxiliary facilities: Dining rooms (resident, 300; employee, 20); auditorium-chapel-social (350); four parlors, fireplaces, kitchenettes, recreation equipment; one lounge (2,000 sq ft); crafts room (1,000 sq ft); tool shop (500 sq ft); automatic laundries; snack kitchenettes; beauty parlor; barber shop; outdoor: three courtyards, different views; wooded hill on site; shuffleboard, croquet, bowling-on-green, flower gardens, horseshoes, putting green
Service facilities: Central kitchen; 220 parking spaces (resident, 120; visitor, 50; institution, 50)
Staff: Total: 71. Administration, 8; health, 3; food, 30; housekeeping, 18; maintenance, 6; gardeners, 6
Charges and services: Entrance fee of $10,500 to $32,000; monthly fee of $185 to $255 covers meals, weekly maid, linen laundry, complete medical care
Construction: Total building area: 183,500 sq ft, 1,675,000 cu ft; building materials: wood stud frame (exterior: walls—wood stud, stucco, gyp board; sash—grey anodized aluminum casements, sliding doors; roofs—asphalt shingles; terraces—precast concrete blocks; walks—concrete, wood deck, steel frame covered; interior: walls — gyp board; floors — carpet; ceilings — sprayed plaster; partitions—wood stud, gyp board; trim—wood; bathrooms—vinyl walls, floors, tile showers); heating: hot water radiant; cooling: air-conditioning in dining room, lounge, administration area; fuel: gas, oil standby
Site development: Off-site sanitary sewer; black-top driveway; landscaped courts, patios
Cost (1960): Total, including site development, buildings, built-in equipment, contractor's fee, but not furnishings: $3,269,971; cost per sq ft, strictly building: $13.50; cost per sq ft, including site development, fire protection system: $18.01; cost per cu ft, above greater coverage: $1.96; kitchen equipment: $35,000
Financing: F.N.M.A.
Special features: Complete health service, including hospitalization, doctors' fees, drugs, etc.; extensive fire protection system: automatic detection equipment each room; direct signal to Fire Department

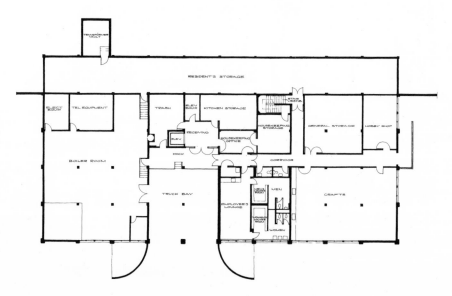

CONGREGATE HOUSING

"THE SEQUOIAS"—*Continued*
(Portola Valley, Calif.; completed 1961)

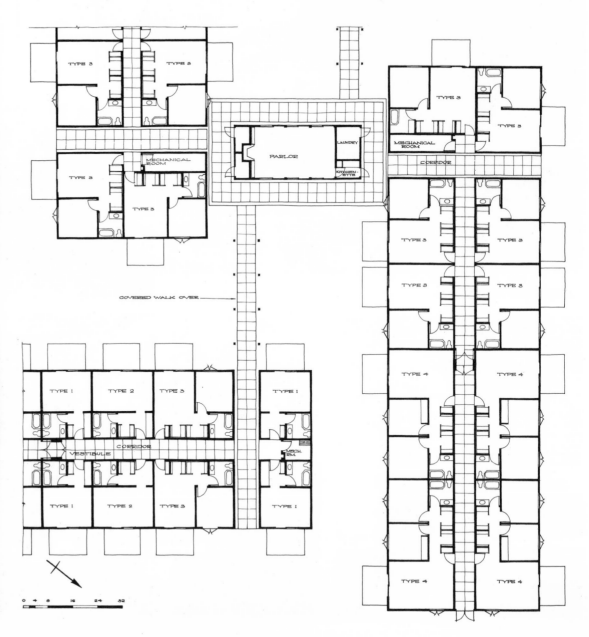

CONGREGATE HOUSING

VETLANDA HOME FOR AGED PEOPLE
(Vetlanda, Sweden)

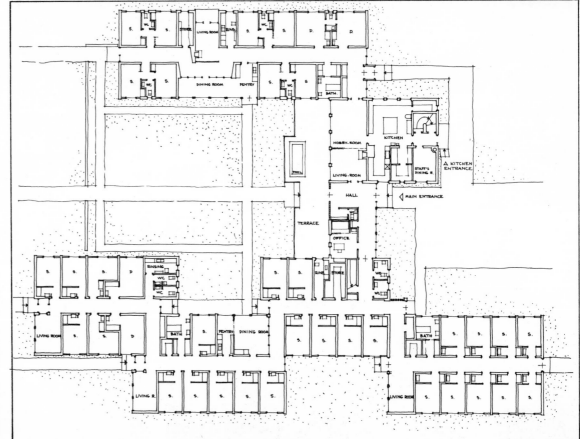

Sponsor: Village of Vetlanda
Architects: Boustedt and Heineman, S.A.R., Kungalv, Sweden
This home is centrally situated on a parklike site in a little town of about 9,000 inhabitants. The home is well adapted to the surrounding houses, mostly small villas for two families. It provides 42 beds.

The main entrance has direct contact with the office, central building, a big terrace, and a sheltered garden.

The ground floor of the two-story central building contains a kitchen with utility rooms, a living room and a hobby room. The latter two rooms can be joined and used as an assembly room. The first floor also contains dwellings for some members of the staff, but the main part of the staff lives outside the home in the town.

All pensioner-rooms face west or east; only secondary rooms face north. One part of the home is divided by a corridor broken down into three parts, all of which are short, well-lighted and provide visual contact with different furnished spaces. Most of the rooms are single rooms, but there are a few double rooms for married couples. The other pensioneers live in small units with six to nine beds in each.

CONGREGATE HOUSING

VETLANDA HOME FOR AGED PEOPLE
(Vetlanda, Sweden)
—Continued

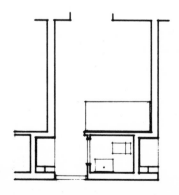

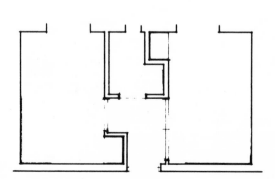

CONGREGATE HOUSING

WESLEY PALMS
(San Diego, Calif.; completed 1962)

Sponsor: Pacific Homes Corporation, an agency of The Methodist Church
Architects: Neptune & Thomas, A.I.A., Pasadena
Consultants: Peterson & Befu, A.S.L.A., landscape architects; Miss Joann Zimmerly, color consultant, interior decorator
Site: 40 acres of suburban hillside with a view of Mission Bay and the Pacific Ocean; 3 miles to Pacific Beach, LaJolla, 10 miles to San Diego
Capacity: 350
People served: Men and women 62 and older, upper income, retired; healthy; ages of applicants, 58 to 92; average, 70½
Buildings: One six-story building containing 137 apartments for 175 people (72 singles; 40 semi-suite [bed alcove]; 19 one-bedroom; six two-bedroom [two-bath] suites; most apartments have kitchenette); 131 cottages for 175 people (60 semi-suites; 49 one-bedroom; 22 two-bedroom [two-bath] suites, all with kitchenette, livingroom, bath; deluxe cottage apartment has two bedrooms, two baths, carport)
Health facilities: Six-bed infirmary; physical therapy; sponsor owns, operates hospital at LaJolla, serving its several homes
Auxiliary facilities: Dining rooms (resident, 350; staff, 100); library; chapel (small); chapel-auditorium; 12 lounges (various sizes); laundries; four solariums; game room (1,197 sq ft); crafts room; tool shop; green thumb room; outdoor: shuffleboard, gardening
Service facilities: Central kitchen; storage (resident, 3,848 sq ft in main building; 32 sq ft in cottages); parking spaces (total 186); electric cart areas
Staff: Estimated total, 100
Charges and services: Accommodation fee of $7,500 to $27,500; monthly fee of $200 covers meals, maid, linen laundry, complete health care; life care, in lieu of monthly fee (based on age and expectancy), for men: $32,050 to $15,446; for women, $35,948 to $17,074
Construction:

	MAIN BUILDING	COTTAGES
Total area:	158,800 sq ft	110,600 sq ft
Building materials:	structural steel frame	wood frame, stucco
exterior—walls:	concrete, plaster	stucco, wood siding
sash:	aluminum	glass louvers
roofs:	gravel	gravel
walks:	concrete	concrete
Interior—walls:	metal stud, plaster	wood stud, plastered
floors:	concrete, carpeted	concrete, carpeted
ceilings:	plaster, acoustic tile	wood, acoustic tile
bathrooms:	tile	tile

Heating: electric baseboard
Cooling: air conditioning for public areas; circulating system for apartments
Site development: Terraces for individual cottages and main building, paved and partially covered; covered main walkways; landscaping, sprinklers
Cost (estimated 1961): Total, including construction, fees, furnishings, site development but not land: $5,500,000; construction only, including mechanical, electrical, elevator: $4,400,000; site development, roads, landscaping: $800,000
Special features: Cottage living is new to retirement homes; outdoor activity will be stressed.

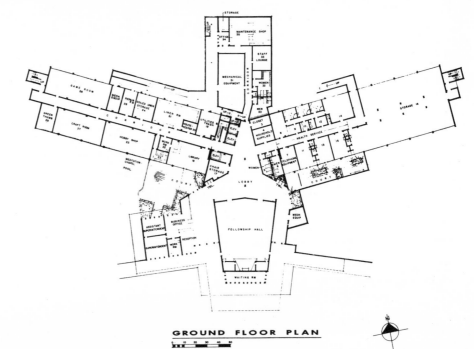

GROUND FLOOR PLAN

0 10 20 30 40 60

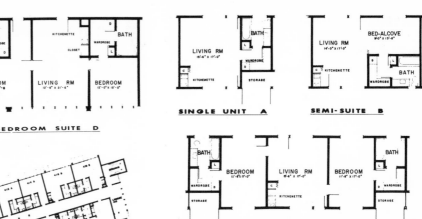

SINGLE UNIT A   SEMI-SUITE B

TWO BEDROOM SUITE D

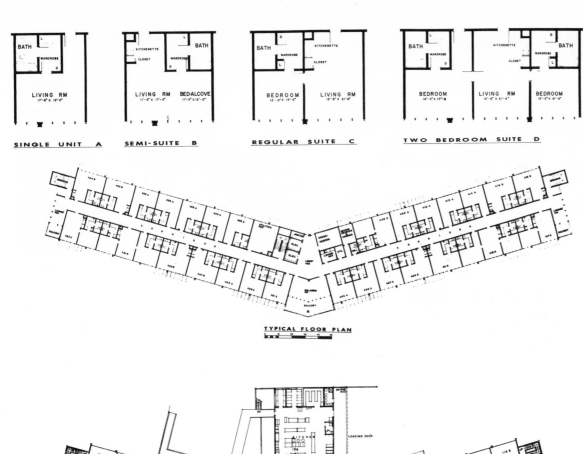

SINGLE UNIT A   SEMI-SUITE B   REGULAR SUITE C   TWO BEDROOM SUITE D

TYPICAL FLOOR PLAN

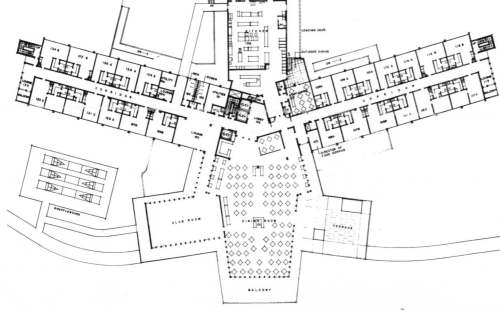

FIRST FLOOR PLAN

CONGREGATE HOUSING

WESLEY GARDENS
(Des Moines, Wash.; completed 1956)

Sponsor: Pacific Northwest Conference, The Methodist Church
Architects: William J. Bain & Harrison Overturf, A.I.A., Seattle
Site: 30 sloping acres in suburban, residential, middle-income neighborhood; 15 miles to Seattle area; near stores, churches; public transportation at site
Capacity: 238 (main building only) plus 56-bed nursing unit
People served: Men and women 65 and over; ambulatory at admission; white, Protestant; current ages, 60 to 98; average age, 79; admission average, 74
Buildings: One multistory building with 214 nonhousekeeping units (190 singles; 24 doubles; 5 with kitchenettes); 37 housekeeping cottages
Health facilities: 56-bed nursing unit, including 40 beds temporary care, 10 chronic, 6 sheltered; occupational therapy
Auxiliary facilities: Four dining rooms (resident, 260; two in nursing unit, 12 each; employee, 16); library (384 sq ft); auditorium (260); five lounges (each 700 sq ft); social room (150); laundry; four crafts rooms (35 each); tool shop (10); beauty parlor (2 chairs); barber (1 chair); recreation room (50); outdoor: croquet, individual flower beds
Service facilities: Central kitchen; central laundry; resident storage (240 cu ft); 126 parking spaces (resident, 50 carports; visitors, 60; institution, 16)
Staff (part-time employees in parentheses): Total: 50 full-time; 29 part-time. Administration, 3 (1); health, 7 (6); food, 26 (20); maid, 5; laundry, 3; maintenance, 4 (1); barber, (1); beauty, 2
Charges and services: For residents in main building: entrance fee of $7,000 to $8,000 for single apartments and $13,500 to $17,000 for two-room suites; monthly fee of $110 covers meals, weekly maid, laundry, limited health care; monthly fee of $195 for long-term patient in nursing unit. For residents of cottages: entrance fee covers full cost of cottage plus $300 maintenance fund fee; monthly fee of $1.00 for water only; care in nursing unit, $5.50 per day; meals available by reservation at current cost
Construction (main building only): Total building area: 148,718 sq ft, 1,390,968 cu ft; building materials: reinforced concrete frame (exterior: walls—concrete; sash—aluminum; roofs—concrete, built-up topping; terraces, walks—concrete; interior: walls —concrete; floors—concrete, carpeted; ceilings—plaster on concrete or suspended acoustical tile; partitions—plaster, solid, or hollow soundproof; trim—hollow metal door jambs; bathrooms— vinyl, metal tile; other—natural birch, lobby); heating: forced hot water; fuel: oil
Site development: Asphalt concrete driveway; landscaping: curved ramp to garden
Cost (1956, main building only): Total, including site development, building, built-in equipment, fees, but not furnishings: $2,372,268; cost per sq ft: $15.95; cost per cu ft: $1.70; furnishings: $37,144; kitchen equipment: $41,232; health: $11,884
Financing: Contributions ($225,000); private conventional loan ($600,000); founders' fees; cottage purchase additional

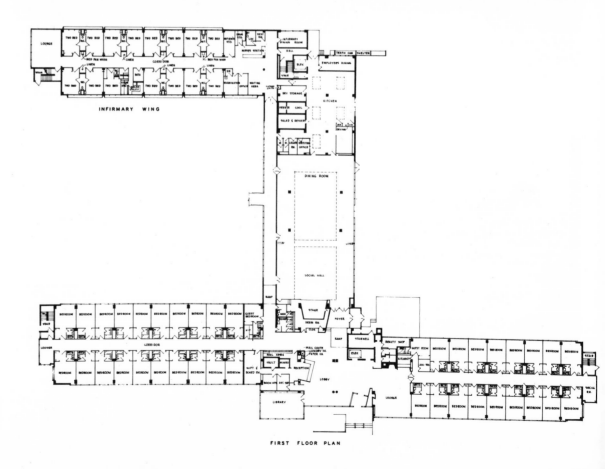

INFIRMARY WING

FIRST FLOOR PLAN

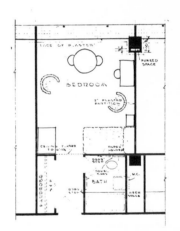

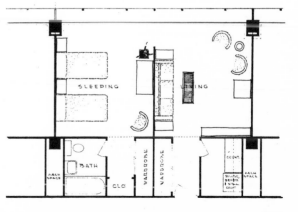

CONGREGATE HOUSING

WESLEY TERRACE
(Des Moines, Wash.; completed 1961)

Sponsor: Wesley Gardens, a Washington Corporation (Pacific Northwest Conference of The Methodist Church)
Architects: William J. Bain & Harrison Overturf, A.I.A., Seattle
Consultants: Beardsley & Brauner, landscape architects
Site: 26.7 acres with view of Puget Sound in suburban, residential, white, middle-class neighborhood; 15 miles to Seattle; near stores, churches; public transportation at site
People served: Men and women 65 and over; ambulatory at admission; white, Protestant; ages of applicants', 60 to 97; average age, 73
Capacity: 283 plus 21-bed infirmary (separate building for nine employees)
Buildings: One multistory building containing 250 units (217 singles; 33 doubles, 8 with kitchenettes)
Health facilities: 21-bed infirmary; seven rooms adjacent to infirmary, limited nursing care; occupational therapy
Auxiliary facilities: Three dining rooms (resident, 284; infirmary, 12; employee, 20); library (1,600 sq ft); auditorium (300); social room (200); six lounges (each 1,152 sq ft); laundry; beauty parlor (3 chairs); four crafts rooms (40 each); one tool shop (12); two recreation rooms (each 100); outdoor: croquet, individual gardening
Service facilities: Central kitchen; central laundry; resident storage (180 cu ft each); 147 parking spaces (resident, 59 carports; spaces for visitors, 70; institution, 18)
Staff (part-time employees in parentheses): Total, 50 full-time, 26 part-time (Administration, 3 (2); health, 7 (2); food, 26 (21); maid, 6; laundry, 3; maintenance, 3 (1); beauty, 2
Charges and services: Entrance fee of $8,000 to $9,000 for single units; $14,000 to $19,000 for double suites; monthly fee of $110 covers meals, maid, laundry, limited health care
Construction: Total building area: 205,020 sq ft, 2,151,904 cu ft; building materials: reinforced concrete frame; (exterior: walls—8″ concrete, painted; sash—aluminum, sliding doors; roofs—concrete, 4-ply and gravel; terraces, walks—concrete; other—marble chip panels in curtain wall; interior: walls—solid plaster; floors—concrete slab, carpeted or vinyl; ceilings—plaster; partitions—hollow soundproof plaster wall; trim—hollow metal door frames; bathrooms—vinyl, Formica, metal tile; other—birch and Flexwood, first floor lobby, library); heating: forced hot water; fuel: oil
Site development: Asphaltic concrete driveway; landscaping features: decorative pierced concrete block walls, benches, plant tubs
Cost (1960): Total, including site development, buildings, built-in equipment, fees, but not furnishings: $3,488,711; cost per sq ft: $17.01; cost per cu ft: $1.62; kitchen equipment: $47,839; health: $11,355; furnishings: $55,040
Financing: Contributions (very little); FHA insured loan and Seattle First National Bank mortgage; founders' fees
Special feature: Seven rooms adjacent to infirmary are for limited nursing care. At some future time, the whole balance of second floor can easily be converted to infirmary usage. The corridors not commanded by existing nurses' station would be served by a newly-added nurses' station centrally located. This change would provide additional infirmary space for a total of 90 beds and lounging and dining areas (21 beds in 11 rooms, original infirmary; 7 private rooms with complete bath; 62 beds in 32 added infirmary rooms)

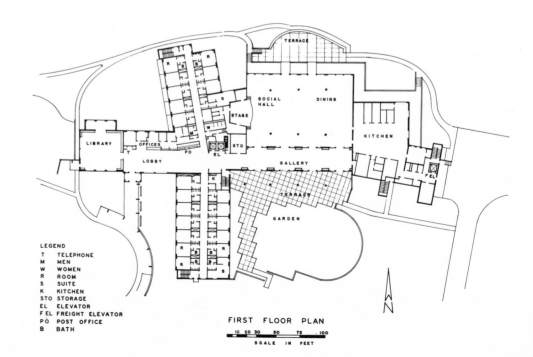

LEGEND
T TELEPHONE
M MEN
W WOMEN
R ROOM
S SUITE
K KITCHEN
STO STORAGE
EL ELEVATOR
F EL FREIGHT ELEVATOR
PO POST OFFICE
B BATH

FIRST FLOOR PLAN

SCALE IN FEET

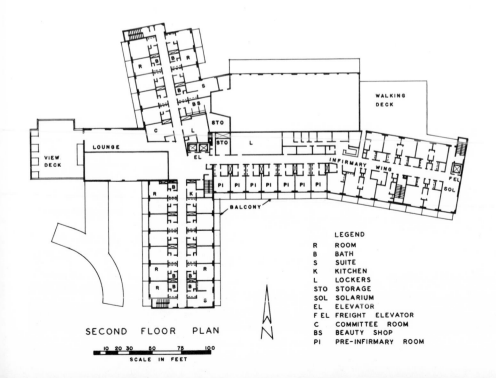

LEGEND
R   ROOM
B   BATH
S   SUITE
K   KITCHEN
L   LOCKERS
STO STORAGE
SOL SOLARIUM
EL   ELEVATOR
F EL FREIGHT ELEVATOR
C   COMMITTEE ROOM
BS   BEAUTY SHOP
PI   PRE-INFIRMARY ROOM

SECOND FLOOR PLAN

10 20 30   50   75   100
SCALE IN FEET

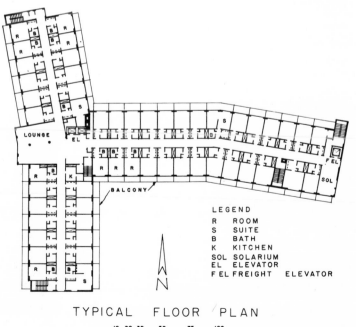

LEGEND
R   ROOM
S   SUITE
B   BATH
K   KITCHEN
SOL SOLARIUM
EL   ELEVATOR
F EL FREIGHT ELEVATOR

TYPICAL FLOOR PLAN

10 20 30   50   75   100
SCALE IN FEET

CONGREGATE HOUSING

WINEBRENNER HAVEN
(Findlay, Ohio; completed 1961)

Sponsor: Ohio Eldership of the Churches of God in North America
Architects: Sullivan, Isaacs & Sullivan, Findlay, Ohio
Site: Approximately 1 acre in middleclass residential neighborhood; ½ to 4 miles to churches; 1½ miles to stores
Capacity: 52 plus six-bed nursing unit
People served: Men and women 65 and over; average income; ambulatory; interracial; interfaith; current ages, 70 to 96; average age, 81; admission average, 81
Buildings: One four-story, containing 48 nonhousekeeping units (44 singles; four doubles)
Health facilities: Six-bed nursing unit, including care, convalescence, chronic, sheltered; clinic; occupational therapy
Auxiliary facilities: Dining room (65); lounge-chapel (1,034 sq ft); recreation-crafts (50); beauty parlor (2 chairs); outdoor: individual gardening, others
Service facilities: Central kitchen; central laundry; storage (resident, 28 sq ft each; institution, 700 sq ft); 28 parking spaces (resident, 3; institution, 5; visitors, 20 on street)
Staff (part-time employees in parentheses): Total, 13 full-time, 7 part-time. Administration, 2; health, 4 (3); food, 4 (3); maid, 1 (1); laundry, 1; beauty operator, 1
Charges and services: No entrance fee; monthly fee of $153 to $220 covers meals, maid, laundry, limited health care
Construction: Total building area of 30,270 sq ft; building materials: steel frame (exterior: walls — brick, porcelain on steel panels, glass; sash—aluminum, awning; roofs—built-up, gravel; terraces, walks—concrete; interior: walls—glazed tile, concrete block; floors—slate, carpet, vinyl asbestos tile; ceilings—acoustical plaster; partitions—concrete block; trim—wood mold, rubber base; bathrooms—terrazzo, glazed tile, plaster); heating: hot water; fuel: natural gas
Site development: Blacktop driveway; landscape features: court with benches, outside dining room
Cost (1958): Total cost, including site development, buildings, built-in equipment, fees, but not furnishings or land: $501,542; cost per sq ft: $16.57; health equipment: $1,200; furnishings: $33,800
Financing: Contributions ($93,500); FHA insured loan

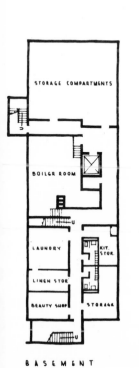

BASEMENT

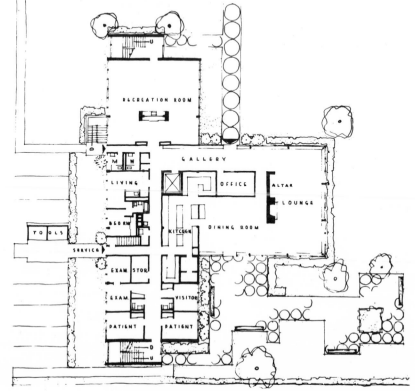

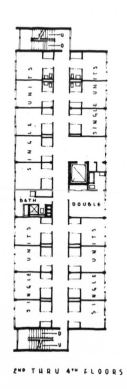

2ND THRU 4TH FLOORS

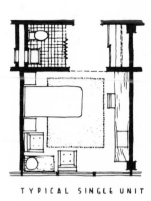

TYPICAL SINGLE UNIT

PROXIMATE HOUSING—PRIVATE: TABLE 1

Explanation of symbols describing health facilities: *Future; Care: Infirmary; Nursing Unit; Hospital; Treatment: Diagnosis; Special (dentist, oculist, podiatrist, psychiatrist); Therapy (physio-, psycho-, occupational); Age figures: Admission average; Average now; Spread of ages.* Data on projects supplied by architects and sponsors.

Name of project	Capacity	Total cost	Cost per sq. ft.	Cost per cu. ft.	Year bid	Health facilities			Ages of residents		
						No. beds	Care	Treatment	Adm.	Av.	Spread
Bradenton Trailer Park	2,600	—	—	—	—	(Community facilities used)			—	70	60-91
El Rancho Trailer Park	760	—	—	—	—	(Community facilities used)			—	65	48-86
Campbell Stone Memorial	103	$590,000	$11.20	$1.40	1958	(Community facilities used)			71	75	62-87
Canterbury Apartments	42	$453,705	$14.90	—	1949	(Community facilities used)			—	—	—
Cottages, Lutheran	120	$60,000	$20.00	$2.18	1961	(Facilities on site)			—	71	68-76
Hudson Guild Apartments	80	$600,000	$25.00	$2.50	1962	—	—	—	—	—	—
Mayflower Home	85	$900,000	$13.50 (average)	—	1953 1955 1959	—	—	—	70	80	61-91
Orange Gardens	240 houses	—	—	—	—	(Community facilities used)			—	62	24-91
Bloomfield Hills Retirement Community	24	$505,000	$20.50	$2.27	1961	—	—	—	—	—	—
Springvale-on-Hudson	700	$3,000,000	$10.00	$1.00	1961	—	N(F)	—	—	—	—
Tenacre Foundation	10	—	—	—	—	(Nursing facilities on site)			—	—	—
Vine Court	38	$138,598	$17.95	$1.63	1959	(Community facilities used)			75	78	72-86
Wilder Apartments (proposed)	80	$731,000	$20.00	—	—	(Nursing home on site)			—	—	—

PROXIMATE HOUSING—PRIVATE: TABLE 2

Explanation of symbols: Parking spaces: *Resident; Institution; Visitor;* Staff allocation: *Administration; Health; Food; Maid; Laundry; Building and grounds maintenance;* part-time staff shown in parentheses. Data on projects supplied by architects and sponsors.

Name of project	Capacity	Parking spaces			Extent of health services	Staff allocation						Fees	
		R	I	V		A	H	F	M	L	B	Entrance	Monthly
Bradenton Trailer Park	2,600	—	—	—	—	4	—	—	—	—	16[1]	$3, 4, 5 weekly	
El Rancho Trailer Park	760	—	—	—	—	1	—	—	—	—	4[1]	$250-300 annually	
Campbell Stone Memorial	103	—	—	—	—	[1]	—	—	—	—	[1]	$600	$50, 65, 83
Canterbury Apartments	42	60 total			—	—	—	—	—	—	1	—	—
Cottages, Lutheran	120	—	—	—	Limited	—	—	—	—	—	—	$14,000 for each cottage	$40
Hudson Guild Apartments	80	—	—	—	—	2	—	—	—	—	1	None	$70-90
Mayflower Home	85	25 total			Limited	2[1]	1[1]	1[1]	1	—	1	$5,750-9,000	$37.50-60
Orange Gardens	240 homes	—	—	—	—	6	—	—	—	—	6	$10,000-15,000 including lot	
Bloomfield Hills Retirement Community	24	2-car garage and 2 V each			—	—	—	—	—	—	1	—	—
Springvale-on-Hudson	700	100%			Limited	8 total						None	$62.50-130
Tenacre Foundation	10	Ample			—	11	57	17	14	—	3	$15,000	$235 and 250
Vine Court	38	5	—	12	—	—	—	—	—	—	1	None	$50-78.50
Wilder Apartments (proposed)	80	On street			Available	[1]	—	—	—	—	1	None	$65-85

PROXIMATE HOUSING — PRIVATE

BRADENTON TRAILER PARK
(Bradenton, Fla.; opened 1936)

Sponsor: Kiwanis Club of Bradenton, Fla.

Site: 1190-lot park (each lot approximately 980 sq ft) located 1 mile from center of city; shopping area, facing park on three sides, includes supermarket, eating places, services, gas stations and small shops; public transportation at site

Capacity: Approximately 2,600

People served: Current ages 16 to 91; average age, 70; approximately 200 single people; largest family size, four

Health facilities: Community services; two-way public address system for emergency aid with 115 speakers strategically located through park

Auxiliary facilities: Auditorium (7,600 sq ft); social hall (dancing, games, potluck meals); laundries, automatic washers and dryers; bath houses; outdoor: picnic and barbecue grounds; shuffleboard; horseshoes; fishing, swimming, water-skiing and boating; Milwaukee Braves spring training field within walking distance

Charges and services: Weekly rates of $3.50, $4.00, and $5.00 (for individual trailer lots; covers unlimited water, 5 kw. electricity, entertainment; special storage rates (six-month period); city tax garbage disposal service, $1.75 monthly for each occupied trailer

Staff: Administration, 4; maintenance grounds and communal buildings, 16 part-time

Site development: 16 asphalt paved streets; perfect drainage

Financing: Kiwanis Club of Bradenton

PROXIMATE HOUSING—PRIVATE

EL RANCHO VILLAGE
(Bradenton, Fla.; opened 1954)

Owners: Mr. and Mrs. George C. McKenney
Site: 76 acres with 400 trailer spaces, each 3,000 to 5,000 sq ft; approximately 1 mile to city, stores and churches; public transportation at site
Capacity: Approximately 760
People served: 360 couples; 40 single people; current ages, 48 to 86; average age, 65; largest family, three
Health facilities: Community medical services (2 miles away); visiting nurse service available from community; nurse in residence; "help-your-neighbor" buzz system for emergency
Auxiliary facilities: Community building: library, crafts rooms, auditorium, social room with kitchen; bath houses; laundry with coin-operated washers and dryers; outdoor: shuffleboard, croquet, horseshoes, bowling-on-green, garden plots, fishing
Charges and services: $250-$300 annual rental for trailer spaces; covers use of communal facilities
Staff: Maintenance of buildings and grounds (residents responsible for care of trailer lots), 4 (one part-time); counseling: 1

CAMPBELL STONE MEMORIAL HOME
(Denver, Colo.; completed 1959)

Sponsor: Association of Christian Churches of Denver
Architects: Ramsey & Reeves, Denver, Colo.
Site: One-third acre in established residential area adjacent to city park; near shops, churches; 10 minutes to downtown; public transportation at site
Capacity: 103
People served: Men and women, 60 and over; moderate income; able to live independently; interdenominational (priority to members of Christian Church); current ages, 62 to 87; average age, 75; admission average, 71
Buildings: One six-story housekeeping apartment building with 66 units (29 buffet; 27 one-bedroom; 10 two-bedroom)
Health facilities: Community health and social services available
Auxiliary facilities: Lounge (approximately 1,300 sq ft); roof deck; laundries equipped with automatic washers and dryers; all electric kitchens with disposals
Service facilities: Parking lot (small extra charge)
Staff: 3 part-time (administration, 1; maintenance, 1; program director, 1)
Charges and services: Entrance deposit of $600 (refundable to resident on severance or to resident's estate on death); monthly rental (buffet apartment, $50; one-bedroom, $65; two-bedroom, $83) covers utilities, trash removal, building and grounds maintenance
Construction: Total building area: 41,162 sq ft, 359,488 cu ft; building materials (exterior: walls—block stucco, face brick; sash — aluminum, sliding; terraces, walks — concrete; trim — metal, wood; bathrooms—textured plaster); heating: hot water; fuel: gas
Cost (1958): Total, including land, site development, fees, but not furnishings: $590,000; cost per sq ft: $11.20; cost per cu ft: $1.40; kitchen equipment: $27,000; furnishings, lounge: $1,400
Financing: FHA insured loan (this was first project of its type in U.S.A. financed by FHA)

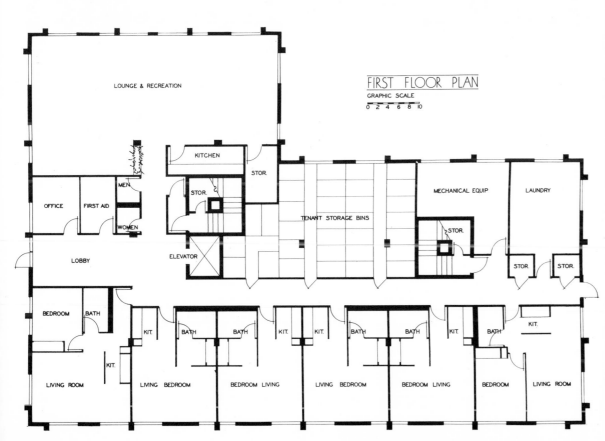

FIRST FLOOR PLAN

GRAPHIC SCALE

0 2 4 6 8 10

LOUNGE & RECREATION

OFFICE

FIRST AID

MEN

WOMEN

LOBBY

BEDROOM

BATH

LIVING ROOM

KIT.

KITCHEN

STOR.

STOR.

STOR.

ELEVATOR

KIT.

LIVING BEDROOM

BATH

BATH

KIT.

BEDROOM LIVING

TENANT STORAGE BINS

KIT.

LIVING BEDROOM

BATH

BATH

MECHANICAL EQUIP

STOR.

KIT.

BEDROOM LIVING

LAUNDRY

STOR.

STOR.

BATH

BEDROOM

KIT.

LIVING ROOM

PROXIMATE HOUSING—PRIVATE

CANTERBURY APARTMENTS
(Upper Arlington, Columbus, Ohio)

Sponsors: The residents (a cooperative corporation)
Architects: Tibbals, Crumley, Musson, A.I.A., Columbus, Ohio
Site: Eight acres on a slight knoll with some trees; middle and upper income suburb; 1 mile to church, shopping center; zoned for two-story buildings only
Capacity: 21 family units
People served: Upper middle income; primarily retired; good health
Buildings: Three buildings: 21 housekeeping apartments, seven in each building (three one-bedroom, 15 two-bedroom, three three-bedroom)
Health facilities: Individual responsibility
Auxiliary facilities: Two blocks to country club with golf, swimming, restaurant, etc.
Service facilities: 30 garages; 30 parking spaces; service yard at each kitchen
Staff: Maintenance and grounds, 1
Construction: Total building area: 30,450 sq ft, 274,050 cu ft; building materials: frame—wood studs and joists (exterior: walls —rough limestone, wood siding; sash—wood casement; roofs— tile; terraces and walks — limestone flagging; garden walls — rough limestone; interior: walls—rough limestone and plaster; floors—oak planks, flagstone, rubber tile; ceilings—plaster; trim —oak; baths—ceramic tile); heating, cooling: forced air; fuel: gas
Site development: Each unit to have private garden surrounded by stone walls or screen planting; one corner of site, not shown, has common picnic area and putting green; garages arranged in screened yards which divide general public area from landscaped entrance courts for groups of three and four units; walled service yard for each unit
Cost (estimate, 1949): Total, building construction including fees, landscaping and site development, but not land or furnishings: $453,705.00; cost per sq ft: $14.90
Architects say: This project was conceived as a cooperative venture at a time when cooperatives for real estate holding were difficult to formulate under the Ohio laws. The obvious advantages it offered retired people were received with enthusiasm, but the legal organization proved too difficult for the people involved to cope with. It would have been a trail-blazing retirement community for Central Ohio.

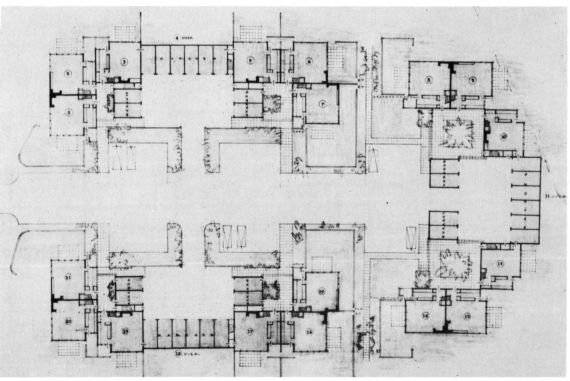

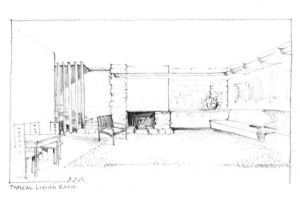

TYPICAL LIVING ROOM

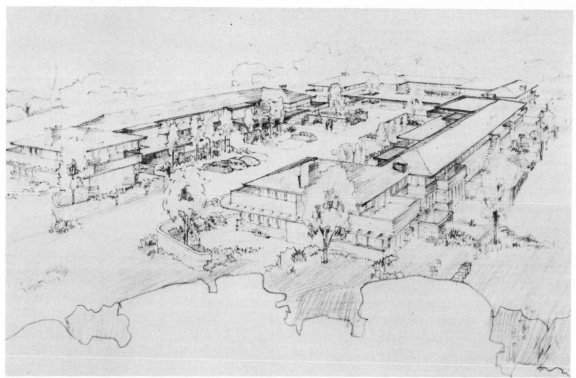

COTTAGE DEVELOPMENT FOR LUTHERAN HOME FOR THE AGED
(Westlake, Ohio; completed 1962)

Sponsor: Lutheran Home for the Aged Association
Architects: Amedeo Leone, A.I.A., and Smith, Hinchman & Grylls, A.I.A., Detroit, Mich.
Site: Approximately 20 level acres in suburban Cleveland; predominantly white, medium-income neighborhood; near churches, stores; public transportation at site
Capacity: 120 (planned, 270 to 320)
People served: Men and women, 65 and over, moderate income; ambulatory, fairly well; interracial, interfaith (priority to white Lutherans); current ages, 68 to 76; average age 71
Buildings: Fifteen one-story cottages containing four efficiency housekeeping apartments each (single or double occupancy). On same site as Lutheran Home for the Aged (capacity, 87 plus nursing unit).
Health facilities: Residents may use nursing unit of Lutheran Home.
Auxiliary facilities: Cottage residents may participate in all programs and activities of Lutheran Home. Meals may be purchased at Lutheran Home dining hall.
Charges and services: Entrance contribution; monthly fee of $40 covers maintenance, repairs, heavy cleaning, limited health services in Lutheran Home nursing unit.
Construction: Area of each building: 2,990 sq ft, 27,600 cu ft; building materials: wood stud frame, plastered (exterior: walls—brick [block back-up]; sash—wood [fixed and casement]; roofs—built-up [white marble chips]; terraces, walks—concrete; interior: walls—plaster; floors—ceramic tile, vinyl; ceilings—plaster [studio]; partitions—wood stud plaster, ceramic tile; trim—wood; bathrooms—ceramic tile); heating: forced warm air; fuel: gas
Site development: Private sewage treatment; asphalt driveway
Cost (1961): Each building, including site development, built-in equipment, fees but not furnishings: $60,000; cost per sq ft: $20; cost per cu ft: $2.18
Financing: Cottage residents pay for individual units; Lutheran Home pays architects' fees, roadways, laying utilities
Special feature: Four apartments clustered around central utility core; flexibility of arrangement permits conversion of two apartments into single large two-bedroom apartment

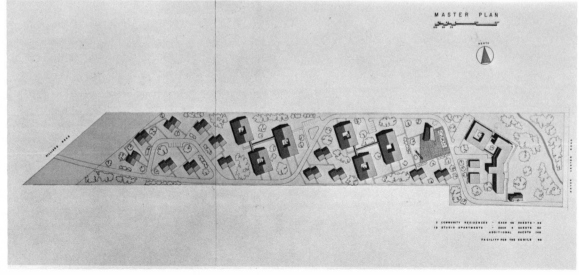

MASTER PLAN

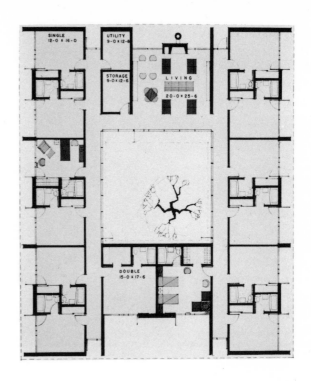

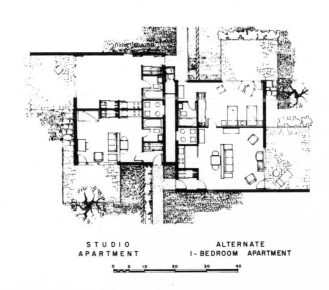

STUDIO
APARTMENT

ALTERNATE
1-BEDROOM APARTMENT

0   5   10   20   30   40

PROXIMATE HOUSING—PRIVATE

HUDSON GUILD APARTMENTS
(New York, N. Y.; anticipated completion 1963)

Sponsor: The Hudson Guild, New York
Architects: Katz, Waisman, Weber, Strauss, A.I.A., Architects Engineers, New York
Consultants: Farkas & Barron, structural engineers; Benjamin & Flack, mechanical engineers; Zion & Breen, landscape design
Site: 3,600 sq ft in center of city; low-middle-class neighborhood, interracial; near churches, stores, public transportation
Capacity: 60 (planned, 80)
People served: Men and women, 60 and over, in good health; interracial; interfaith
Buildings: One 11-story building containing 41 housekeeping units (20 singles; 20 doubles); superintendent's residence
Health facilities: Provided by Hudson Guild, within walking distance
Auxiliary facilities: Social room—lounge (30); laundry facilities; outdoor: shuffleboard; other facilities provided by Hudson Guild
Service facilities: Storage: 9 sq ft each resident
Staff: Administration, 2; maintenance, 1
Charges and services: Entrance fee: none; monthly rent of $70 to $90
Construction: Total building area: 28,800 sq ft, 249,000 cu ft; building materials: reinforced concrete frame (exterior: walls—brick; sash—aluminum; roofs—built-up tar, gravel; walks—concrete; interior: walls—concrete block; floors—concrete, asphalt tile finish; ceilings—concrete, plastered; partitions—plaster; trim—wood, metal; bathrooms—tile); heating: steam; fuel: oil
Site development: Landscaping: small pool
Cost (1962): Total, site development, building and built-in equipment, fees but not furnishings or land: $600,000; cost per sq ft: $25; cost per cu ft: $2.50; kitchen equipment: $3500; furnishings: $5000
Financing: FHA insured loan, #231 program
Architects say: "The Hudson Guild, one of New York's leading neighborhood houses, devoted to serving the welfare of its Chelsea Community, and desiring to provide housing for its elderly residents through the FHA 231 program, has embarked on a building program with a prototype apartment dwelling unit for 40 families. This first project will allow opportunity for careful analysis of construction and administrational problems prior to proceeding with additional units.
"The problems of finding land at a reasonable cost located in such a dense urban area resulted in a vertical solution on the first tiny site available.
"The major public social facilities at the Hudson Guild are within walking distance. The residential social functions are provided for on the ground level by a social room and garden. These areas, plus the combined superintendent's office-laundry center off the lobby, and the tenants' storage and service areas in the cellar, are all supervised by a resident concierge. The concierge maintains a continued contact with residents by electronic means.
"The apartments are planned to center around the living and dining areas with the dining spaces designed as intimate porches in the sky with large screened windows opening out to the surrounding neighborhood view."

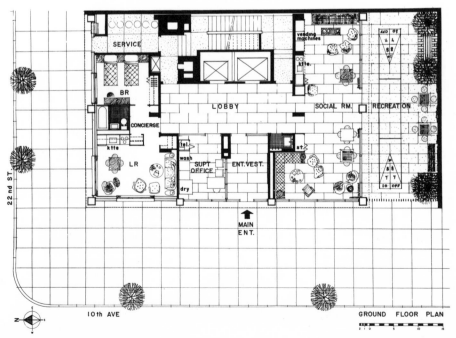

GROUND FLOOR PLAN

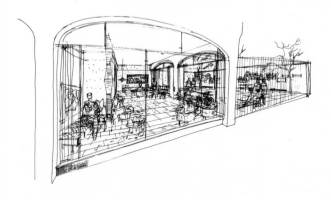

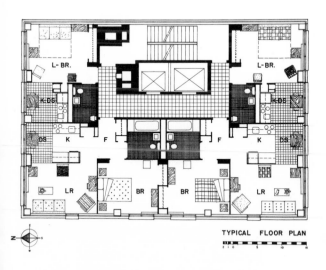

TYPICAL FLOOR PLAN

MAYFLOWER HOME
(Grinnell, Iowa; completed 1959)

Sponsor: Congregational Christian Conference of Iowa
Architects: Wetherell-Harrison-Wagner, A.I.A., Des Moines, Iowa
Site: 1½ acres of level, wooded land; four blocks to downtown area; near First Congregational Church
Capacity: 85 (planned, 170)
People served: Men and women, 60 years and over; ambulatory, in good general health on admission; interfaith (priority to members sponsoring church); fifteen apartments reserved for retired clergy of sponsor; current ages, 61 to 91; average age, 80; admission average, 70
Buildings: One two-story housekeeping apartment building and two one-story housekeeping apartment buildings with seven efficiencies; 25 one-bedroom apartments, three two-bedroom apartments, 15 one-room apartments
Health facilities: four-bed infirmary (current cost $5 per day); 24-hour nursing service; service in resident's apartment available at cost; two community hospitals (resident pays all costs)
Auxiliary facilities: Dining room (community, 32; planned, 100); library; chapel, meeting room, 125 (planned, 200); lounges, small meeting rooms; recreation, hobby, craft, woodworking room; outdoor: individual gardens
Service facilities: Kitchen for community dining room; resident storage lockers each building; parking spaces, 25 (planned, 50)
Staff (part-time in parentheses): Total: 6 (3). Administration, 2 (1); health, 1 (1); food, 1 (1); maid, 1; maintenance, 1
Charges and services: Entrance fee of $5,750 to $9,000; monthly fee of $37.50 to $60, including all utilities; meals extra (main meal available daily on reservation); infirmary, $150 per month
Construction: Total area (three buildings): 53,740 sq ft; building materials: concrete frame (exterior: walls—masonry, 4" brick, 2" insulation, 4" tile, plaster; sash—aluminum double-hung, aluminum storm, screens; roofs—concrete deck, 2" insulation, 20-year built-up; interior: walls—tile, plastered; floors—composition tile, carpet; ceilings—acoustical tile, plaster; bathrooms—ceramic tile, plaster); heating: hot water, individual control; cooling: air conditioners in meeting rooms only; fuel: gas, oil standby
Cost (Unit #1, 1953; Unit #2, 1955; Unit #3, 1958): Total, including land, fees, site development, but not furnishings: $900,000; cost per sq ft: unit #1, $12.62; unit #2, $13.03; unit #3, $16.79 (architectural fees not included); equipment: community kitchen, $5,000; infirmary, $1,500; apartment kitchens, $15,000; other, $20,000
Financing: Endowment; contributions of churches and individuals; private loan; Mayflower Home Bonds
Architect says: "The challenge has been to provide an adventure in apartment type retirement living where the resident has the opportunity to be original, independent, useful, and constructive. The emphasis on continued active living rather than retiring has been stressed. The happiness of the present residents and need for additional units point out soundness of basic design concept. Increasing interest in this type of retirement living has been indicated by others who have visited Mayflower Home."

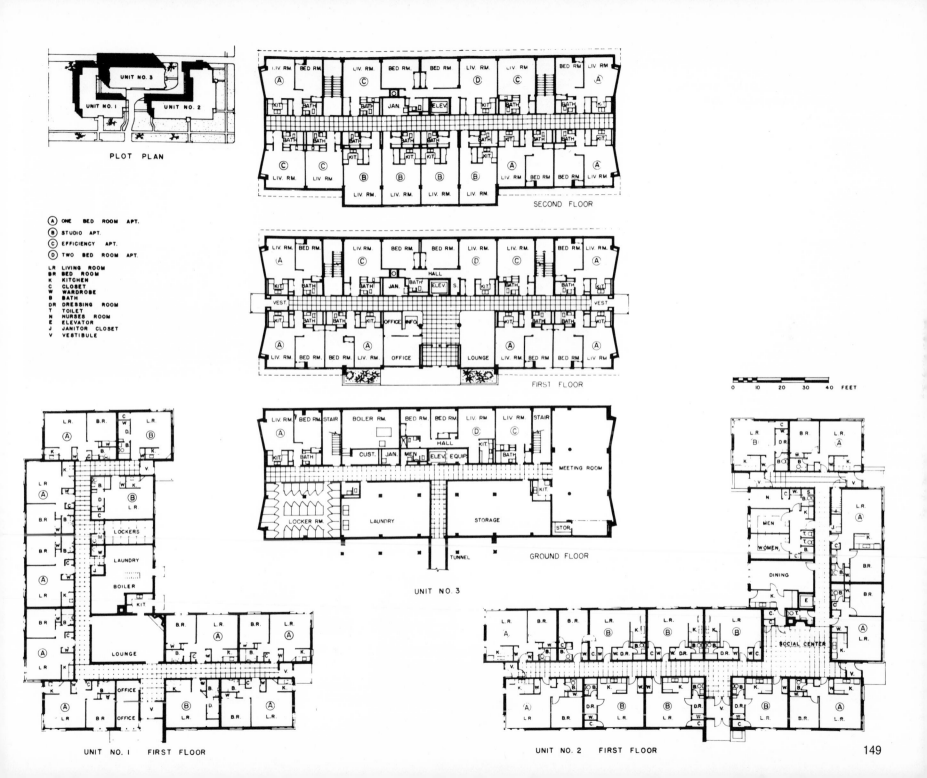

PLOT PLAN

UNIT NO. 3
UNIT NO. 1
UNIT NO. 2

Ⓐ ONE BED ROOM APT.
Ⓑ STUDIO APT.
Ⓒ EFFICIENCY APT.
Ⓓ TWO BED ROOM APT.

LR LIVING ROOM
BR BED ROOM
K   KITCHEN
C   CLOSET
W   WARDROBE
B   BATH
DR DRESSING ROOM
T   TOILET
N   NURSES ROOM
E   ELEVATOR
J   JANITOR CLOSET
V   VESTIBULE

SECOND FLOOR

FIRST FLOOR

0   10   20   30   40 FEET

GROUND FLOOR

UNIT NO. 3

UNIT NO. 1   FIRST FLOOR

UNIT NO. 2   FIRST FLOOR

149

PROXIMATE HOUSING—PRIVATE

MENLO PARK RETIREMENT APARTMENTS
(Menlo Park, Calif.; completed 1961)

Sponsor: Peninsula Volunteers, Inc., Menlo Park, Calif.
Architects: Skidmore, Owings & Merrill, San Francisco, Calif.
Consultants: Thomas Church, landscape architect
Site: Approximately ⅔ acre of flat land with very large walnut, olive, magnolia, evergreen trees; middle-income, residential neighborhood; near churches, stores, public transportation
Capacity: 54
People served: Men and women 62 and over, limited income; good general health; white, interfaith; current ages, 62-88; average age, 68; average on admission, 67
Buildings: One consisting of four two-story structures around a large landscaped quadrangle with 30 housekeeping units (six singles, 24 doubles)
Health facilities: Community; occupational therapy at Little House, a Senior Citizen Activity Center, under same sponsorship, two blocks distant
Auxiliary facilities: Individual balcony or patio; laundry (two washers, two dryers, lawn area); wood screens for privacy; fire protection and alarm system
Available to tenants at Little House, a Senior Citizen Activities Center, two blocks distant, under same management: Dining room; library (300 sq ft); auditorium (250 capacity); three social rooms (total 500); lounge (375 sq ft, plus patio); crafts (20); toolshop (5); lapidary, weaving rooms
Service facilities: Parking: 10 garages
Staff: Maintenance, 1; employment counseling, retraining, and placement service available at Little House
Charges and services: Entrance deposit (refundable) $20; monthly rentals, $65, $75, and $100, cover water, garbage service, garden maintenance; garage rental (optional), $8
Construction: Total building area, 11,952 sq ft; building materials: wood frame (exterior: walls—wood shingles; sash—wood; roofs—built-up; terraces, ground floor—brick; second-floor balconies—wood; walks—brick; interior: walls—dry wall construction; floors—concrete, carpeted; ceilings—exposed wood; partitions—gypsum wallboard; trim—wood; bathrooms—ceramic tile, sheet vinyl); heating and cooling: electrical; fuel: electric power
Site development: Concrete driveway; fences, pergolas, gardens, large planters; landscaped central court
Cost (1961): Total, site development, buildings and built-in equipment, fees, but not furnishings: $315,000; cost per square foot: $16.90
Financing: Federal Program, Section 202 (direct loan, Housing and Home Finance Agency); funds allocated by sponsoring Peninsula Volunteers, Inc.
Design objective: "To meet the need for small groups of ... apartments where older people in good health can live comfortably in their familiar surroundings and within their retirement income."

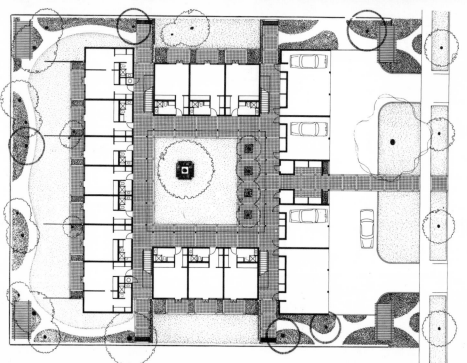

ORANGE GARDENS
(Kissimmee, Fla.; opened 1955)

Owner: George Beauchamp, Kissimmee, Fla.
Land plan by: F.H.A. (Atlanta Office)
Site plan by: F.H.A. (Atlanta Office)
Landscaping: Hollybrook Nurseries, Davenport, Fla.
Residence designs: K. C. Moore, Jr.
Site: 240 acres, 70 to 80 ft above sea level, many five-year-old long leaf pines, good top soil; residential area within ½ to 1½ miles of churches and stores; low-fare taxi service to town
Capacity: 220 families (Site has space for 600 additional homes)
People served: 85 per cent men and women 60 and over; (15 per cent young families with children); white; interfaith; current ages: youngest family head, 24; oldest resident, 91; average age of adults, 62; average income, $250 to $500 per month
Home types: 200 two-bedroom houses, 20 three-bedroom houses
Health facilities: Kissimmee hospitals within 1½ miles; regular clinics in two hospitals; nursing home in Kissimmee; several doctors make house calls in Orange Gardens
Auxiliary facilities: Community building with kitchen for group activities of all kinds; outdoor: shuffleboard, swimming, boating, picnicking
Staff (part-time employees in parentheses): Administration, 6; maintenance of grounds and community building, 6; sales, (7)
Cost (1961): Range in price of homes, $10,000 to $15,000 including lot; range in price of lots, $2,750 to $3,950 (average size of lot 70' x 110')
Construction: Building materials: concrete block frame (exterior: walls—concrete block; roofs—built-up; terraces—seeded; walks—concrete; interior: walls—drywall; floors—terrazzo or tile; ceilings—drywall; partitions—drywall; bathrooms—tile); heating and cooling: all types; fuel: oil, electricity or gas
Site development: Driveway: limerock, concrete; lots individually landscaped; parks

The Value of Work to the Older Citizen

Some persons nominally retired continue to work, at least part-time, in order to supplement their retirement income. . . . Many older people continue to work today, however, not primarily because of the income, but because they enjoy working, and want the sense of personal significance which a job furnishes them. This is partly good and partly bad.

It is highly desirable that men and women who possess skills and abilities, and who want to use them, should be permitted to do so. . . . But I feel it is bad when any person feels worthless and insignificant unless he is holding down a job and bringing in a paycheck. Some retirees are working at dull and routine jobs because they are unable to think of other ways to justify their continued existence. No man's worth, at any age, should be measured simply by his paycheck.

For this reason, although I am happy that retirees have been so able to find work at Orange Gardens when they want it, I am much more pleased at the extent to which other retirees, both men and women, have participated in a multitude of community volunteer services, the Red Cross and similar drives, library and adult education activities, welfare programs, and all the many unpaid ways by which an American community enriches the lives of its citizens.

—George E. Beauchamp, President of Orange Gardens
Vice-President, Florida Council on Aging

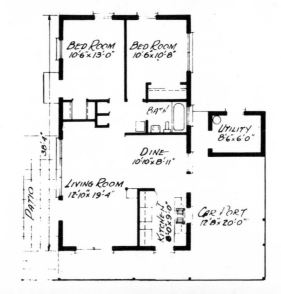

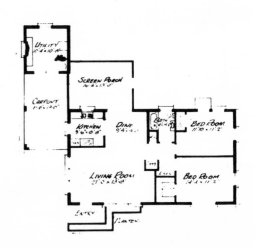

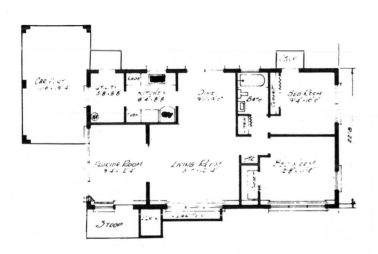

PROXIMATE HOUSING—PRIVATE

TIVERTON COURTS
(Bloomfield Hills, Mich.; anticipated completion 1963)

Sponsors: The residents
Architects: Begrow & Brown, A.I.A., Bloomfield Hills, Mich.
Site: 5.4 rolling acres, with many tall pine trees in suburban neighborhood of wealthy executives; 1 mile to churches; near stores, public transportation
Capacity: 12 couples
People served: White citizens; income level, $25,000 to $50,000 annually; in good health; interfaith
Buildings: Six one-story buildings with 12 housekeeping apartments (2 apartments each building)
Health facilities: Each resident provides his own
Auxiliary facilities: Swimming pool; golf putting green; sun terraces
Service facilities: Parking: two-car garage each apartment; two spaces each apartment for visitors
Staff: Maintenance, 1 (all other services contracted)
Construction: Total area per living unit: 24,600 sq ft, 20,500 cu ft; building materials: wood stud frame, joists (exterior: walls—brick, redwood; sash—wood, casement; roofs—ranch roofing, asphalt shingles; terraces—flagstone cedar deck; walks—precast concrete; other—cathedral colored glass; interior: walls—plaster brick, wall paper, walnut plywood; floors—oak, paving brick, concrete in garage; ceilings—plaster, some exposed timbers; partitions—plaster; trim—laun mahogany; bathrooms—ceramic tile); heating, cooling: year around forced air; fuel: gas
Site development: Well water supply; asphalt driveways; courtyards richly landscaped, pools, fountains
Cost (1961): Total, including site development (including swimming pool), buildings, built-in equipment, fees, but not furnishings: $505,000; cost per sq ft: $20.50; cost per cu ft: $2.27; kitchen equipment: $7,500
Architects say: "A beautiful estate of rolling terrain and shade trees provides the setting for an exclusive cooperative village for wealthy retired couples who seek a responsibility-free home. The village will consist of six two-family one-story residences orientated in close proximity to each other and paired to alleviate any serious emergencies that are so often found with elderly people. The homes will be built around a central mall consisting of a swimming pool, putting green, and rose gardens. Each pair of homes will have its own private garden courts and separate covered entrance walks. All twelve units will have a similar plan and elevation with only subtle differences. The roofs will be copper with skylights in the living room and garage. Colonial brick and white woodworking will provide a dignified exchange for estate luxury."

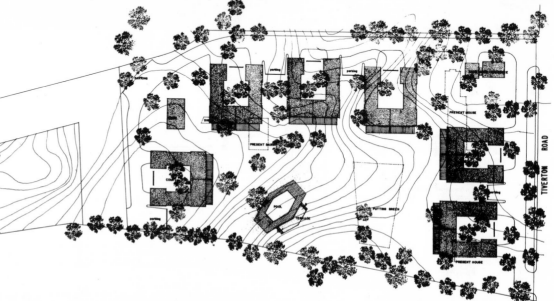

154

PROXIMATE HOUSING—PRIVATE

SPRINGVALE-ON-THE-HUDSON
(Cortlandt, N. Y.; completed 1962)

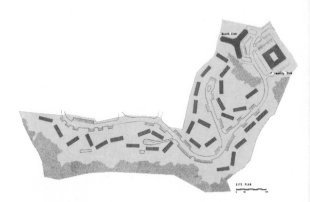

Sponsor: Van Cortlandt Ave. Corp., Pleasantville, N. Y.
Architects: Luders & Associates, A.I.A., Irvington-on-Hudson, New York
Consultant Engineers: T. Lewis Buser, P.E.
Site: 35 acres, high plateau, precipitous perimeter, overlooking Hudson River; suburban neighborhood; 3 miles to churches; 1 mile to stores (regular deliveries); public transportation at site; project private bus
Capacity: 700, plus future 60-bed nursing unit and 150 room resident hotel
People served: Men and women 55 and over; good general health; interfaith
Buildings: 30 two-story; 450 housekeeping apartments
Health facilities: Proposed 60-bed nursing unit; diagnostic equipment; therapy: physio- , occupational; proposed resident hotel will have health club and medical clinic
Auxiliary facilities: Laundry facilities; outdoor: shuffleboard, croquet, bowling-on-green, gardening; future community club (adjacent residential hotel for senior citizens) will contain lounge, library, chapel, cafeteria, health club, shops, cocktail bar, plus 150 resident rooms
Service facilities: Parking spaces for all residents and visitors
Staff: Estimated total, 8
Charges and services: No entrance fee; monthly rentals, $62.50 to $130, including utilities
Construction: Total building area, 287,000 sq ft, 5,161,000 cu ft; building materials: wood frame (exterior: walls—brick veneer and wood siding; sash—aluminum, sliding; roofs—built-up; terraces—cement-asbestos and concrete; walks—concrete; interior: walls—alternating concrete block, wood frame, plasterboard finish throughout; floors—wood frame, flexible tile; ceilings—plasterboard; partitions—plasterboard, sound insulated; trim—wood; bathrooms—ceramic tile); heating: hot water; fuel: gas
Site development: Sewage treatment: private plant; 33-foot blacktop road through project, 1 mile long
Cost (1961): Total, site development, buildings, built-in equipment, fees, but not furnishings, land, nursing home, or hotel: $3,000,000; cost per square foot: $10.00; cost per cubic foot: $1.00
Financing: Private loan, Savings & Loan Bank

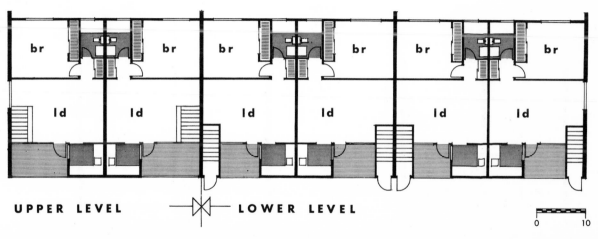

UPPER LEVEL ──────── LOWER LEVEL

0   10

PROXIMATE HOUSING — PRIVATE

SPRINGVALE-ON-THE-HUDSON—*Continued*
(Cortland, N.Y.; completed 1962)

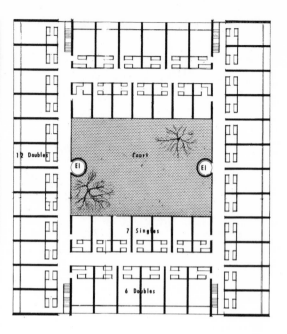

2nd and 3rd FLOORS

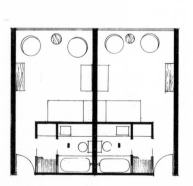

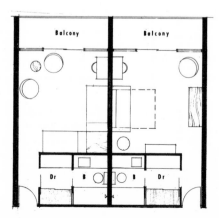

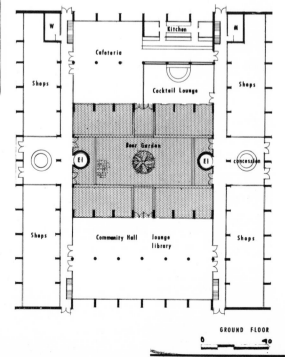

GROUND FLOOR

PROXIMATE HOUSING—PRIVATE

TENACRE FOUNDATION
GARDEN APARTMENTS
(Princeton, N.J.; first apartments completed 1961)

Sponsor: Tenacre Foundation, Princeton, N. J.
Architect: Kenneth Kassler, F.A.I.A., Princeton, N. J.
Site: 45 acres, reasonably level, wooded, stream; high class neighborhood; 2½ miles to churches, stores, public transportation; private bus provided (about 10 trips to town daily)
Capacity: 10 (planned, 42)
People served: Men and women; members of Christian Science churches
Buildings: Present, 3. Total will be 21 apartments or units in nine buildings; all housekeeping units
Health facilities: Tenacre is primarily a state-licensed facility offering nursing care in accordance with the tenets of the Christian Science Church; included are separate departments for (1) sheltered care, (2) nursing home or hospital-type infirmary, (3) full care of the mentally ill. There is also a program of training for Christian Science nurses. Aim of project is to render hostess or visiting nurse assistance or full time, round-the-clock special nursing in the private apartments as long as the practical problems involved are surmountable; then institutional care in the appropriate department is available
Auxiliary facilities: Cafeteria; Christian Science Reading Room; multiple purpose room: chapel, social, crafts, community dining room; outdoor: croquet, gardening
Service facilities (serving also nursing unit): Central kitchen; central laundry; storage facilities; ample parking; carports optional
Specific staff required for 21 apartments, attached to the existing 60-bed nursing facility: Administration, 1; food delivery, 2; maid, 3; maintenance, 2 part-time
Charges and services: Entrance fee, $15,000; monthly fee, $235 and $250, covers meals, maid, linen laundry. Individually prepared meals are delivered to the apartment. Residents may use the staff cafeteria for any of the three meals or the resident dining room for the noon meal). Hostess, visiting nurse, or full infirmary care is provided at $1.50 per hour, with resident paying for only the first 66⅔ hours, or $100. Care beyond 66⅔ hours, for whatever period required, is supplied without further charge.
Construction: Total area, 9,731 sq ft; building materials: wood frame; (exterior: walls—wood; sash—wood; roofs—asphalt shingles; terraces—wood; walks—concrete, exposed aggregate; interior: walls, ceilings, partitions—two layers of ⅜-in. sheetrock; floors—wood, carpeted; trim—wood; bathrooms—tile, painted sheetrock); heating, cooling: hot water convector with fan, thermostat control; back unit capable air conditioning; fuel: oil
Site development: Private sewage plant; blacktop driveway; landscaping, including rocky terrain along brook
Cost: Total, site development, buildings, built-in equipment, fees, but not land or furnishings: $139,156.57; cost per square foot: approximately $14.30
Financing: Current funds and loans from residents
Design objective: Tenacre Foundation Garden Apartments have appeal for those who have means for their own support and for whom the following features have special significance: (a) To be part of an active group of dedicated Christian Scientists while, at the same time, having access to the cultural advantages of the university town of Princeton, within easy distance of New York and Philadelphia; (b) to be able to contribute a portion of their free time to important volunteer work; (c) the security of a life-care contract guaranteeing Christian Science care should it ever be necessary

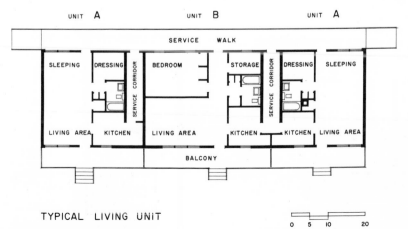

TYPICAL LIVING UNIT

0 5 10   20

PROXIMATE HOUSING—PRIVATE

TENACRE FOUNDATION GARDEN
APARTMENTS—*Continued*
(The Great Road, Princeton, N.J.)

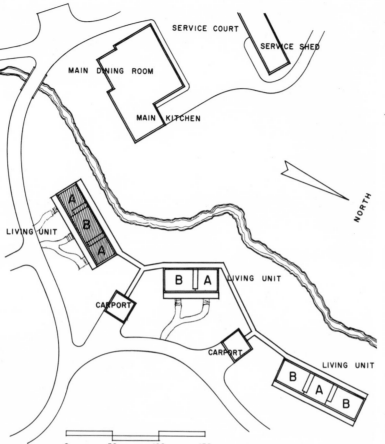

PROXIMATE HOUSING—PRIVATE

VINE COURT APARTMENTS
(Hartford, Conn.; completed 1959)

Sponsor: Church Homes, Inc., Hartford, Conn.
Architects: Jeter & Cook, A.I.A., Hartford, Conn.
Site: Adjacent Horace Bushnell Congregational Church; near stores, library, public transportation
Capacity: 38
People served: Men and women 65 and over; moderate income; able to manage for themselves; priority to members of sponsoring churches and those in greatest need; current ages, 72 to 86; average age, 78; admission average, 75
Buildings: One-floor row arrangement around court (4,000 sq ft) with 20 housekeeping apartments (2 singles, 8 doubles, 10 singles or doubles)
Health facilities: Community health and social services available
Auxiliary facilities: Lounge, kitchen, complete bath; may be reserved for overnight guests; utility room: washers, dryers, garbage disposals, trash receptacles
Service facilities: Parking spaces: five on site; church parking lot adjacent
Staff: Maintenance, 1
Charges and services: No entrance fee; monthly rentals: singles, $50 plus $6.50 utility; single/double, $60 plus $6.50 utility; doubles, $78.50 plus $8 utility
Construction: Total building area: 8,100 sq ft, 89,000 cu ft; building materials: wood stud frame (exterior: walls—frame, stained shingles; sash—wood, double-hung; roofs—mineral surfaced roofing; walks—concrete; interior: walls—sheetrock; floors—asphalt tile; ceilings—sheetrock; partitions—sheetrock, studs; trim—wood; bathrooms—ceramic tile); heating: hot water; fuel: oil
Site development: Bituminous concrete driveway; landscaping: lawn, garden, court, walks to all apartments
Cost (1958): Total, including site development, buildings, built-in equipment, fees, but not furnishings: $138,598; cost per sq ft: $17.95; cost per cu ft: $1.63
Financing: Contributions of cooperating churches and individuals; FHA insured loan ($160,000)
Special feature: This is a pilot venture by the sponsor. Several future projects are contemplated

GENERAL FLOOR PLAN

GRAPHIC SCALE, IN FEET

WILDER APARTMENTS
(A Proposed Project)
(St. Paul, Minn.)

Sponsor: The Wilder Foundation, St. Paul, Minn.
Architect: Ralph Rapson, A.I.A., Minneapolis
Site: On east side of 13½-acre site of Wilder Residences, over-looking St. Paul Loop and Mississippi River Valley; near churches, stores, library, public transportation
Capacity: 106
People served: Men and women 62 and over, residents of St. Paul area; limited income specified for each size apartment
Buildings: Nine one-story structures with 26 efficiencies, 18 one-bedroom, six two-bedroom apartments
Health facilities: Nursing service at cost in own apartment by staff of infirmary of Wilder Residences; access to 141-bed Wilder Residence Infirmary; physio- and occupational therapy
Auxiliary facilities: Resident laundry each building; each apartment has screened porch, yard; central paved court, 80' x 80', for social activities; 12 apartments have enclosed outdoor courts; Craft and Recreation Center Building, Wilder Residences; coffee shop in infirmary, cost basis, for emergency needs
Service facilities: On-street parking
Charges and services: $65 monthly rental for efficiency apartment ($250 income limitation); $75 monthly rental for one-bedroom apartment ($300 income limitation); $85 monthly rental for two-bedroom apartment ($400 income limitation)
Construction: Total building area: 35,000 sq ft, 433,000 cu ft; building materials: frame — masonry-bearing lateral walls (exterior: walls—brick or block; sash—casements, large areas fixed glass, awnings; roofs — dead level pitch and gravel, shingled pyramid roofs; terraces—enclosed courts seeded, main court of precast concrete pavers; walks—concrete; interior: walls—lath, plaster, sheet rock, exposed masonry; floors—carpet, resilient tile, concrete; ceilings—sheetrock or plaster; partitions—lath and plaster or sheetrock; trim—wood; bathrooms—plastered lath, sheetrock, ceramic tile); heating (and future cooling): heat from central mechanism to unit fan coil heaters, individually controlled; fuel: gas with oil standby
Site development: Brick-top driveway construction; central paved court will have large trees in large planters; other landscaping in future development
Cost (estimate, 1961): Total, including site development, buildings, built-in equipment, fees, but not furnishings: $600,000; cost per sq ft: $17.00; cost per cu ft: $1.45
Financing: Wilder Foundation Endowment; loan under Section 202 Housing and Home Finance Agency

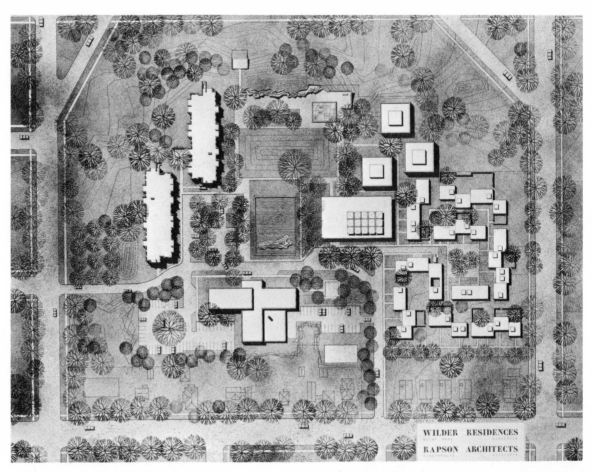

WILDER RESIDENCES

RAPSON ARCHITECTS

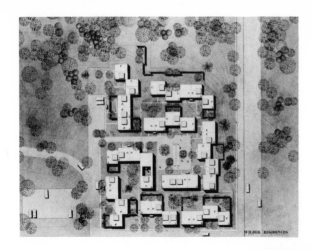

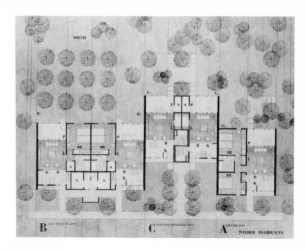

PROXIMATE HOUSING—PUBLIC: TABLE 1

Explanation of symbols describing health facilities: *Future*; *Care: Infirmary*; *Nursing Unit*; *Hospital*; *Treatment: Diagnosis*; *Special (dentist, oculist, podiatrist, psychiatrist)*; *Therapy (physio-, psycho-, occupational)*; Age figures: *Admission average*; *Average now*; *Spread* of ages. Data on projects supplied by architects and sponsors.

Name of project	Capacity	Total cost	Cost per sq. ft.	Cost per cu. ft.	Year bid	Health facilities			Ages of residents		
						No. beds	Care	Treatment	Adm.	Av.	Spread
Cedar Apartments Extension	570	$1,992,749	$15.74	—	1953	(Community facilities used)			—	75	60-94
Cedar Gardens	96	$462,000	$13.97	—	1961	(Community facilities used)			70	70	65-95
Haverhill Housing	104	$556,338	$17.33	—	1959	(Community facilities used)			70	71	65-86
Hawthorne Square	152	$6,895,736	—	—	1958	(Community facilities used)			—	—	—
Lyndale Homes	132	—	$13.44	$1.43	1958	(Community facilities used)			71	75	51-86
Morton Circle	72	$382,000	$17.30	$1.44	1958	(Community facilities used)			71	72	66-82
New Jersey Projects: No. 22-4, New Brunswick (Samuel Hoffman)	108	$738,286	$15.50	$1.65	1960	(Community facilities used)					
No. 52-1, Boonton	28	$150,000	$13.50	$1.57	1961	(Community facilities used)			—	—	—
Anthony M. Webbe Apartments	266	$1,588,500	$12.61	$1.37	1961	(Community facilities used)			72	73	60-87
Gaylord White Homes	496	—	—	—	—	(Community facilities used)			—	—	—

PROXIMATE HOUSING—PUBLIC: TABLE 2

Explanation of symbols: Parking spaces: Resident; Institution; Visitor; Staff allocation: Administration; Health; Food; Maid; Laundry; Building and grounds maintenance; part-time staff shown in parentheses. Data on projects supplied by architects and sponsors.

| Name of project | Capacity | Parking spaces | | | Extent of health services | Staff allocation | | | | | | Fees |
		R	I	V		A	H	F	M	L	B	Minimum monthly rent
CedarApartments Extension	370	Lot			—	Housing Authority personnel						$30
Cedar Gardens	96	10	2	10	—	2	—	—	—	—	2(2)	$45
Haverhill	104	15 total			—	—	—	—	—	—	—	$52
Hawthorne Square	76					5(1)	—	—	—	—	19(1)	$32 ($24 entrance deposit)
Lyndale Homes	132	100%			—	1	—	—	—	—	1	$32
Morton Circle	72	16			—	(1)	—	—	—	—	(1)	$52
New Jersey Projects: No. 22-4, New Brunswick (Samuel Hoffman)	108	30 total plus lot			—	Housing Authority personnel						$32
No. 52-1, Boonton	28	22 total			—	2	—	—	—	—	—	—
Anthony M. Webbe Apartments	266	60%			—	Housing Authority personnel						$40 ($20 entrance deposit)
Gaylord White Homes	496	—			—	—	—	—	—	—	—	—

CEDAR APARTMENTS EXTENSION
GOLDEN AGE BUILDING
(Cleveland, Ohio; completed 1955)

Sponsor: Cleveland Metropolitan Housing Authority
Architects: Dalton-Dalton Assoc., A.I.A.; Damon, Worley, Samuels & Assoc., A.I.A.; George B. Mayer, A.I.A.; Mellenbrook, Foley & Scott, A.I.A.; Walker & Weeks; Weinberg & Teare, A.I.A.
Site: Part of level 17.7-acre public housing estate; near downtown area, stores, public transportation
Capacity: 350
People served: Approximately two-thirds of residents are men and women 62 and over, low income, able to live independently; some younger families (when children reach four years, family is moved to different building on same estate); interdenominational; interracial
Buildings: One 14-story building with 104 one-bedroom and 52 two-bedroom unfurnished housekeeping apartments (practice of converting one-bedroom apartments to two living-bedroom units for two unrelated single persons sharing kitchen and bath has not proved satisfactory)
Health facilities: Chiropodist comes weekly; community health and social services available; St. Vincent's Charity Hospital nearby
Auxiliary facilities: Cafeteria, operated by residents five days each week; social room—chapel—reading room (public library across street); craft, educational and recreational programs operated by professional staff of Golden Age Center; coin-operated washers and dryers in basement
Charges and services: Minimum rent of $30, including utilities; annual membership in Golden Age Center of $2 per person, $3 per couple
Staff: Part time of the staff of entire housing estate (appreciable time required for protection of elderly residents, counseling, emergency referrals to health and social agencies)
Construction: Total building area: 126,557 sq ft; building materials: reinforced concrete frame (exterior: walls—concrete block, brick facings; sash—steel casement; roofs—concrete slab, fiber glass, built up tar and gravel; interior: walls—concrete block, plaster; ceilings—concrete slab; bathrooms—tile, plaster); heating: hot water; fuel: coal
Cost (estimated, 1953): Construction cost, including mechanical, electrical, elevator, fees: $1,992,749; cost per sq ft: $15.74; apartment kitchen equipment: $23,251.80; furnishings and equipment for Golden Age Center: approximately $35,000 (donated)
Financing: Metropolitan Housing Authority, Cleveland (bonds to private investors)
Manager says: "Skip-stop elevator service should be avoided. Both elevators should stop on all floors."

CEDAR APARTMENTS
NEIGHBORHOOD
CLEVELAND METROPOLITAN HOUSING AUTHORITY

·THESE LARGE-SCALE PLANS SHOW
HOW THE I BEDROOM DWELLINGS
ARE CONVERTIBLE INTO 2 LIVING-
BEDROOM DWELLINGS·

GRAPHIC SCALE

·ONE-2 PERSON FAMILY USE DWELLING·
·LIVING RM·BED RM·KITCHEN & BATH·

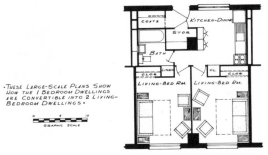

·TWO-I PERSON FAMILY USE DWELLING·
AS CONVERTED INTO 2 LIVING-BEDROOMS
·WITH SHARED KITCHEN & BATHROOM FACILITIES·

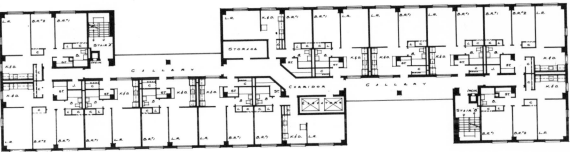

·TYPICAL DWELLING FLOOR OF 14 STORY BUILDING·

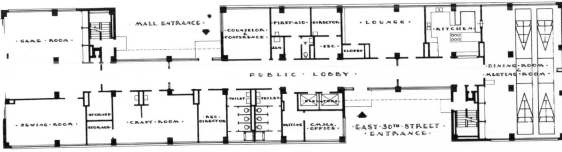

GOLDEN-AGE CENTER

FIRST FLOOR OF 14-STORY APARTMENT BUILDING

CEDAR APARTMENTS EXTENSION

CEDAR GARDENS
(Natick, Mass.; completed 1959)

Sponsor: Housing Authority of Natick, Mass.
Architects: Tekton Assoc., Joseph P. Staniunas, Chief Architect, Natick, Mass.
Site: 3 acres of high, wooded land, 1 mile away from center of city; 1 mile to churches, stores; near public transportation (special taxi rate to project same as bus fare)
Capacity: 96 (planned, 64 additional)
People served: Men, 65, women, 62, and over; low income; ambulatory and able to care for themselves; interracial; interfaith; current ages, 65 to 95; average age, 70; admission average, 70
Buildings: One two-story building with eight units; three two-story buildings with 12 units; one one-story building with four units; total, 48 housekeeping apartments, each single or double occupancy; one community building
Health facilities: Emergency alarm system (special cord on switches activates buzzer in hall and electric door opener of apartment); community facilities
Auxiliary facilities: Recreation room, 200, adjoining kitchen (meeting place of Golden Age Club of Natick); laundry, coin-operated washers and dryers; clothes-drying yard, decorative glazed tile screen enclosure; outdoor: croquet, individual flower beds
Service facilities: Storage (resident, 25 sq ft each; institution, 1,800 sq ft); 22 parking spaces (resident, 10: visitors, 10; institution, 2)
Staff: Administration, 2; maintenance, 2 part-time
Charges and services: Minimum rent of $45 covers heat, hot water (resident pays separately metered electricity)
Construction: Total building area: 31,000 sq. ft; building materials: wood stud frame (exterior: walls—brick veneer; wood stud; plywood spandrels; sash—steel, sliding, double glazed; roofs—asphalt shingles; terraces—concrete, brick, bituminous concrete; walks—bituminous concrete; other—terracotta screen at drying yards; fiberglass canopies; interior: walls—wood stud, concrete block stair wells; floors—asphalt tile; ceilings—plaster; partitions—plaster, prefinished plywood; trim—wood; bathrooms—ceramic tile); heating: hot water; fuel: gas
Cost (1958): Total, including site development, buildings, built-in equipment, fees, but not land or furnishings: residence buildings, $434,000; community building, $28,000; cost per ft, buildings; $13.97; cost per dwelling unit: $8,458
Financing: Housing Authority of Natick, Mass.

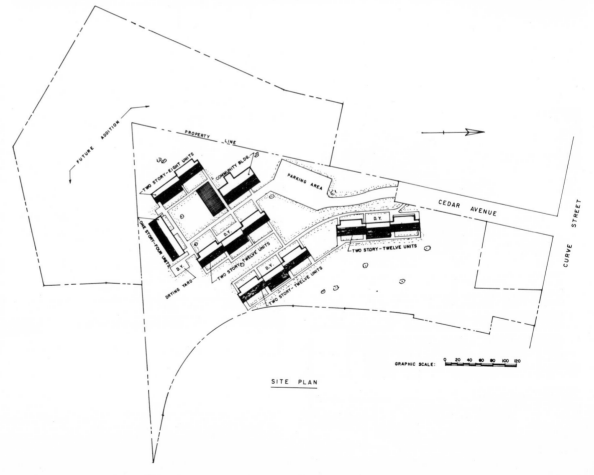

SITE PLAN

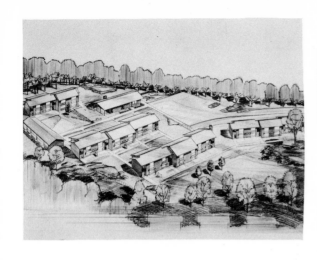

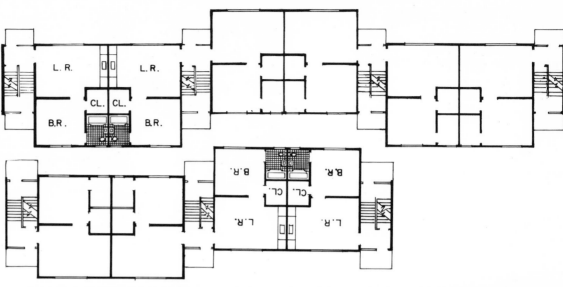

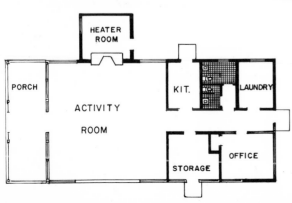

PROXIMATE HOUSING—PUBLIC

HAVERHILL HOUSING FOR ELDERLY, PROJECT 667—1
(Haverhill, Mass.; completed 1960)

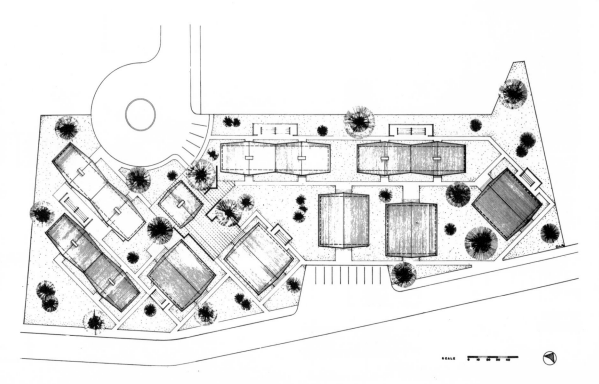

Sponsors: Housing Authority of Haverhill, Mass., and Commonwealth of Massachusetts State Housing Board
Architects: Drummey, Rosane, Anderson, A.I.A., Boston
Site: 2 acres on gentle slope in residential area; near stores, churches, public transportation
Capacity: 104
People served: Men and women, 65 and over, of low income; able to care for themselves; interracial, interfaith; current ages, 65 to 86; average age, 71; admission average, 70
Buildings: Five one-story and four two-story buildings with 52 one-bedroom apartments; community building
Health facilities: Community services; emergency alarm systems
Auxiliary facilities: Commons room with canteen; concession operated laundry room; balconies on two-story buildings protecting front porches; recessed entrances on one-story buildings, making front porches; fire alarm detectors connected with city fire department; electric door-openers activated by fire system; emergency call switches in bedrooms and baths unlock main apartment doors
Service facilities: Screened drying yards; trash disposal containers; parking spaces, 15
Staff: Housing Administration
Charges and services: Monthly rent based on family income (minimum, $46.50) covers gas heat, hot water, cooking
Construction: Total building area, 32,686 sq ft; building materials: post and beam frame, laminated wood (exterior: walls—brick veneer, cement; sash—steel; roofs—asphalt shingles; terraces [community center]—flagstone; walks—bituminous concrete; interior: walls—plaster, prefinished wood paneling; floors—prefinished oak strip; ceilings—plaster; partitions—plaster; bathrooms—ceramic tile); heating: forced hot water; fuel: gas
Site development: Landscaping: flagstone terrace, concrete benches, blue stone-capped brick sitting walls; trees, shrubs, ground cover
Cost (1959): Total, construction only: $566,338.02; cost per sq ft; $17.33; landscaping: $3,500
Financing: Housing Authority of Haverhill Finance notes and bonds guaranteed by Commonwealth of Massachusetts under provision of Chapter 667
Architect says: "All commons facilities and exterior sitting areas were designed to draw the occupants into contact with each other. This is done for each building and for the community center."

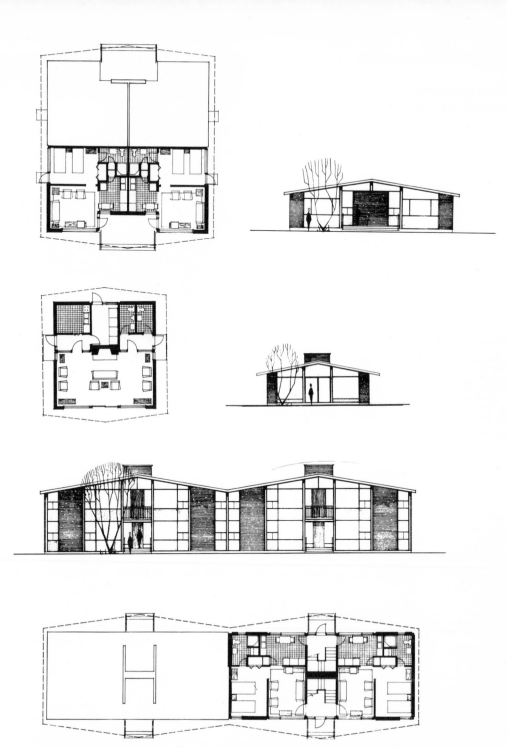

PROXIMATE HOUSING—PUBLIC

HAWTHORNE SQUARE
(Philadelphia, Pa.; completed 1960)

Sponsor: The Philadelphia Housing Authority
Architects: Carroll, Grisdale & Van Alen, A.I.A., Philadelphia
Consultants: George Patton, landscape architect
Site: In new public housing community near central city; near schools, churches, shopping, public transportation
Capacity: 76 units for elderly out of total of 576
People served: Men and women 62 or over; low income; ambulatory
Buildings: Three, 11 stories each; one, 15 stories; housekeeping apartments for various sized families, all ages; round, one-floor community building
Health facilities: Community facilities
Auxiliary facilities: Community building includes social room with kitchen and three craft rooms; laundry facilities in each building
Service facilities: Maintenance building for total project; storage for residents; parking spaces: residents, 153 plus street parking; staff, 8 (none specifically allocated for elderly)
Staff, total project (part-time employees indicated in parentheses): Administration, 5 (1); maintenance, 19 (1); counseling, private agency
Charges and services: Entrance deposit, $24; rentals based upon family income, minimum $32 per month; covers basic utilities (quarterly billing for excessive use of gas, electricity)
Construction: Building materials: reinforced concrete frame (exterior: walls—brick block 10-in. cavity wall; sash—aluminum; roofs—tar and gravel; walks—concrete, bituminous; interior: walls—block, plaster, painted; floors—asphalt tile, concrete; ceilings—concrete block; partitions—concrete, metal strip, plaster; trim—metal; bathrooms—plaster, painted); heating: hot water; fuel: oil
Site development: Bituminous concrete driveway construction; landscaping: minimum lawn and planting raised 18 in. above walks, generous use of trees
Cost (date bid, 1958): Actual total, $6,895,736
Financing: Housing Authority of Philadelphia
Architect says: "We consider the room layout (for apartments for elderly) in this project very good for an efficiency apartment in that the end units have cross ventilation, and all have a dining space in connection with the kitchen out of the area of the living-bedroom."

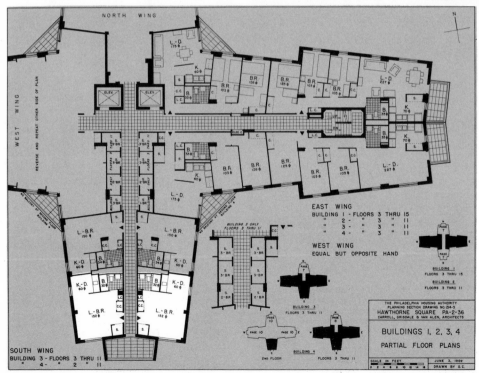

170

PROXIMATE HOUSING—PUBLIC

LYNDALE HOMES
(Minneapolis, Minn.; completed 1959)

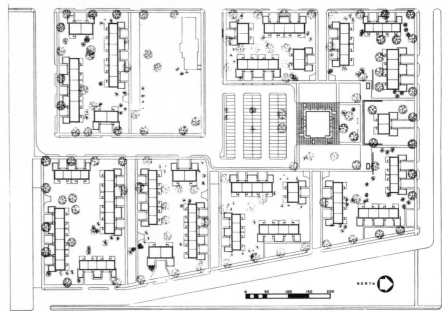

Sponsor: Housing and Redevelopment Authority in and for the City of Minneapolis, Minn.
Architects: Thorshov & Cerny, A.I.A., Minneapolis
Landscape architect: Norrill and Nicolls, Minneapolis
Site: 2½ level acres near downtown Minneapolis; adjacent to public housing project for families all ages; near stores, churches, public transportation
Capacity: 132
People served: Men 65 and over; women 62 and over; low income; able to care for themselves; interracial; interfaith; current ages, 51 to 86; average age, 75; admission average, 71
Buildings: One 12-story building with 88 housekeeping units (44 efficiencies, 44 one-bedroom apartments)
Auxiliary facilities: Community room (1,200 sq ft) with piano and kitchen; laundry facilities; crafts room; outdoor: patio, lawn recreation area
Health facilities: Community facilities; tenant organization assumes responsibility for periodic checking to detect accidents or illness; also assists in special problems, for example, blindness. Housing Authority furnishes leadership and social worker.
Service facilities: Maintenance shop; parking spaces for all (85% used by housing development adjacent)
Staff: Housing Authority
Construction: Total building area: 56,920 sq ft, 533,600 cu ft; building materials: reinforced concrete frame (exterior: walls—4" brick veneer, 4" clay tile back; sash—aluminum; roofs—built-up, pitch, gravel; interior: walls—4" clay tile; floors—asphalt tile; ceilings—plaster; partitions—plaster); heating: steam; fuel: gas, oil standby
Cost (1958): Total, including site development, but not land, fees or furnishings: $764,971; cost per sq ft: $13.44; cost per cu ft: $1.43
Financing: Housing and Redevelopment Authority in and for the City of Minneapolis

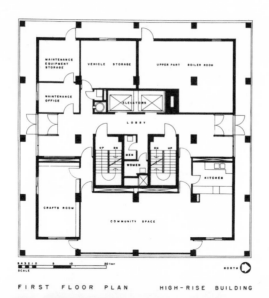

FIRST FLOOR PLAN   HIGH-RISE BUILDING

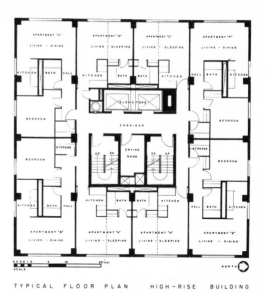

TYPICAL FLOOR PLAN   HIGH-RISE BUILDING

MORTON CIRCLE
(Wellesley, Mass.; completed 1959)

Sponsor: Wellesley Housing Authority
Architects: Bastille Halsey Associates, 120 Tremont Street, Boston
Engineers: Cleverdon, Varney & Pike
Planting: Wellesley Garden Club
Site: Approximately 1½ acres, generally flat, with shade trees; adjacent town park; white neighborhood; near churches, stores; transportation at site
Capacity: 72
People served: Men and women, 65 and over; low income; ambulatory, good general health; interracial; interfaith; current ages, 66 to 82, average age, 72; admission average, 71
Buildings: Six two-story buildings, three with four units each, three with eight units each (all housekeeping); one one-story community building
Health facilities: Emergency signal system (switches in bedroom and bath that activate gong and release apartment door lock); community health and social services (clinics, visiting nurse, etc.)
Auxiliary facilities: Community building social room (460 sq ft) with adjoining kitchen; terrace; individual flower gardens
Service facilities: Resident storage, 18 sq ft in unit; parking spaces: 16
Staff: Administration, 1 part-time; maintenance, 1 part-time
Charges and services: No entrance fee; monthly rent of $52, including utilities
Construction: Total building area of 22,050 sq ft, 265,050 cu ft; building materials: wood frame (exterior: walls—face brick, cinder block, back-up; sash—sliding steel; roofs—asphalt shingles; terraces—concrete paving blocks; walks—bituminous concrete; other — sliding aluminum door, community room; bituminous concrete drying yards; interior: walls—plaster, coated masonry, load-bearing; floors — oak strip; ceilings — plaster; partitions — masonry at stairs [others, wood stud]; trim—wood, steel; bathrooms—ceramic tile, linoleum floors; other—hardwood kitchen cabinets, flush steel doors); heating: forced hot water; fuel: gas
Site development: Bituminous concrete driveway; landscaping: existing trees retained; planting
Cost (1958): Total cost, including site development, buildings, built-in equipment, fees, but not furnishings: $382,000; cost per sq ft: $17.30; cost per cu ft: $1.44
Financing: State-aided (State guarantees return of principal in 40 years)
Architect says: "Our design concept . . . was based upon a desire to develop . . . a living center in which each individual resident would feel the maximum sense of dignity and the least sense that he was living in an institutional development. . . . We devoted great attention to the creation of a series of smaller houses, and to relating them on the limited site in such a manner as to preserve to the maximum this feeling of individuality and independence. In the variety of exterior spaces, in the preservation of existing trees, and in such details as the selection of paint colors, this concept was carried out, and we believe that all of the persons living in the project share the pride which we hoped they would develop."

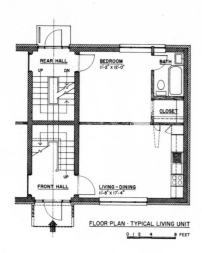

REAR HALL
UP DN

BEDROOM
11'-2" X 12'-0"

BATH

CLOSET

FRONT HALL
UP

LIVING – DINING
11'-8" X 17'-4"

FLOOR PLAN · TYPICAL LIVING UNIT

0 1 2 4   8 FEET

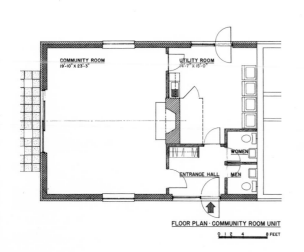

COMMUNITY ROOM
19'-10" X 23'-3"

UTILITY ROOM
14'-7" X 15'-0"

WOMEN

ENTRANCE HALL   **MEN**

FLOOR PLAN · COMMUNITY ROOM UNIT

0 1 2 4   8 FEET

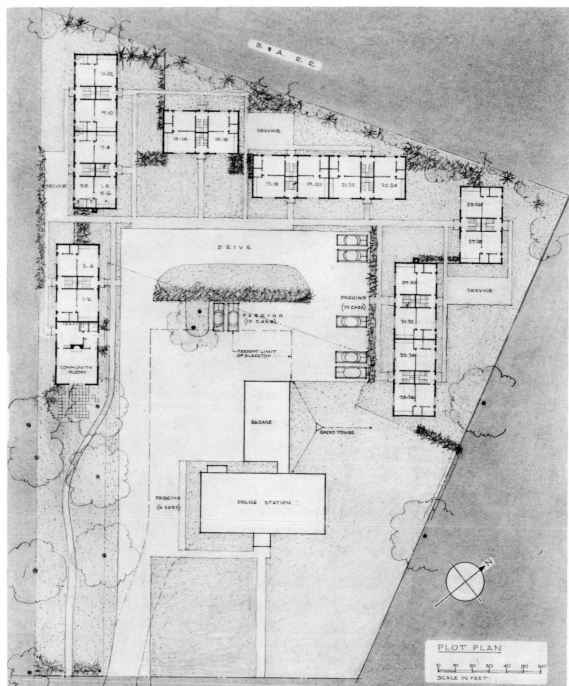

B. & A. R. R.

11-12

9-10

7-8

SERVICE

13-14 15-16

17-18 19-20 21-22 23-24

SERVICE

D.R.
L.R.
5-6
K.

25-26

27-28

3-4

DRIVE

SERVICE

1-2

PARKING
(10 CARS)

PARKING
(10 CARS)

29-30

COMMUNITY
ROOM

PRESENT LIMIT
OF BLACKTOP

31-32

33-34

35-36

GARAGE

RADIO TOWER

PARKING
(6 CARS)

POLICE STATION

N

PLOT PLAN

0 10 20 30 40 50 60

SCALE IN FEET

PROXIMATE HOUSING—PUBLIC

PROJECT NEW JERSEY 22-4
THE SAMUEL D. HOFFMAN PAVILLION
FOR THE ELDERLY
(New Brunswick, N. J.; completed 1962)

Sponsor: Housing Authority of the City of New Brunswick, N. J.
Architect: E. N. Turano, A.I.A., New York, N. Y.
Site: 6-acre trapezoidal, sloping tract adjacent large public housing project, heart of downtown; near stores, churches, public transportation
Capacity: 108 (planned, 100 additional)
People served: Men and women, 65 and over; low income; ambulatory; interracial; interfaith
Buildings: One multi-story with 60 housekeeping units (12 singles, 48 for couples)
Health facilities: Community
Auxiliary facilities: Social room (120) with kitchen; laundry facilities; outdoor: sitting areas for group games, croquet, individual flower beds
Service facilities: Resident storage: 5 sq ft in apartment; 25 sq ft, central area; parking spaces: resident, 30; visitors in lot and on street
Staff: Total: 23. Administration, 10; maintenance, 13 (Housing Authority staff manages total of 598 units, including this home)
Charges and services: Minimum rent of $32 (maximum, 20 per cent of gross income) covers utilities
Construction: Total building area: 47,200 sq ft, 440,800 cu ft; building materials: concrete frame (exterior: walls—brick, glass, metal panels; sash—aluminum; roofs—built-up; terraces, walks —concrete; interior: walls—3" gypsum block; floors—asphalt tile; ceilings—concrete, painted; partitions—2-in. gypsum; trim— metal; bathrooms—plaster); heating: steam; fuel: oil
Cost (1960): Total cost of site development, building, built-in equipment, but not land, fees, furnishings: $738,286; cost per sq ft: $15.50; cost per cu ft: $1.65; kitchen equipment: $6,000; furnishings: $19,800
Financing: Housing and Home Finance Agency, U. S. Public Housing Administration
Architect says: "In evolving a concept of living for the elderly in public housing, the architects strove (1) to provide a quality and quantity of space that would yield a simple, informal, and pleasant mode of living that most housing developments seem to lack; and (2) to achieve an aesthetic that would erase the stigma generally associated with public housing design. . . .
"Development of the concept is based on the living unit's central core, an efficient, compact mechanical and storage hub. The basic module is a one-bedroom unit. The combination of two modules can be readily converted into a no- and two-bedroom unit by the closing of two soundproof doors or wall panels. This affords . . . flexibility in apartment size and distribution . . . without construction or alteration. . . .
"Community and hobby rooms will be located on the entry level with direct access to exterior landscaped sitting areas and several adult recreational areas. The articulated relationship of this project to the existing PHA project will help to integrate the elderly with family groups of all sizes, yet provide the type of privacy necessary and desired for the elderly."

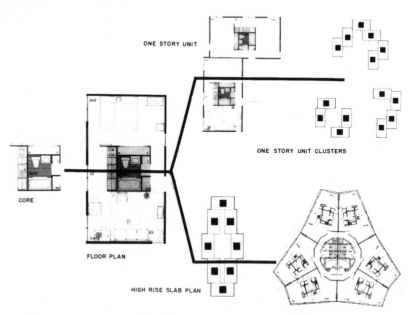

ONE STORY UNIT

ONE STORY UNIT CLUSTERS

CORE

FLOOR PLAN

HIGH RISE SLAB PLAN

HIGH RISE TOWER PLAN

DEVELOPMENT OF CONCEPT - HOUSING FOR THE AGED

PROXIMATE HOUSING—PUBLIC

PROJECT NEW JERSEY 52—1
(Boonton, N. J.; anticipated completion 1963)

Sponsor: Housing Authority of the Town of Boonton
Architect: E. N. Turano, A.I.A., N. Y., N. Y.
Site: 1.02 acres of level ground in middle-class interracial residential area; near center of town, churches, stores and public transportation
Capacity: 28
People served: Men and women, 65 and over; low income; ambulatory; interracial; interdenominational
Buildings: Three one-story buildings with 14 housekeeping apartment units
Health facilities: Community facilities
Auxiliary facilities: Resident laundry; community room, capacity 30, with kitchen; outdoor sitting areas for cards, games, etc.; croquet on lawns; shuffleboard; individual gardening
Service facilities: 5 sq ft storage space in each unit; 25-35 sq ft space in central area; maintenance shop; parking: 22 spaces
Staff: Not yet established
Charges and services: Not yet established
Construction: Total building area: 10,400 sq ft, 92,000 cu ft; building materials: wood frame (exterior: walls—brick veneer; sash—wood projected; roofs—shingles; terraces—concrete; walks—concrete; interior: walls—drywall; floors—asphalt tile; ceilings—drywall; partitions—drywall; trim—wood; bathrooms—ceramic tile); heating: individual gas units
Site development: Blacktop driveway; sitting areas; screen walls
Estimated cost (1961): Total cost, including site development, buildings and built-in equipment, fees, but not furnishings: $145,000; cost per sq ft: $13.50; cost per cu ft: $1.57; kitchen equipment: $1,300
Financing: Public Housing Administration
Architect says: "The development of this concept focuses about the central core, an efficient, compact mechanical and storage hub. . . . The basic module is a one-bedroom unit. The combination of modules permits many variations of building forms. Two modules can be readily converted into a no- and a two-bedroom unit by the closing of two soundproof doors or wall panels. The obvious advantage of this is the ability to achieve a flexible apartment size distribution without additional construction or alteration nor any need to change the basic core."

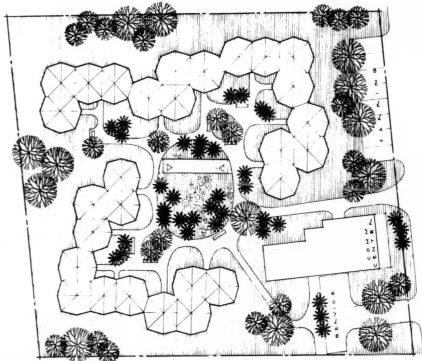

177

ANTHONY M. WEBBE APARTMENTS
(St. Louis, Mo.; completed 1961)

Sponsor: St. Louis Housing Authority
Architects: Hellmuth, Obata & Kassabaum, A.I.A., St. Louis
Site: 14 acres in south central St. Louis; part of large public housing project occupied by families of all ages; near stores, sports, civic, social activities, public transportation
Capacity: 266
People served: Men 65, women 62, and over; interracial; interfaith; current ages, 60 to 87; average age, 73; admission average, 72
Buildings: One eight-story (two elevators, all stops) building with 84 one-bedroom and 28 two-bedroom housekeeping units (allowing elderly persons to live with younger relatives)
Health facilities: "Help-your-neighbor" buzzer, flashlight system; city hospital, welfare agencies
Auxiliary facilities: Library; large social room, kitchen; consulting, crafts, meeting rooms; coin-operated washers, dryers; outdoor sitting area surrounded by pierced masonry screen; three small outdoor sitting areas each floor
Service facilities: Resident storage (900 sq ft); parking spaces, 60 per cent
Staff: Part of staff for entire housing project
Charges and services: Deposit fee of $20; minimum rent of $40 (few exceptions) covers all utilities
Construction: Total building area: 92,000 sq ft, 592,000 cu ft; building materials (exterior: walls — brick; sash — aluminum; roofs—tar, gravel; walks—concrete; interior: walls—plaster; ceilings—concrete; floors—asphalt tile; partitions—solid plaster; trim—wood; bathrooms—cement plaster); heating: steam; cooling: provision for installation of individual units; fuel: gas, oil
Cost (1961): Total, including land, site development, fees, but not furnishings: $1,588,500; cost per sq ft: $12.61; cost per cu ft: $1.37; equipment and furnishings, total: $32,700
Financing: St. Louis Housing Authority
Architect says: "The restrictions that age places upon activity require the liberal use of enlivening colors, to enhance the spaces within which such curtailed activity takes place. Infirmities dictate use of grab bars and supporting rails, ramps instead of stairs, close proximity to buzzer and flashing light systems. "Above all, aging people should not be isolated from other people. They should live close to hospital facilities, to be sure, but community — the sense of belonging — dictates not only that older people be in communication with younger ones, but that they be physically close to them. . . . Within the limits of a tight budget, these are some of the considerations that went into our planning for the Webbe Apartments—as indeed they enter into any planning for housing the aging."

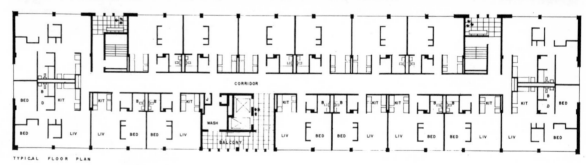

TYPICAL FLOOR PLAN

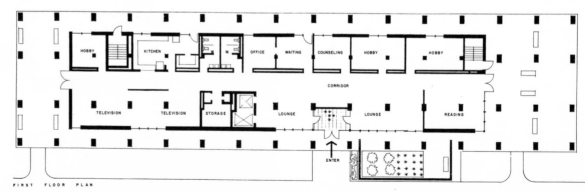

FIRST FLOOR PLAN

SCALE

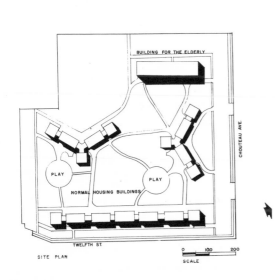

SITE PLAN

SCALE

BUILDING FOR THE ELDERLY

NORMAL HOUSING BUILDINGS

PLAY

PLAY

CHOUTEAU AVE.

TWELFTH ST.

0   100   200

GAYLORD WHITE HOUSES
(New York Public Housing)
New York, N. Y.

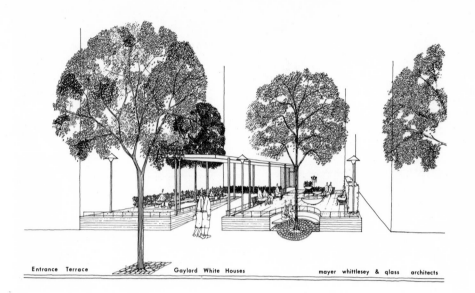

Entrance Terrace   Gaylord White Houses   mayer whittlesey & glass   architects

Sponsor: City of New York Housing Authority
Architect: Albert Mayer, F.A.I.A., New York
Site: Densely populated urban area
People served: Men and women 65 and 62 and over, respectively; low income; interracial; interfaith
Buildings: One eight-story, plus tower to twenty stories (248 units)
Health facilities: Community
Auxiliary facilities: Complete community and recreation center, operated by Union Settlement, for people of the larger neighborhood, closely geared in with special spaces and facilities for the elderly: (a) entrance terrace on ground floor, combination of main entrance and small sitting plaza (a lively link with busy, noisy street); (b) usual social and activity rooms on ground floor (elderly also have access to facilities of adjoining Union Settlement Community Center); (c) recreation garden (small enclosed court off main social area), raised gardens easily cared for by elderly and well lighted for summer evenings; (d) "community stage" located off main activity room; multipurpose; daytime use as child care center; evening use as community space for pictures, performances (elderly may be participants or spectators); (e) ninth floor sun deck, solarium; semi-private niches for intimate groupings; laundry off solarium, encouraging sociability while machines do work (Note: architect would prefer small sitting and chatting area on **each** floor with minimum kitchen and equipment and with laundry facility adjoining)
Charges and services: Minimum rental
Architect says: "This presentation concentrates its attention not so much on the essential creature comforts such as easy-to-operate windows, non-slip surfaces in bathrooms, grab bars, etc., nor on room layout or arrangement, nor on the 'standard' facilities such as craft rooms and equipment, but rather on the equally essential but usually less stressed elements of satisfactory individual and social relationships and on social facilities and their placement and the variety of choices they can offer.

The older people are in an easy and an 'optional' relationship with the rest of the community and its stimuli. Their own living quarters and recreational elements are quite separate, to provide privacy when needed, yet so closely related and adjacent to the sociable street, the general community, and child care facilities, that there is no kind of imposed withdrawal. Joining in the life and entertainment of the rest of the community is made the simplest possible and most natural thing; as is withdrawal when that is the mood."

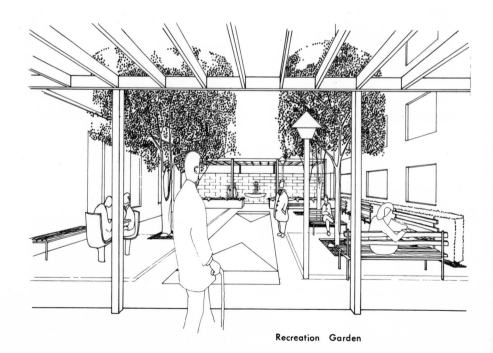

Recreation Garden

MAYER WHITTLESEY & GLASS ARCHITECTS Don Mallow

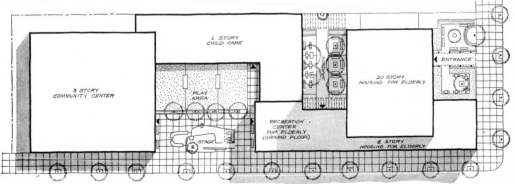

3 STORY
COMMUNITY CENTER

1 STORY
CHILD CARE

PLAY
AREA

STAGE

RECREATION
CENTER
FOR ELDERLY
(GROUND FLOOR)

ENTRANCE

20 STORY
HOUSING FOR ELDERLY

6 STORY
HOUSING FOR ELDERLY

CONGREGATE AND PROXIMATE HOUSING: TABLE 1

Explanation of symbols describing health facilities: *Future*; Care: *Infirmary*; *Nursing Unit*; *Hospital*; Treatment: *Diagnosis*; *Special* (dentist, oculist, podiatrist, psychiatrist); *Therapy* (physio-, psycho-, occupational); Age figures: *Admission average*; *Average now*; *Spread* of ages. Data on projects supplied by architects and sponsors.

Name of project	Capacity	Total cost	Cost per sq. ft.	Cost per cu. ft.	Year bid	Health facilities			Ages of residents		
						No. beds	Care	Treatment	Adm.	Av.	Spread
East Ridge	396	$3,458,090	$14.65	$1.72	1961	27	N	T	—	74	65-82
First Community Village	496	$4,797,720	$18.47	—	1962	28	N	D,S,T	—	—	—
Mt. San Antonio Congregational Homes	331	$4,000,000	$14.80	—	1960	40	N	D,S,T	—	—	—
Presbyterian Village	140	$1,175,000 $1,250,000	$20.34	$2.00	1953 1961	50(F)	N	T	—	78	62-98
Rockynol	108	$2,022,700	—	—	1962	50	N	D,S,T(F)	—	—	—
Royal Oaks Manor	225	$3,000,000	$13.80	$1.30	1959	6	I	(Contract with hospital)	74	74	61-93
Schowalter Villa	54	$557,605	$15.20	—	1961	4	I	T	—	72	65-79
Wesley Manor Retirement Village	380	$3,859,642	$14.78	$1.18	1961	24	N	D,S,T	—	—	—

CONGREGATE AND PROXIMATE HOUSING: TABLE 2

Explanation of symbols: Parking spaces: *Resident; Institution; Visitor;* Staff allocation: *Administration; Health; Food; Maid; Laundry; Building and grounds maintenance;* part-time staff shown in parentheses. Data on projects supplied by architects and sponsors.

Name of project	Capacity	Parking spaces			Extent of health services	Staff allocation						Fees	
		R	I	V		A	H	F	M	L	B	Entrance	Monthly
East Ridge	396	310 total			Limited	5	12	4	9	—	6	$8,800-16,875	$110-150
First Community Village	496	—	—	—	Limited	12	9	45	12	—	6	None	$124-330
Mt. San Antonio Congregational Homes	331	—	—	—	Limited	15	10	30	—	—	3	$10,000-20,000	$175
						75 total (est.)							
Presbyterian Village	140	3 lots			Limited	1(1)	8(7)	23	—	1	4(1)	None	$85-165
Rockynol	108	10	30	25	Complete	60 total (est.						Life care based on expectancy	
Royal Oaks Manor	225	108 total			Complete	5	5	30	6	—	7	$5,900-23,000	$175
Schowalter Villa	54	12	17	21	Minimum	1	5	1(1)	2	—	1(1)	$5,000-7,500	$75-180
Wesley Manor Retirement Village	380	78	41	50	Complete	8	26	24	16	3	12	$5,000-20,000	$170

CONGREGATE AND PROXIMATE HOUSING

EAST RIDGE RETIREMENT VILLAGE
(Biscayne Bay, Fla.; completed 1962)

Sponsor: A Federation of Lutheran Churches for Welfare within the Florida-Georgia District, The Lutheran Church (Missouri Synod)

Architects: Steward-Skinner Associates, A.I.A., Miami, Fla.

Site: 73½ acres in South Dade County; 2½ miles to stores, public transportation; 1 to 3 miles to churches

Capacity: 396 (planned, 204 more; ultimate, 1,000)

People served: Men and women, 65 and over; ambulatory; interfaith (priority to Lutherans); ages of current applicants; 65 to 82; average, 74

Buildings: 97 one-story buildings (12 single-unit; 65 multi-unit); 242 housekeeping units (162 singles, 80 doubles); 76 single non-housekeeping units with kitchenettes

Health facilities: 27-bed nursing unit (expandable to 40); physio- and occupational therapy

Auxiliary facilities: Dining rooms (resident, 150; nursing unit, 40; employee, 10); chapel, 40; library; auditorium, 400; two social rooms (400, 50); 14 lounges; nine group laundries; recreation room; four crafts rooms; barber shop; beauty shop; outdoor: shuffleboard, croquet, bowling-on-green, putting green, swimming pool, gardening

Service facilities: Central kitchen; resident storage (20 sq ft each); parking (total spaces, 310); security building, one ambulance, one fire truck

Staff: Estimated total, 45 (Administration, 5; food, 4; health, 12; maids, 9; maintenance, 6; counseling, 3; other, 6)

Charges and services: Entrance fee of $8,800 to $16,875; monthly fee of $110 or $150 (without/with meals) covers maid, limited health services

Construction: Total building area, 236,131 sq ft; 2,007,119 cu ft; building materials (exterior: walls—concrete block, stucco; sash —aluminum, sliding glass doors, jalousies; roofs—built up; terraces—walks, concrete; interior: walls—concrete block, plaster; floors—concrete, terrazzo, tile; ceilings—plaster; partitions—concrete block, wood stud; trim—metal; bathrooms—ceramic tile; doors—wood); heating: hot water and steam; cooling: wall air conditioners controlled by occupants; fuel: oil, gas

Site development: Landscaping: tropical plants added to existing pines

Cost (1961): Total, including site development, buildings, built-in equipment, fees, but not land or furnishings: $3,458,090; cost per sq ft: $14.65; cost per cu ft: $1.72

Financing: Endowment, for expansion; contributions for partial operation; FHA insured loan (No. 231) for construction

Architect says: Special features include: (1) visiting health service, supporting residents in home; (2) rehabilitation occupational therapy includes opportunity to do remunerative piecework; (3) safety measures: ambulance and firetruck housed on site; (4) hospitality shop carries variety items, for convenience of residents; (5) shuttle bus operates within project grounds

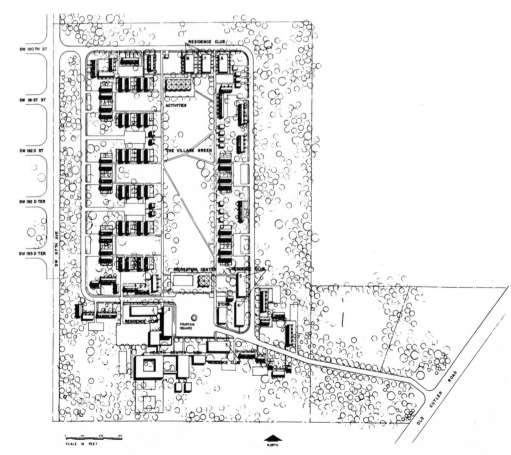

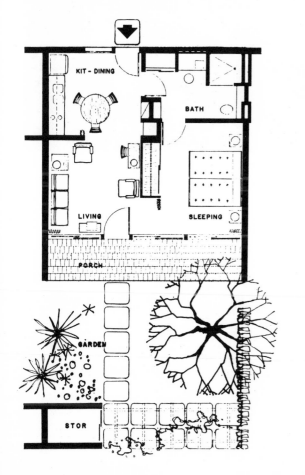

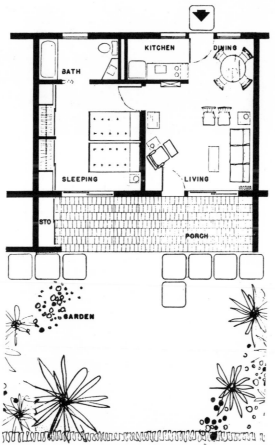

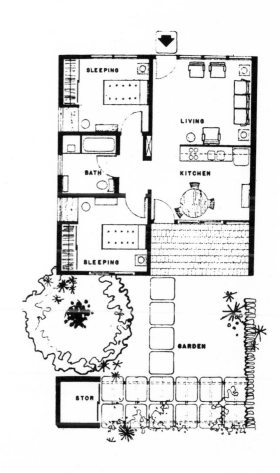

KIT - DINING

BATH

LIVING

SLEEPING

PORCH

GARDEN

STOR

BATH

KITCHEN

DINING

SLEEPING

LIVING

STO

PORCH

GARDEN

SLEEPING

LIVING

BATH

KITCHEN

SLEEPING

STOR

GARDEN

CONGREGATE AND PROXIMATE HOUSING

FIRST COMMUNITY VILLAGE
(Columbus, Ohio; anticipated completion, 1963)

Sponsor: First Comunity Church, Columbus, Ohio
Architects: Tibbals, Crumley, Musson, A.I.A., Columbus, Ohio
Consultants: Site plan: Tibbals, Crumley, Musson; interior design: Interior Design Section of Tibbals, Crumley, Musson; mechanical and electrical engineers: Drake & Ford, Columbus, Ohio
Site: 28 acres on wooded bluff, meadow below; upper-middle, suburban neighborhood; approximately two miles to churches, stores; one mile to public transportation
Capacity: 496 plus 28-bed nursing unit
People served: Men and women, 65 and over; minimum income, $4000; good general health; interfaith
Buildings: One multi-story structure and 30 one-story structures (414 single units; 38 doubles; 65 housekeeping units; 387 non-housekeeping units; non-housekeeping cottages arranged around garden courts and connected by enclosed walks to dining rooms)
Health facilities: 28-bed nursing unit; treatment: dentist, oculist, podiatrist; rehabilitation: physio- and occupational therapy; psychiatrist
Auxiliary facilities: Dining rooms (four resident, capacity of each approximately 125; staff, 12; employees, 15); chapel; library; 24 lounges (each 576 sq ft); resident laundry facilities; 12,000 sq ft in multi-purpose rooms of various sizes for auditorium, crafts, tool shops, social gatherings, recreation, etc.; shop for drugs, gifts, candy; snack bar; beauty parlor (2); barber shop (2); outdoor: shuffleboard, croquet, flower beds; possibly greenhouses, bowling-on-green
Service facilities: Central kitchen; maintenance shop; storage (institutional, 2,500 sq ft; resident, 3,000 sq ft); parking spaces: 290
Staff (part-time in parentheses): Total: 90 (4). Administration, 12; health, 9; food, 45; housekeeping, 12; maintenance of grounds and buildings, 6; counseling, 2; barber, 2 (2); beauty parlor, 2 (2)
Charges and services: Entrance fee, $1,500; monthly fee of $125 to $330 covers meals, maid, linen laundry, limited health services
Construction: Total building area, 259,700 sq ft; building materials: frame, wood trusses, steel columns (exterior: walls—metal curtain wall, brick veneer; sash—aluminum; roofs—asphalt shingle, tar, gravel; terraces—concrete; walks—concrete, asphalt; interior: walls—dry wall, masonry; floors—concrete with resilient tile; ceilings—dry wall, concrete; partitions—dry wall; trim—metal, wood; bathrooms—ceramic walls, vinyl floor); heating: hot water (cooling proposed for public rooms, administration area); fuel: gas
Site development: Asphalt driveway construction; landscaping: reflecting pools, shrubs, trees
Cost (date bid, 1961): Total, site development, buildings, built-in equipment, fees, but not furnishings: $4,797,720; cost per sq ft: $18.47
Financing: FHA insured loan
Architect says: "First Community Village was conceived as an extension of the rich and varied program of First Community Church, not only for the seniors of the church but of the community. It was designed as a residential club to offer a variety of living arrangements and a broad selection of amenities. Any resident may have as much privacy or as much sociability as he chooses, in housekeeping or non-housekeeping accommodations. It is impossible to make such a large development look or feel like a private residence, but the residential quality was sought by every device to create privacy, intimacy, variety and livability, and to provide for all sorts of recreational, social, creative and cultural activities for groups of every size. The court yards, patios, walks in the woods, and vista from the hilltop have been conceived as an extension, visually and physically, of the life lived in the buildings, just as that life will interact with the life of the community around."

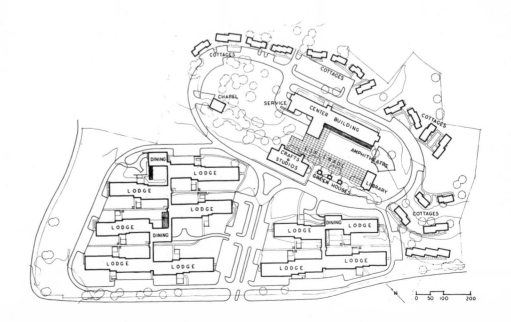

CHAPEL

LIBRARY

CONGREGATE AND PROXIMATE HOUSING

FIRST COMMUNITY VILLAGE—*Continued*
(Columbus, Ohio; anticipated completion 1963)

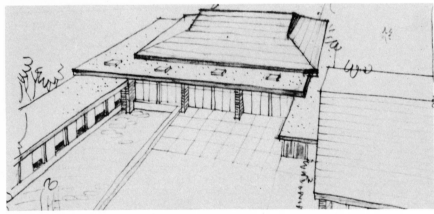

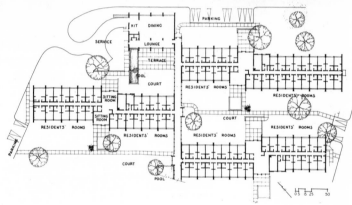

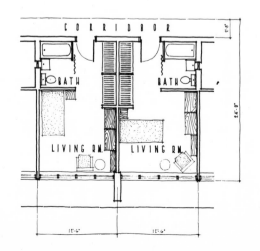

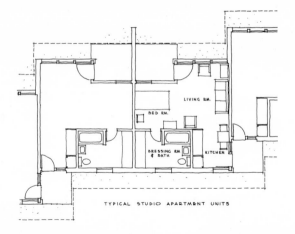

TYPICAL STUDIO APARTMENT UNITS

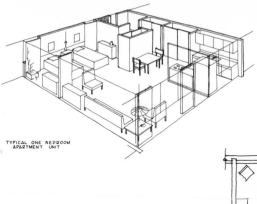

TYPICAL ONE BEDROOM
APARTMENT UNIT

CONGREGATE AND PROXIMATE HOUSING

MT. SAN ANTONIO
CONGREGATIONAL HOMES
(Pomona, Calif.; completed 1961)

Sponsor: Congregational Homes, Claremont, Calif.
Architects: Kenneth Lind Associates, A.I.A., Los Angeles
Site: 13½ acres in residential area; non-denominational church on site, others 1 mile away; 1 mile to major shopping center; near public transportation
Capacity: 331 plus 40-bed nursing unit (planned, 35 duplex cottages)
People served: Men and women, 62 and over; interfaith; current ages, 62 to 88; average, 73½
Buildings: 12 one-story multi-unit buildings; two three-story buildings with 201 housekeeping units and 78 non-housekeeping units, with individual or shared kitchenettes (227 singles, 52 couples); each unit has private patio or balcony
Health facilities: 40-bed nursing unit (planned, six-bed protected care); clinic: diagnostic, rehabilitation equipment; special treatment: dentist, oculist, podiatrist; therapy
Auxiliary facilities: Dining rooms (main, 300; one each in three buildings, 60; staff, 20); library; chapel and meditation rooms; auditorium; small meeting rooms; recreation (covered area 17,020 sq ft, open all sides; covered terrace under three-story personal service building; large social room; lounges (one each in six buildings, 1,200 sq ft; fireplace; adjacent snack kitchen; personal laundry); crafts and tool rooms; shops; beauty parlor, barber shop; men's smoking and game room, adjoining terrace; outdoor: shuffleboard, croquet, bowling-on-green, gardening, fishing; planned swimming pool, greenhouse
Service facilities: Central kitchen; individual resident storage (360 sq ft); 190 parking spaces (resident, 160; visitors and staff, 30)
Staff: Estimated total, 75
Charges and services: Entrance fee of $10,000 to $20,000; monthly fee of approximately $200 covers meals, maid, linen laundry, health services excluding surgery
Construction: Total building area: 270,000 sq ft; building materials (exterior: walls—masonry; sash—aluminum; roofs—built-up; terraces, walks—concrete; interior: walls—masonry; floors—concrete; ceilings—acoustical; partitions—wood stud, plaster; trim—wood, metal; bathrooms—tile); cooling: central air conditioning; fuel: gas
Site development: Automatic sprinkling system
Cost (1961): Total, including land, site development, fees, but not furnishings: $4,000,000; cost per sq ft: $14.80; furnishings: $210,000
Financing: FHA insured loan, Title 231
Special feature: Many cultural resources and activities offered by Associated Claremont Colleges
Architect says: "The plan has been developed with a village rather than an institutional approach. Its aim is a practical well-run facility with a homelike atmosphere in which the individual can maintain his identity and feeling of ownership while benefiting from group housing and central accommodation buildings."

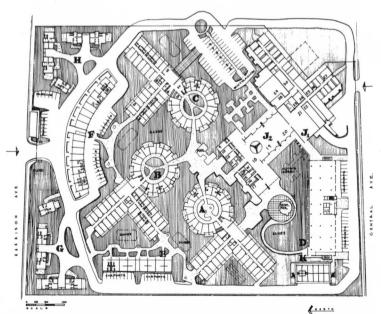

Legend

A, B, and C—Congregate buildings
D—Personal service building
E—Apartments
F—Efficiency apartments and apartments
G—Cottages
J-1—Central administrative and medical service
J-2—Central resident facilities
K—Staff quarters/lounge and kitchen

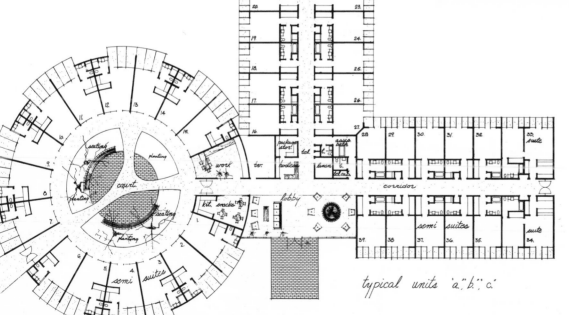

suite 21. 22. suite

20. 23.

19. 24.

18. 25.

17. 26.

16. 27.

package stor. tel. 28. 29. 30. 31. 32. 33. suite

work tor. toolen. linen asso bath cl. clo.

kit snacks lobby corridor

semi suites suite

semi suites 39. 38. 37. 36. 35. 34.

typical units 'a', 'b', 'c.'

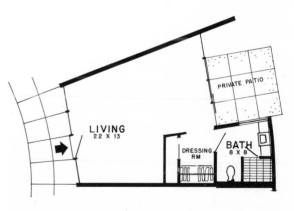

PRIVATE PATIO

LIVING
22 x 13

DRESSING
RM

BATH
8 x 8

**MT. SAN ANTONIO
CONGREGATION HOMES—**Continued
(Pomona, Calif.)

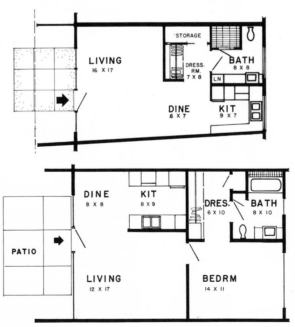

LIVING
16 X 17

STORAGE

DRESS.
RM.
7 X 8

BATH
8 X 8

LN

DINE
6 X 7

KIT
9 X 7

DINE
8 X 8

KIT
8 X 9

DRES.
6 X 10

BATH
8 X 10

PATIO

LIVING
12 X 17

BEDRM
14 X 11

CONGREGATE AND PROXIMATE HOUSING

PRESBYTERIAN VILLAGE
(Detroit, Mich.; completed 1962)

Sponsors: The Presbytery of Detroit

Architects: Smith, Hinchman & Grylls, A.I.A., Detroit, Mich.

Site: 33 acres of level, wooded land in suburban, residential neighborhood; near shopping center, churches; public transportation at site

Capacity: 142 plus 12-bed nursing unit (planned 50-bed medical, nursing center)

People served: Christian men and women 60 and over; financially able; ambulatory, in good general health; interracial; interdenominational (priority to Presbyterians)

Buildings: Six one-story buildings: in three are ten unfurnished housekeeping apartments (eight one-bedroom, two two-bedroom); in one are four unfurnished studios for one and two persons; in two are 90 furnished single rooms, four doubles

Health facilities: 12-bed nursing unit; clinic, twice weekly (nominal charge); physio- and occupational therapy (charge materials only); planned 50-bed medical-nursing center for chronic disease, complete rehabilitation, sheltered care

Auxiliary facilities: Dining rooms (two resident); chapel-social-lounges; three smaller lounges; library shelves in corridors, all lounges; crafts rooms; barber shop, beauty parlor; laundry

Service facilities: Two kitchens (one diet kitchen); central laundry; maintenance building; parking (three large lots)

Staff (part-time in parentheses): Total: 35 (8). Administration, 1 (1); health, 5 (5) (2 doctors on call); food and maid, 23; laundry, 1; maintenance, 4 (1); recreation, 1 plus 47 volunteers; counseling, (1) plus assistance of 176 ministers in Detroit area

Charges and services: No entrance fee; $85 to $100 a month for one- and two-bedroom apartments, with utilities; $113 a month for studio, with utilities, one main meal daily; $165 a month single, $265 double, for community residence room: maid, meals, linen, laundry; all village facilities available to all residents

Construction: Total building area: plus or minus 59,000 sq ft, 600,000 cu ft; building materials: wood frame (exterior: walls—brick veneer, wood trusses; interior: walls—wood stud, plastered; floors—cork tile, vinyl asbestos; ceilings—acoustical tile, plaster, flexicord; bathrooms—ceramic tile); heating: hot water; fuel: gas, oil

Estimated cost (from 1953 to 1961): Total cost of all buildings, including construction in progress, between $1,175,000 and $1,250,000; cost per sq ft, $20.34 average plus or minus; cost per cu ft, $2.00 average plus or minus; furnishings between $94,000 and $105,000

Financing: Contributions from churches, individuals; FHA insured loan

Special feature: Facilities of nursing unit available to community

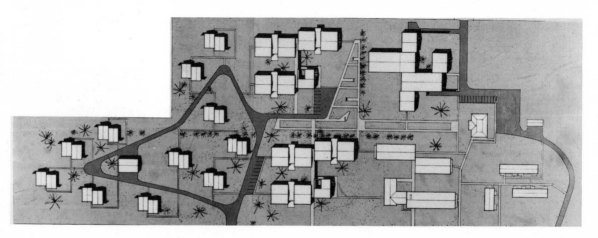

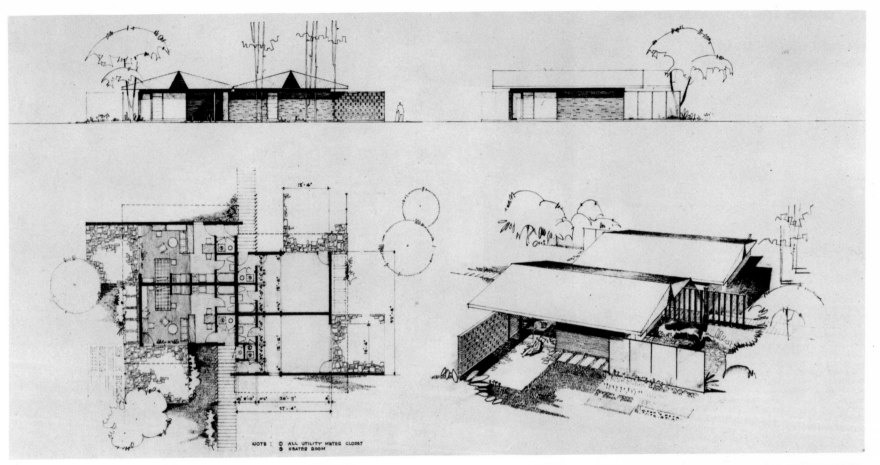

NOTE: ① ALL UTILITY METER CLOSET
② HEATER ROOM

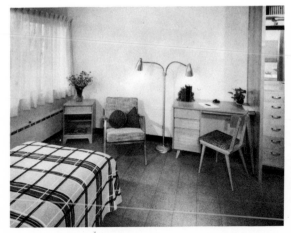

CONGREGATE AND PROXIMATE HOUSING

ROCKYNOL
(Akron, Ohio)

Sponsor: The Ohio Presbyterian Homes owned and operated on a non-profit basis by the Synod of Ohio of the United Presbyterian Church in the United States of America
Architects: Samborn, Steketee, Otis & Evans, Toledo, Ohio
Site: 11 acres of rocky, rolling land with three small lakes; old high-class residential neighborhood; near public transportation, churches; ½ mile to stores
Capacity: 108 plus 50-bed nursing unit (planned, 100 additional)
People served: Men and women 70 and over
Buildings: One one-story building (lobby, lounge, offices) connecting two other buildings; one six-story, residential structure containing 108 single units, with provision for converting some to double units; one four-story nursing unit
Health facilities: 50-bed nursing unit; treatment: dentist, podiatrist, (future) psychiatrist; rehabilitation: physio-, occupational therapy; (future) diathermy, hydro-therapy; diagnostic: (future) e.k.g., b.m.r.
Auxiliary facilities: Dining rooms (resident, 120; staff, 30); three libraries (12 each); chapel; three lounges (one large, two small); resident laundries; resident snack kitchens; crafts; recreation room: shuffleboard; shops; two beauty parlors (four stations each); outdoor: shuffleboard, croquet, gardening, greenhouses, fishing
Service facilities: Central kitchen; central laundry; maintenance shop; resident storage; 65 parking spaces (resident, 10; staff, 30; visitors, 25)
Staff: Estimated total, 60
Charges and services: Cost of life care, based on life expectancy, covers meals, maid, laundry, complete health services
Construction: Total building area: 852,000 sq ft; building materials: concrete frame (exterior: walls—glass, concrete, native stone; sash—aluminum; roofs—built-up; terraces, walks—concrete; interior: walls, partitions—plaster on metal lath, concrete block; floors—concrete, cork, carpet, tile, asphalt, vinyl; trim—metal; bathrooms—ceramic tile, plaster); heating and cooling: steam, hot water, tempered air, steam absorption cooling; fuel: gas
Site development: Asphalt driveway
Cost (estimated, 1962): Total, including land, furnishings, equipment: $2,022,700
Financing: Private loan for construction. To be paid from contributions and founders' gifts for rooms

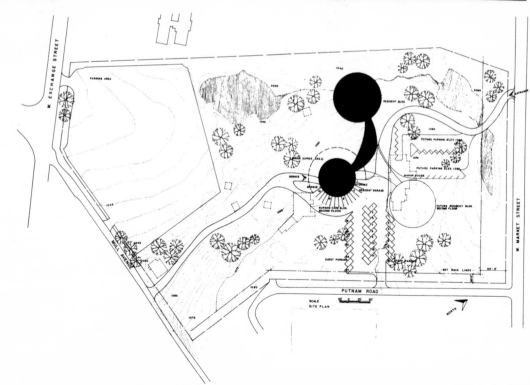

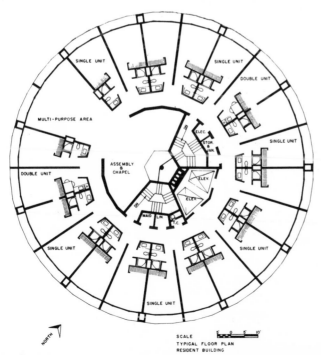

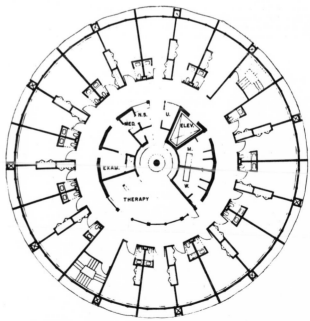

CONGREGATE AND PROXIMATE HOUSING

ROYAL OAKS MANOR
(Duarte, Calif.; completed 1959)

Sponsor: Southern California Presbyterian Homes, Los Angeles
Architects: Orr, Strange, Inslee & Senefeld, A.I.A., Los Angeles
Consultants: Kenneth Mitchell, landscape architect; Margo Graham, interior design
Site: 18½ rolling acres in foothills of San Gabriel Mountains, outside limits of small town; near stores, churches, public transportation
Capacity: 225 plus six-bed infirmary
People served: Christian men and women, 60 and over; middle income; ambulatory at entrance; interfaith; current ages, 61 to 93; average age, 74; admission average, 74
Buildings: One four-story building with 159 nonhousekeeping units (78 singles, 81 doubles; some with kitchenette); five one-story cottages with 24 units (20 one-bedroom; four two-bedroom)
Health facilities: Six-bed infirmary, 24-hour registered nurse; contract with community hospital for complete care including major surgery, long-term hospitalization
Auxiliary facilities: Dining rooms (resident, 200; employee, 35); library (1,056 sq ft); chapel-auditorium (2,925 sq ft in separate building on site); four lounges: one reception (4,800 sq ft, adjacent resident-operated canteen), one (600 sq ft), two (192 sq ft), all with kitchen; hobby, crafts, sewing rooms; six laundry units; recreation; beauty parlor (two chairs); outdoor: shuffleboard, croquet, individual gardens, greenhouse, trout fishing in nearby lake
Service facilities: Central kitchen; parking: resident carports, 33; 75 spaces
Staff: Total: 54. Administration, 5; health, 5; food, 30; maid, 6; maintenance, 7; beauty shop, 1
Charges and services: Entrance fee of $5,900 to $23,000; monthly fee of $175 covers bi-weekly maid, meals, complete medical service
Construction: Total building area: 170,000 sq ft, 1,800,000 cu ft; building materials: steel frame (exterior: walls—brick, front faced with stone, plaster; sash—steel, aluminum; roofs—paper, rock; terraces, walks—concrete; interior: walls—brick, plaster; floors—concrete; ceilings—acoustical plaster; partitions—plaster, metal lath; trim—brick, aluminum; bathrooms—tile, plaster); heating and cooling: hot water, chilled water; fuel: gas, standby oil
Site development: Asphalt driveway; landscaping: park-like grounds, beautiful lawns, unusual trees
Cost (1959): Total, including site development, buildings, built-in equipment: $2,700,000; kitchen and infirmary equipment: $300,000; cost per sq ft of main building: about $13.80; cost per cu ft: $1.30
Financing: Corporation funds; private loan; FHA insured loan, (Title 213)
Architect says: Primary purpose is to provide a maximum service at minimum cost to persons who desire a Christian atmosphere, pleasant surroundings, and a meaningful daily fellowship. The building is so designed that residents may get to any place in entire project without climbing steps. Royal Oaks Manor received a "Beautiful Building Award" from the Los Angeles Chamber of Commerce, 1961.

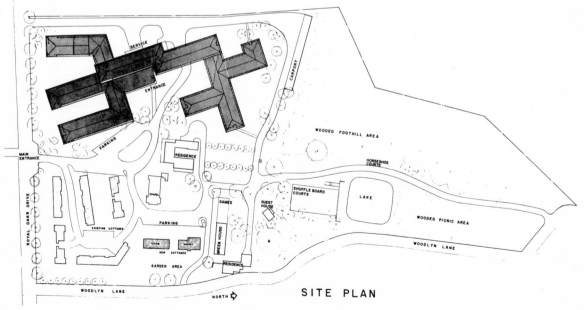

SITE PLAN

SCHOWALTER VILLA HOME
FOR THE AGING
(Hesston, Kans.; completed 1961)

Sponsor: Mennonite Board of Missions and Charities, Elkhart, Ind.

Architects: Miller, Hiett, Hockett, Dronberger & Arbuckle, Architects and Engineers, Hutchinson, Kans.

Site: Approximately ⅞ acre at city limits of farming Mennonite community; near campus chapel of Mennonite College, stores

Capacity: 54 plus four-bed infirmary (planned, 144)

People served: Men 65 and over, women 62 and over; ambulatory, in good health, no chronically ill admitted; income level: average for farmers, moderately low for clergy; interracial; members of Mennonite faith and those able to live compatibly in Christian atmosphere; current ages, 65 to 79; average age, 72

Buildings: One one-story building with 28 nonhousekeeping units (26 singles, two doubles); three one-story buildings, each with four double housekeeping apartments

Health facilities: four-bed infirmary (planned, 22 beds); clinic; occupational therapy in hobby area; several community hospitals available

Auxiliary facilities: Dining room (70); library (413 sq ft); chapel (208 sq ft for sanctuary, plus 1,470 sq ft for nave); hobby room—crafts (576 sq ft, 20); tool shop (10); two lounges (1,470; 300 sq ft); coffee bar; snack kitchen; laundry; interior greenhouse; outdoor: shuffleboard, gardening

Service facilities: Central kitchen; central laundry; storage (resident, 15 sq ft; institution, 399 sq ft); 50 parking spaces (resident, 12; visitors, 21; institution, 17)

Staff (part-time in parentheses): Total: 10 (3). Administration, 1; health, 5; food, 1 (1); maid, 2; maintenance, 1 (1); counseling, (1)

Charges and services: Entrance gift of $5,000 to $7,500; monthly fee of $75 to $180 (some charity or limited fee) covers meals, maid, laundry, limited health care

Construction: Total building area: 31,916 sq ft; building materials: frame—laminated beams, steel columns (exterior: walls—brick, curtain wall; sash—aluminum-wood casements; roofs—built-up marble chip; terraces, walks—concrete; interior: walls—concrete block, plaster [duplexes, plaster on studs]; ceilings—exposed tectum, fissured mineral tile [duplexes, exposed wood decking]; floors—concrete, carpet, vinyl asbestos, slate; partitions—concrete block plastered, structural tile, face brick, ceramic tile; trim—metal bucks, birch doors; bathrooms—ceramic tile, plaster); heating and cooling: hot and chilled water; fuel: gas

Cost (estimated, 1961): Total, including site development, buildings, built-in equipment, fees, but not furnishings: $557,605; cost per sq ft, $15.20; kitchen equipment: $14,379; laundry: $9,010; health: $2,000

Financing: Endowment (Schowalter family gift for preplanning); contributions (some from estates); private loan ($200,000 Mennonite Church; $200,000 Savings and Loan); balance from entrance gifts

Architects say: "Each individual is to be given independence in relation to his desires and needs. This is physically accomplished with three major building types: cottages, duplexes, or private rooms in the main building. . . . It is planned that the typical couple could start their residence in either the cottages or a duplex, and then as age and the loss of their loved one change their requirements, they would move into the main building where dining facilities, companionship and other help was more readily available. . . . A major consideration was control and operation of the main building with the least amount of personnel. . . . The major design element of the main building is the interior greenhouse and fireplace located centrally in the public area. With a large skylight over it, it becomes the focal point upon entering the building. The adjoining lounge, dining room, hobby room, etc., adjoin or have views of this feature. The skylight floods the interior with extra light and airiness, and it is hoped this will set the theme or feeling for the entire project as one enters."

FIRST FLOOR PLAN

SITE PLAN

WESLEY MANOR RETIREMENT VILLAGE
(Jacksonville, Fla.; anticipated completion 1963)

VIEW OF AUDITORIUM AND RECREATION
PAVILION FACING BOAT HARBOR

Sponsor: Jacksonville Methodist Home, Inc., Jacksonville, Fla.
Architects: Broward & Warner, Associated Architects, A.I.A., Jacksonville, Fla.
Consultants: Edward L. Daugherty, landscape architect, Atlanta; Gomer E. Kraus, structural engineer, Jacksonville; Frank B. Wilder & Associates, mechanical engineers, Jacksonville
Site: 42 gently sloping acres with beautiful trees in rural area 12 miles from city; 3 miles to stores, churches; 6 miles to public transportation
Capacity: 348, plus 24-bed nursing unit (planned, 100-bed nursing unit)
People served: Men and women 62 and over; middle-upper income; good health; interfaith
Buildings: Thirteen one-story duplexes with 26 double housekeeping units; eleven one-story row houses (one with 36 single nonhousekeeping units; five with 20 single, two double nonhousekeeping units; five with 20 single, four double nonhousekeeping units)
Health facilities: 24-bed nursing unit, including eight beds for sheltered care; diagnostic: x-ray, e.k.g., b.m.r.; rehabilitation: physio- and occupational therapy; special treatment: dentist, podiatrist, E.N.T.; contract with local hospital for acute care, surgery
Auxiliary facilities: Four dining rooms (resident, 300; infirmary, 16; staff, 15; employee, 30); library (580 sq ft); chapel (1,256 sq ft); auditorium (400, including wheelchair space for 20); 11 lounges (2,279 sq ft each); snack kitchens; laundries; hobby rooms (crafts, 35; tools, 10); recreation room; trading post and snack bar, sidewalk cafe overlooking river; beauty parlor (3 chairs); barber shop (1 chair); outdoor: croquet, bowling-on-green, gardening, shuffleboard, greenhouses, fishing, golf putting green, boating
Service facilities: Central kitchen (4,300 sq ft); central laundry (2,880 sq ft); maintenance shop (1,440 sq ft); storage (resident, 60 sq ft each; institution, 4,926 sq ft); parking spaces (resident, 78; visitors, 50; institution, 41)

Staff (estimated; part-time in parentheses): Total: 90 (4). Administration, 8; health, 26; food, 24; maid, 16; laundry, 3; maintenance, 12; counseling, 1; barber, (1); beauty, (3)
Charges and services: Entrance fee of $5,000 to $20,000 or, in lieu of entrance fee, $500 earnest fee and $75 to $115 per month rent for debt retirement; monthly fee of $170 covers meals, maid, laundry, complete health service
Construction: Total building area: 261,000 sq ft, 3,262,500 cu ft; building materials: precast-prestressed concrete frame (exterior: walls—brick, glass, concrete; sash—aluminum, awnings, sliding aluminum doors; roofs—tectum, 3-in. wood deck, concrete; terraces—concrete; walks—concrete, sand; interior: walls—brick; floors—terrazzo, carpet, concrete; ceilings—tectum, 3-in. wood deck, sheetrock, acoustical tile; partitions—sheetrock on metal studs, paneling, structural glazed tile; trim—rubber base; bathrooms—terrazzo floor, tile); heating: fan-coil units, individual control; cooling, same; fuel: oil, gas
Site development: Aerobic-digestion type sewage treatment; private water system; macadam driveway; landscaping
Cost (1961): Total, including site development, buildings, built-in equipment, fees, but not furnishings: $3,859,642; cost per sq ft: $14.78; cost per cu ft: $1.18; kitchen equipment: $60,000; health: $150,000; drapes, carpet: $80,000
Financing: Endowment; contributions ($100,000); FHA loan ($4,825,000 plus three future floors, health center)
Architect says: "Wesley Manor has been designed with one basic goal in mind: to provide an environment that will keep each individual involved in daily life. The elderly must remain involved in daily controversy as well as daily security, retaining privacy and freedom while being afforded comfort and protection formerly found in the three-generation family home. A so-called home for the elderly fails in its mission if it becomes merely a repository for those whom society refuses to accept as valuable citizens. Wesley Manor is intended to be a place of beauty, dignity, and purpose. The architecture is a result of this approach."

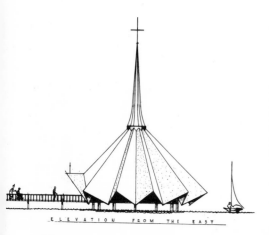

ELEVATION FROM THE EAST

INTERIOR PERSPECTIVE

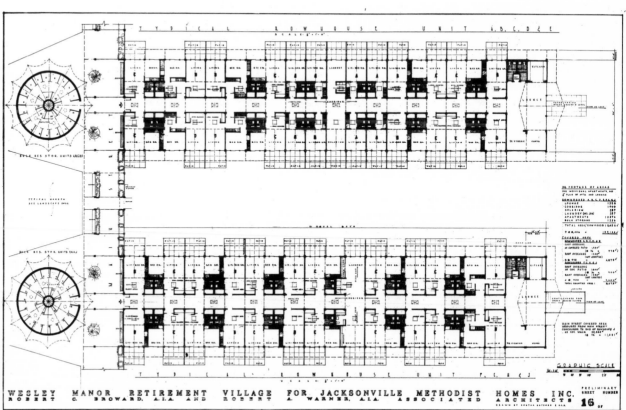

WESLEY MANOR RETIREMENT VILLAGE FOR JACKSONVILLE METHODIST HOMES INC.
ROBERT C. BROWARD, A.I.A. AND ROBERT A. WARNER, A.I.A. ASSOCIATED ARCHITECTS

SECTION VII

ARCHITECTURAL CHECK LIST

At the Brookings Institute Conference Study on Housing for the Aged, the well-known architectural writer Frederick Gutheim said, "A substantial literature of rule-of-thumb recommendations on the design of housing for the elderly has been created. The implicit assumption of such literature is that, with such assistance, an ordinary architect without special experience or insight into the matter would be able to design satisfactory housing for the elderly, and with such aids it would be possible for clients to specify the housing they need, and public officials would be able to approve such designs. The basic objective, in other words, is to substitute handbook knowledge for competence—for the professional skill, experience, and creative ability of a talented architect. This is the wrong direction in which to proceed."

Facts are nothing in and of themselves. They need a context to acquire sense, to have value or import. Facts are only information. There is a marked distinction between information and meaning, between meaning and significance. Information can be useless or even dangerous if we are unable to understand its meaning or evaluate its significance.

What follows in this chapter is a compilation of information. It is a check list of things to think about, not rules to follow, a set of cues rather than a collection of standards. If the need which prompted the "standard" is not understood, the standard is meaningless. The data buff can become the fanatic Santayana describes as one who "redoubles his effort after having lost sight of his objective."

The designer may observe any or almost all the following and produce a residence or he may produce an institution. It is not so much what he does as how he does it. He should design for the following objectives:

1. For safeguarding life and limb, but not for a policy of paternalism
2. For cleanliness and easy care and maintenance, but not for the janitor
3. For comfort and meaningful activity, not simply for ease of administering
4. For the creation of a residence, not an institution.

Items that will be appropriate to a project can be intelligently selected from this check list if we first determine whether we are dealing with the young old, the middle-aged old, or the very old. Our image of the user of the building defines the problem and illuminates the solution. If everything on this list is observed, we are designing for the very old.

Regarding carrying protective devices too far, *Architectural Forum* (August, 1958) says it is "difficult to draw the line between imperative services and demoralizing protection." But this line must be drawn, and is drawn in every thought the architect has about his project. He must identify the people he is designing for and from this determine to what degree he must compensate for the following: limited mobility, declining vigor and strength, vertigo, disturbed sense of verticality, reduced sense of sight, hearing, touch, and smell, forgetfulness, and confusion.

Architect Joseph Douglas Weiss puts it bluntly: the elderly are "handicapped people." But the variety and degree of the handicaps, or lack of them, is so infinite as to beggar generalization. Weiss says that we must remember that the residents we design for:

"1. Fall easily when they change direction, stumble, or bump into an object
2. Need twice as much light as a young person, but are sensitive to glare
3. Have impaired hearing; play their radios loud—but do not want to hear the neighbor's radio
4. May have impaired sense of smell and not be aware of a gas leak
5. Must have draftless ventilation and a warmer home than young people
6. Want privacy but need community services which must not invade it
7. Are exacting, critical, and impatient (everything was better in the old days) but many are very kind."

The result of these characteristics is a psychological withdrawal caused by reduced mobility and a sense of insecurity. Dressing, bathing, rising and sitting down are difficult. Stairs are a mental hazard as well as a physical one. Many accidents occur at night because of poor vision. Sight must compensate for other deficiencies. Escaping gas and incipient fire are not detected by smell. Reduced sensitivity of hearing makes noises less easily identified and therefore annoying or even alarming. Traffic street noises can be shattering; doorbells, telephone, and alarm bells may go unheeded. Radio and television are turned up, yet the sound of someone else's television is annoying.

The nucleus of this chapter is a paper prepared by architect Weiss for the National Council on Aging, Mohawk Lake Conference on Housing for the Elderly, in June, 1960. It includes additions from many other sources including the authors' own research.

Site planning
General

- Plan landscape as an extension of interior functions and concepts.
- Activities and inactivities need careful study and design.
- Walks and paths should have many cross walks.

- Avoid dead-end walks.
- Don't funnel traffic from entrance directly into busy street.
- Place benches and other facilities for group gatherings wherever possible.
- Use level walks and gentle ramps.
- Allow space for wheelchairs to pass each other and the bench-sitters.
- Terraces, walks, and paving are cheaper to maintain than grass and flowers.
- Movement in landscape design is very desirable—fountains, brooks, fish, waterfalls (water needs safeguards), mobiles, bird feeders, swans.
- Plan drinking fountains and water closets at a maximum of 500 feet from building if possible.
- Separate vehicular and pedestrian traffic, but do not segregate.
- Provide terraces and protected sitting or walking areas that overlook project or street traffic.
- Drives and roads need wide curves, good visibility without blindspots, easy flow into main traffic.
- Plan parking for residents, visitors, staff.
- Bus stop may require shelter.
- Keep in mind access for big trucks, fire equipment.
- Check airport flight patterns.

Proximate housing
- Design roadways and drives carefully for visibility and maneuverability.
- Keep lots small.
- Provide for sociability and privacy.
- Use attached garages or provide parking as near entrance as possible.
- Keep walks short to minimize snow removal.
- Keep gardens out of main view (they run down after a while).
- Ambulance entrance and hearse exit should both be inconspicuous.

- Provide shelter at entrances; consider watchman service.
- Consider maintenance shops, a ground superintendent's shop, and sheds.
- Place incinerator near all apartments, 40 feet away maximum.

Congregate Housing
- Plan should be simple and easily comprehended so that no one gets lost.
- Shelter at entrances.
- Lobby friendly, inviting—a furnished parlor which invites traffic watching.
- Mailboxes located for socializing.
- Drinking fountains.
- Entertainment space for several groups.
- Special kitchen and dining room for family group entertainment by resident.
- Hobby space flexible.
- Lavatories near all public spaces.
- Concealed hearse or ambulance exit.
- Building maintenance shop and storage (furniture, venetian blinds, etc.).
- Grounds maintenance shop and storage.
- Watchman check points.
- Employees' and staff dining rooms, lounge and rest rooms, time clock.
- Package and drycleaning delivery spot.
- Safe for residents' valuables.
- Fire-resistant construction desirable; fire extinguisher, hose.
- Management visible but not obtrusive.

Living room

Used much more extensively and intensively than by younger people because of the extra leisure time of the elderly or as result of their confinement. As it is a large part of the old person's world, it should be designed to help him keep up appearances (concealment should be provided for cooking mess, unmade bed).

- Plan for sufficient wallspace to accommodate large old furniture and large pictures.

- A window to sit by, with a wide sill for plants.
- Book shelves.
- Lamps, radio, television.
- Variation in furniture arrangement.
- Closet for general storage.

Dining room
- If in kitchen, must provide easy movement around tables without the necessity of moving chairs for cooking or access to storage.
- If in living room, should be available for eating without the necessity of moving floor lamps or other furniture.
- Drop leaf table is all right only if its use does not require rearrangement of the room (table best near or at window with good view).
- Electric outlet at table-top height for lamp, radio, sewing machine.
- Needs good light day and night.

Bedroom
- 18 in. on three sides of bed for bedmaking.
- 36 in. between beds.
- Large bed tables for lamp, night light, water, medicine, teeth, tissues, radio, books.
- View out of window for confined residents.
- Short, direct path to bathroom.

Living room—bedroom (efficiency apartment)
"Efficiency apartments are all right for efficient people," says Joseph Weiss, but they make it harder to keep up appearances.

- Allow bed to be screened (alcove?); if not, a long wall is required so that the bed may become a couch.
- Kitchen should be screened; entry makes a good location.
- Catch-all closet for quick tidying up.
- Provide for a full, comfortable existence, including sitting, eating, sleeping, cooking, work, hobby.
- Adequate storage for clothing, linen, kitchen supplies and equipment, books, personal gear.

Baths

Accidents are frequent in bathrooms; they are hazardous places, small, crowded, slippery, full of hard-to-reach necessities, dangerous projections. All these hazards become greater when stamina is lowest. A place of emergency use, they are especially dangerous at night when one is in a hurry, dizzy, weak, confused.

- *Ideal access* is provided by the straightest path without unnecessary turns; avoid intervening rooms and especially stairs to pass.
- Emergency call bell or cord should be accessible from tub if possible.
- Windows are unnecessary and even undesirable if located over tub where curtain or shade is hard to reach or if they cause draft (an exhaust fan will do).
- Recess hamper or scales.
- Ceiling heat lamp provides safest and most economical auxiliary heat.
- Avoid small rugs and mats.
- Communal bathing facilities feasible, but toilet down the hall is unthinkable because of night problems of emergency, confusion, poor vision.

Tub

- Useful for soaking.
- Easy-to-grasp faucet handles.
- Non-skid surfaces, including that of seat if built-in (a spray-on anti-skid is available).
- Portable seats are dangerous.
- Grab bars for getting in and out (old-fashioned free-standing tub provided a grip that built-in tubs don't afford).
- Mixing faucet, with one handle, reachable without stooping too much.
- Recessed soap dish.
- Spray hose useful.
- Shower in tub dangerous to unsteady bather.
- Tubs for bathing the handicapped may be at normal level if removable grating (aluminum) over small pit trench allows attendant to step down instead of lifting patient by hoist.

Shower

- Preferred by many after first use, especially wheel chair users and their attendants. Easier to get in and out of. Appeals to those who have greatest difficulty with tub. It is cleaner and more invigorating and there is no danger of drowning, but it is also more expensive to install and maintain.
- Needs seat, non-skid floor, grab bars on two walls, single valve, recessed soap dish.
- Valves should be located so they can be reached from a wheel chair.
- Towel bars should take 300- to 500-lb. pull (heavy weight applied suddenly).
- Use door, not curtain; translucent plastic safer than glass; if curtain used, rod should take 300- to 500-lb. pull.

Lavatory

- Avoid legs; they cause stumbling and block wheelchair.
- Avoid projection over the basin.
- Recess soap and tumbler holders; projecting holders break off.
- Water temperature should not exceed 115 deg. F. at faucet.

Toilet

- If placed next to tub, it provides seat for soaking feet.
- Arched grab bars, if needed, but these may interfere with foot soaking.
- Paper-holder mounted so as to obviate undue twisting or reaching.
- Avoid low style seats common now.
- Sturdy seat lid.

Medicine cabinet

- Flush, non-projecting type.
- Sliding doors good.
- Spacious (to hold extra medicine).
- Avoid glass shelves.

Grab bars

- ¾" to 1-in. diameter, no more.
- Should take 300- to 500-lb. pull.

Doors

- Should open out, never in (a person who has fainted inside may block door).
- Folding doors might do.
- No inside locks or dead bolts.
- Light switch should be on outside and have built-in night light in plate.

Kitchen

Kitchens are another danger spot with dangerous equipment.

- Locate near front door and near dining space with direct path between.
- Window desirable, but not mandatory with mechanical ventilation.
- Limit reaches to 66 in. in an upward and 18 in. in a downward direction to offset dizziness and poor vision. Drawers may be a little lower. No storage should be permitted that must be reached from a stool or chair.
- Cabinet doors are a hazard to persons with poor vision. Sliding doors are better than swinging doors if they won't pinch fingers. No doors would be best.
- Electric range (with elements that glow) is safer than gas. Keep range away from curtains. No storage over range. Controls should be on front of range and extra legible.
- Wall ovens are excellent but are usually set too high.
- Double sink, swing faucet. Should allow hand laundering. Easy-to-grip faucet handles with single control are best. Hot water not over 115 deg. F. at faucet.
- Provide mounting for can opener, etc.
- Self-defrosting refrigerator is desirable; under-counter type unsatisfactory; freezer compartment allows less frequent marketing.
- Broom closet.
- Garbage pail and trash basket space away from traffic. Easy trash and garbage disposal important.

- Superior lighting for work spaces needed. Dark storage cabinets should be avoided.
- Pullman or 5-ft. package kitchens are especially unsatisfactory for the elderly. They have no work space; refrigerator is too low; storage is poor and hard to reach; sink is inadequate, there is no place to hide a mess if the kitchen is visible from the living room.

Doors

- 3-ft. room doors and exterior doors desirable for wheelchair and crutch users, but these are relatively few.
- Avoid interior thresholds; if unavoidable, keep low and bevel if possible.
- Avoid interference of one door with another.
- Large, hexagonal, or octagonal door knobs better than round; lever type good.
- Swinging closet doors are a hazard to poor vision, and sliding doors pinch fingers. Bi-fold or accordian doors are better and cost no more.
- Avoid protruding door stops.
- Fit carefully and check regularly for binding.
- Revolving doors hazardous.
- Door closers usually act too quickly.
- Key apartment and building entrances alike.
- Master-key all doors for warning and assistance.
- Prohibit chain devices and dead bolts.
- Peephole on exterior doors good psychology.
- Card holder on outside door with emergency data on back side of card.
- Combination screen and louvered doors are good in a warm climate.

Windows

- Must open and close easily; cranks are difficult.
- Sliding metal and old fashioned double-hung can be made to operate well.
- Most awning types too hard to operate.
- Bottom vent panel O.K.
- Ventilation desirable but elderly don't like

drafts and are less sensitive to stale-smelling atmosphere. Cross ventilation rarely liked. Mechanical ventilation is a good alternative.
- Double glazing, storm sash, and weatherstripping very important in cold climates. Sash should be washable and removable from inside.
- Pleasant view has high priority; scenes of activity desirable to hold interest for long periods of time.
- Glare shading on exterior to be considered. Direct sunlight usually recommended, but north window with view of sunlit scene may have less glare, less heat. Large windows reduce glare through better distribution of light in room.
- Venetian blinds are flexible in use; roller shades less so, and are hazardous to retrieve.
- Heavy pull draperies useful; weighted pull cord.
- Sills should be wide for plants, knicknacks, and low enough to look over without strain while seated (or from bed).
- Insect screens needed. Should be removable from inside.
- Hazards abound around windows. Operation of windows, blinds, and curtains awkward, especially over a wide radiator. On upper floors sash should have a guard rail at 42 to 48 in. height. Avoid stair windows that are hard to reach.

Corridors

- 5-ft. minimum width.
- Keep short or design to seem short.
- Light colors for visibility.
- Treat acoustically.
- Handrail at hazardous points, 36 in. above floor.
- Ventilate.

Gallery balconies (as corridors to apartments)

- 7-ft. width allows sitting out.
- High rail.
- Not good in wet or freezing climates.

Stairs

Some say to avoid stairs if possible because they are tiring and dangerous. Others say they are good exercise, safe if well designed, and not as difficult to manage for most elderly as many other activities.

- Wide treads, low rises, short runs, with handrails.
- Well lighted day and night (10 foot-candles minimum).
- Avoid glare.
- Frequent landings (every 8 to 12 risers) with a seat if possible.
- Continuous handrail around both sides.
- Avoid open risers and too open railings.
- Avoid circulation directly across top of stairs.
- Non-slip treads, not just non-slip edges or tacked-on pads.
- Use easy proportion and keep consistent throughout project. Seven-inch risers probably maximum.
- Don't use a single step except at entrances.
- No winders.
- No locking devices in stairs except at exterior door.
- Contrast top and bottom step with adjoining floor.
- Avoid out-of-reach windows.
- Study monumental stairs (and others) so that design avoids feeling of danger, lack of support to grasp.
- Open metal fire escapes are terrifying to many.

Ramps

- Too long to be used for any but slight change of level. Bad for wheelchairs, crutches, and the unsteady unless very gradual.
- 1 in. to the foot absolute maximum pitch.

Elevators

- One large enough for a stretcher with access to inconspicuous exit.
- Automatic, self-leveling.

- Slow-acting doors (to accommodate wheel-chairs, crutches).
- Safety edge or electric eye doors.
- Emergency alarm.
- Low controls and call buttons for wheelchairs.
- Large numerals, buttons, floor indicators.
- Fan, light (15 foot-candles at floor), handrail all around, seat or package shelf if possible.
- Bench and/or package table in lobby.

Floors

- Smooth and level with minimum change in level.
- Should not only be non-skid but should *look* non-skid. Appearance of slipperiness is psychologically dangerous if it causes person to walk with undue care.
- Avoid thick rugs, fringed rugs, throw rugs which cause slipping and tripping. Carpets O.K.
- Avoid terrazzo, polished marble, highly buffed asphalt tile, etc.
- A broad lobby of polished terrazzo, and a gleaming wide stair with open risers and sparse handrails can be a nightmare to an elderly person.

Interior finishes

- Should encourage cleanliness.
- Should encourage safety.
- Should maintain "hominess."
- Consider carpet for traffic areas. (Use of carpet in schools and public lobbies seems to indicate it is easier and cheaper to maintain than other floor materials.)
- Wallpapers can be washable.

Lighting

Many elderly require more light than normal. But they also require carefully designed light that eliminates glare and avoids marked changes in brightness level because of difficulty they have in adapting to such changes. Seeing is used to compensate for re-

duced hearing and the restricted ability to move and feel.

- Uniform levels of illumination (but not without shadows), shielded light sources, and careful illumination of surface for work movement, etc., are all desirable.
- Public spaces require double the normal light. It should be turned on early.
- Corridors require up to 10-foot candles at floor.
- Stairs require 10 to to 15 foot-candles.
- Entrances to building and at elevators require 10 to 15 foot-candles at floor.
- Exit signs should be large and legible.
- Mailboxes, building directories, and pay phones frequently require more than normal illumination.
- Outside lighting should be generous and should be turned on early. Use low fixtures for walks and steps; these must be shielded for person going up steps as well as down.
- Light at outside door (to find keyhole).
- Individual quarters require more than normal illumination.
- Ceiling lights are a hazard if resident must rebulb himself. Some designers use pull-down style.
- Switch all fixtures.
- Switch paths of travel carefully, from front door to bed, with 3-way switches to avoid fumbling and confusion in the dark.
- Switch at bed (3-way).
- Bathroom switch on outside of door with night light under plate.
- Corridor outlets for night light between bath and bed.
- Generous amount of outlets.
- Outlets 18 in. to 24 in. above floor.
- Outlets above table tops where tables will be used.
- Locate circuit breakers for easy accessibility.

Color

Must function as an aid to poor eyesight as well as psychological tool.

- Color contrast can make hazards "read" easily. Contrast floor with wall, furniture with floor, stairs with corridor, treads with risers.
- Where artificial light levels are low, avoid light-absorbing colors.
- In any room, one dark wall may be fine, but not all four.
- Keep cheerful.
- Use patterns functionally.

Heating

Comfort requirements change in the person and vary with individuals.

- Draftless, uniform distribution.
- 80 deg. F. possible in all weather.
- Individual temperature control.
- Warm floors, but not radiant panels for total job of heating; these aggravate foot troubles.
- Quick-acting system.
- Insulate hot water and steam pipes to avoid burns. Baseboard heating has proved excellent.
- Convector tops should be non-staining, rust-proof (for potted plants, etc.).
- Windows should be blanketed with heat as well as double-glassed or storm-sashed (for winter sitting).
- Ventilation is important. Corridors may be held under slight pressure forcing air under doors or through door louvers and out through kitchen and bath vents. This keeps corridors fresh.
- Cooling not needed or liked by very elderly except in extreme climates.

Sound

As hearing acuteness is reduced, the reduced ability to identify sounds is annoying, disturbing, even frightening. Immediate and recognizable sounds are more resented than distant, anonymous sounds. Invasion of naps, illness, sedentary occupations are particularly resented. Excessive sound is especially distracting. Annoying sounds include those from public corridors, garbage chutes, elevators, playgrounds, excessive traffic. Elderly neighbors are also noisy, talk loudly, and turn up the T.V. and radio.

- Reasonable sound isolation of private quarters is important.
- Insulate against impact and airborne noises.
- Bells, signals, and intercom need to be low pitch sound.
- Special ear pieces or head phones may be had for radio and T.V.
- Carpet is a prime sound deadener for corridors.

Alarms and intercoms

- Alarm sounds should carry low frequencies as well as high.
- Signal button for intercom call may have extension cord to permit bed to be located in various places.
- Individuals may install emergency signals to friendly neighbors.
- Emergency signals are desirable in bath and at bed.
- Apartments and the like need warning signals for fire, etc.
- Group housing or connecting homes may have intercom systems (1) for announcing visitors to residents in their rooms, (2) for piped music and religious services, (3) for warnings, (4) for resident emergency calls, (5) for night listening by nurses in case of temporary illness.
- A typical system provides a master station in the main office and in the infirmary. These are interconnected and connected with all resident rooms. Two-way conversations are originated at the master station but not at the residents' rooms. Residents' rooms have call buttons connected to both masters.
- Submasters, which are interconnected and connected with the master, are located in the kitchen, housekeeper's office, and maintenance engineer's quarters. These are completely two-way.
- Paging system from main office to public rooms.

Telephones

- Outlet at bedside table.
- Public phones: open station better than booth; seat required; should be designed with height and clearance for wheelchair use; good light needed for directory and dial.
- Special bells and amplifier sets may be needed for the hard of hearing.
- Lower pitch sounds usually required.

Infirmary

To care for temporary illness, convalescence, chronic conditions requiring assistance but not hospital or nursing home care.

- Motorized beds keep patient down for safety, raise him for bathing, etc.
- Intercom-connected
- Incinerator for paper goods
- Nurses' station: intercoms, telephone, drug closet, records, files.
- In a large project, sub-nurse stations for temporary use may be located conveniently and inconspicuously in several places for short time use to care for residents in their own rooms.
- Utility room: clinical sink, washer and dryer, counter, trash hamper.
- Kitchen: hotplate, sink, shelves, refrigerator.
- Health service (clinic): counseling, preventive medicine, examination, diagnosis (lab work, X-ray, other elaborate procedures to be contracted out); office, reception, interviews; waiting room; lavatory; dressing room; records; social worker; treatment (medication, podiatrist, dentist, oculist); therapy.

Resident laundry

- Automatic machines.
- Double sink for hand laundering.

- Ironing board.
- Sitting space for socializing.
- Scatter in small units not over 500 ft. apart.

Social hall

- Should accommodate twice the number of project population.
- Toilet facilities.
- Convenient, well-lighted kitchen.
- Service entrance.
- Storage for ice cream, etc.
- Locked storage for projector, screen, etc.
- Space for dispensing machines, partly concealed.

Storage

- Institutional and individual, best near point of use.

Wheelchair requirements

The percentage of users is small, but their requirements are specific. Wheelchairs with 8-in. wire spoke wheels on front are safer than those with 5-in. hard coasters and are easier to operate. According to Dr. Burk, "As the age average rises in a group, more people require wheelchairs and there is a tendency to make all facilities such as door sizes, kitchen spaces, bathrooms, and room dimensions to accommodate wheelchairs. While all doors can be made 3 ft. wide, many other requirements for wheelchair residents may be so expensive that it is advisable to have a small number of really well designed apartments with special bathroom sizes instead of standardizing on a compromise layout. A wheelchair requires 4 ft. 7 in. to turn around, which is considerably more than is ordinarily used in a bathroom between fixtures. A safe new design for wheelchairs which could maneuver around in a small space would be a real contribution to the cause of the elderly and would make the life of architects a lot simpler." (See Bibliography for wheelchair studies.)

- 60 in. at one side of bed.
- 36-in. doors and pathways.

- 55-in. diameter for turning.
- Omit legs from lavatory.
- Wall-hung toilet lets projecting foot of chair come up close, as do a few floor-mounted models.
- Kitchen counter 30 in. high with 30-in. openings under, where needed.

Hotel conversions

Joseph Weiss says: "As far as physical requirements are concerned, ideally this type of building should approach in its standards any new high-rise type of accommodations. It is difficult to adjust any existing building to new standards. Without expensive rebuilding, it is usually possible to provide hotel type facilities augmented by central organized food, social, health and other services. Individual cooking arrangements run into problems of code and ventilation. Closets are not adequate. Despite these difficulties, several individual and chain organizations are successfully doing conversions, mostly for the use of the well segment of the elderly."

- Check and improve fireproofness of building.
- Eliminate all transoms above corridor doors into rooms.
- Install sprinklers in corridors, storage spaces, shafts.
- Enclose all open shafts, stair shafts, elevator shafts.
- Open fire escapes must be real open fire stairs 4 ft. wide; no ladders; full railings and landings available without climbing over sills.
- Install fire alarm and watchman system.
- Provide window cleaning service.
- Telephone between each unit and switchboard.

TERMINOLOGY

In the text of this book appear certain words of a mildly technical nature which perhaps need definitions to show how the authors have used them in reference to the elderly.

Living arrangements for individuals or family units:

"Independent living": Self-sufficient, unassisted, unsupervised housekeeping

"Assisted living": Non-housekeeping with a management providing various services and perhaps mild supervision

"Sheltered living": Assisted living for the senile with care, mild supervision, and protection

"Protected living": Completely supervised living with all services provided and the elderly guarded for treatment or protection of self or others

Residence types:

"Dispersed residences": Independent living units for the elderly scattered among units for the non-elderly

"Proximate residences": Independent living units for the elderly clustered in a group

"Congregate residences": Assisted living units for the elderly clustered in a group, under a management and usually under one roof complex

"Institutional living": Protected living units for the elderly under one roof for care, treatment, or surveillance

"Foster homes": Private families who take in non-related elderly for pay

Services:

"Homemaker service": Assistance with housekeeping, shopping, etc., provided by a visiting worker

"Home care service": Periodic care of individual in his own home provided by a visiting nurse

"Home medical service": Treatment and assistance, usually during a convalescence, provided by a visiting team of doctor, nurse, social worker

"Out-patient service": Clinical and therapeutic treatment of non-residents provided by a home for the elderly in its own facilities

Facilities:

"Infirmary": Facility for minimum care of temporary illness or during convalescence; no laboratory facility

"Nursing unit": Facility for complete nursing during convalescence or of a temporary or chronic illness; simple laboratory facility

"Hospital": Facility for complete diagnosis, care, and treatment of acute illness including surgery; complete laboratory facility

"Clinic": Examining rooms and offices for minor diagnosis and treatment

"Diagnostic facilities": Complete equipment for diagnosis such as in a hospital, including X-ray, EKG, BMR, fluoroscope, clinical laboratory, etc.

"Therapy": Space for non-medical treatment and rehabilitation procedures: physiotherapy, occupational therapy, psychotherapy

"Special treatment": Dentist, oculist, ENT, podiatrist, psychiatrist

Health Care:

"Minimum care": Care of temporary illness only (infirmary)

"Limited care": Care of convalescent, temporary, chronic, or terminal illness, sometimes including senility but not surgery

"Complete care": Complete treatment, nursing care, hospitalization, surgery, X-ray, etc., including doctor bills

"Sheltered care": For senility

Treatment:

"Rehabilitation": Therapeutic procedures for restorative purposes

Sociology:

"Integrated elderly": Mixed with non-elderly

"Segregated elderly": Separated from non-elderly

"Isolated elderly": Out of contact with other elderly or non-elderly

"Insulated elderly": Groups of elderly in a living situation which provides for all their needs, social and other, without necessity of contact with general public

SELECTED READING

Books

Burgess, Ernest W., ed., *Retirement Villages*, University of Michigan Press, Ann Arbor, 1961.

Donahue, Wilma, *Housing the Aged*, University of Michigan Press, Ann Arbor, 1954.

Environmental Planning for the Elderly, Proceedings—8th Planning Conference for Architects, University of Illinois, Urbana.

Mathiasen, Geneva, and Noakes, Edward H., *Planning Homes for the Aged*, F. W. Dodge Corp., New York, 1959.

Pamphlets

"Aged Home Care Patients in New York City. Housing and Related Facilities Needed," New York State Division of Housing, 1958.

"Aging Americans, Their Views and Living Conditions," Report by Subcommittee on Problems of the Aged and Aging of Committees on Labor and Public Welfare, U. S. Senate, Washington, D. C., Dec. 1960.

"Aging with a Future, Reports and Guidelines from the White House Conference on Aging," U. S. Department of Health, Education, and Welfare, Washington, D. C., April, 1961.

"Background Paper on Housing," Nelson, Walter C., chairman, Planning Committee on Housing for the White House Conference on Aging, U. S. Department of Health, Education, and Welfare, Washington, D. C., 1960.

"Background Studies Prepared by State Committees for The White House Conference on Aging," U. S. Department of Health, Education, and Welfare, Washington, D. C.

"Federal Programs for Senior Citizen Housing Fact Sheet," U. S. Housing and Home Finance Agency, Washington, D. C., Feb. 1962.

"Guide to Community Action in the Field of Aging," Diamond, Beverly, National Council on the Aging, 1961.

"A Guide for Lutheran Homes Serving the Aging," National Lutheran Council, Division of Welfare, New York, June 1957.

"Housing and the Social Health of Older People," Donahue, Wilma, and Ashley, E. Everett, 3rd, U. S. Housing and Home Finance Agency, Washington, D. C.

"Housing for the Elderly, Architect's Check List," Public Housing Administration, H.H.F.A., Washington, D. C.

"Housing Requirements of the Aged—A Study of Design Criteria," New York State Division of Housing, 1958.

"How to Make and Use Local Housing Surveys," prepared by The Bureau of Business and Social Research, University of Denver, U. S. Housing and Home Finance Agency, Washington, D. C., 1954.

"How to Provide Housing Which the Elderly Can Afford," New York State Division of Housing, 1958 (reprinted 1961).

"Income, Retirement, and Security for the Aging," Epstein, Lenore A., 1961 Proceedings, 8th Planning Conference for Architects, University of Illinois, Urbana.

"Kitchens for Women in Wheel Chairs," Circular No. 841, University of Illinois College of Agriculture, Extension Service in Agriculture and Home Economics, Urbana, Nov. 1961.

"More than Bread. Social Services in Public Assistance and Community Resource," Social Security Administration, Bureau of Public Assistance, U. S. Department of Health, Education, and Welfare, Washington, D. C., 1958.

"New Population Facts on Older Americans, 1960," staff report of The Special Committee on Aging, U. S. Senate, Washington, D. C., 1961.

"Planning a Non-profit Retirement Home," Stanton, Willard E., Wesley Gardens, Des Moines, Wash.

"Programs for Older People—Activities, Resources, Dollar Dimensions," Federal Council on Aging, Washington, D. C., 1960.

"Report of Missouri Committee for the 1961 White House Conference," Kassabaum, George, Governor's Commission on Aging.

"Report of the White House Conference on Aging, January 9-12, 1961," Federal Council on Aging, Washington, D. C.

"Source Book of Health Insurance Data," Health Insurance Institute, New York, 1961.

"The 1961 White House Conference on Aging, Basic Policy Statements and Recommendations," Special Committee on Aging, U. S. Senate, Washington, D. C.

"The 1961 White House Conference on Aging Chart Book," Federal Council on Aging, Washington, D. C., 1961.

Articles

"Building Types Study Number 214—Buildings for the Aged," *Architectural Record*, Sept. 1954.

Cowgill, Clinton H., "Facilities for the Aging and Infirm, Part I," *A.I.A. Journal*, May 1960.

Cowgill, "Facilities for the Aging and Infirm, Part II," *A.I.A. Journal*, July 1960.

Epstein, Lenore A., "The Aged in the Population in 1960 and their Income Sources," *Social Security Bulletin*, July 1961.

"Housing for the Aged," *Architectural Record*, August 1961.

"Housing for the Aged," *Progressive Architecture*, March 1961.

"Housing for the Elderly," *Architectural Forum*, May 1961.

Kassabaum, George, "Design of Old Aged Homes," *A.I.A. Journal*, July 1961.

Kassabaum, "Housing for the Elderly, Technical Standards of Design," *A.I.A. Journal*, Sept. 1962.

Loring, William C., "A New Housing Market: The Old," *Architectural Forum*, December 1960.

Loring, "Design for a New Housing Market: The Old," *Architectural Forum*, May 1961.

Mathiasen, Geneva, "Better Buildings for the Aging," *Architectural Record*, May 1956.

Mead, Margaret, "New Thoughts on Old People," *Council Woman*, October 1960.

"Retirement House, A Prototype House, Rental and Co-op Apartments," *House and Home*, February 1961.

Rienow, Robert, and Train, Leona, "The Desperate World of the Senior Citizen," *Saturday Review*, Jan. 28, 1961.

Turano, E. N., "Four Old Age Homes," *Progressive Architecture*, March 1961.

Weil, Helen K., "An Out-Resident Program in a Home for the Aged," *Jewish Social Service Quarterly*, Spring 1953.